OPERA AS SOUNDTRACK

ASHGATE INTERDISCIPLINARY STUDIES IN OPERA

The *Ashgate Interdisciplinary Studies in Opera* series provides a centralized and prominent forum for the presentation of cutting-edge scholarship that draws on numerous disciplinary approaches to a wide range of subjects associated with the creation, performance, and reception of opera (and related genres) in various historical and social contexts. There is great need for a broader approach to scholarship about opera. In recent years, the course of study has developed significantly, going beyond traditional musicological approaches to reflect new perspectives from literary criticism and comparative literature, cultural history, philosophy, art history, theatre history, gender studies, film studies, political science, philology, psycho-analysis, and medicine. The new brands of scholarship have allowed a more comprehensive interrogation of the complex nexus of means of artistic expression operative in opera, one that has meaningfully challenged prevalent historicist and formalist musical approaches. The *Ashgate Interdisciplinary Studies in Opera* series continues to move this important trend forward by including essay collections and monographs that reflect the ever-increasing interest in opera in non-musical contexts. Books in the series will be linked by their emphasis on the study of a single genre – opera – yet will be distinguished by their individualized and novel approaches by scholars from various disciplines/fields of inquiry. The remit of the series welcomes studies of seventeenth century to contemporary opera from all geographical locations, including non-Western topics.

Opera as Soundtrack

JEONGWON JOE
University of Cincinnati, USA

ASHGATE

Published by
Ashgate Publishing Limited
Wey Court East
Union Road
Farnham
Surrey, GU9 7PT
England

Ashgate Publishing Company
110 Cherry Street
Suite 3-1
Burlington, VT 05401-3818
USA

www.ashgate.com

British Library Cataloguing in Publication Data
Joe, Jeongwon.
　Opera as soundtrack. – (Ashgate interdisciplinary studies in opera)
　1. Motion pictures and opera. 2. Film soundtracks.
　I. Title II. Series
　781.5'42-dc23

The Library of Congress has cataloged the printed edition as follows:
Joe, Jeongwon.
　Opera as soundtrack / by Jeongwon Joe.
　　pages cm. – (Ashgate interdisciplinary studies in opera)
　Includes bibliographical references and index.
　ISBN 978-0-7546-6718-6 (hardcover : alk. paper) 1. Opera in motion pictures.
　2. Motion pictures and opera. I. Title.
　ML2100.J64 2013
　791.43'6578–dc23

2012049941

ISBN 9780754667186 (hbk)
ISBN 9781472411310 (ebk – PDF)
ISBN 9781472411327 (ebk – ePUB)

MIX
Paper from
responsible sources
FSC   FSC® C013985
www.fsc.org

Printed in the United Kingdom by Henry Ling Limited, at the Dorset Press, Dorchester, DT1 1HD

To my canine children,
Tamino and Gustav

Contents

List of Figures and Tables

Figures

Tables

Series Editor's Preface

Ashgate Interdisciplinary Studies in Opera provides a centralized and prominent forum for the presentation of cutting-edge scholarship that draws on numerous disciplinary approaches on a wide range of subjects associated with the creation, performance, dissemination, and reception of opera and related genres in various historical and social contexts. The series includes topics from the seventeenth century to the present and from all geographical locations, including non-Western traditions.

In recent years, the field of opera studies has not only come into its own but has developed significantly, going beyond traditional musicological approaches to reflect new perspectives from literary criticism and comparative literature, cultural history, philosophy, art history, theater history, gender studies, film studies, political science, philology, psychoanalysis, and even medicine. The new brands of scholarship have allowed a more comprehensive and intensive interrogation of the complex nexus of means of artistic expression operative in opera, one that has meaningfully challenged prevalent historicist and formalist musical approaches. Today, interdisciplinary, or as some prefer cross-disciplinary, opera studies are receiving increasingly widespread attention, and the ways in which scholars, practitioners, and the public think about the artform known as opera continue to change and expand. *Ashgate Interdisciplinary Studies in Opera* seeks to move this important trend forward by including essay collections and monographs that reflect the ever-increasing interest in opera in non-musical contexts.

Opera as Soundtrack clearly stakes out its territory, the use of operatic segments within film, and makes an original contribution by systematically addressing opera as a scoring practice. Jeongwon Joe's critical inquiry into this specific type of intersection between opera and cinema explores a variety of the effects that opera creates in film, differentiated from those of other types of soundtrack music. It does so from diverse perspectives including qualities of the operatic voice, properties, concepts, and themes commonly associated with opera; and tensions between the two art forms of film and opera—for instance, opera as live, embodied, high art and cinema as technologically mediated, popular entertainment. The author thus shows the manner in which, during the end of the twentieth century and beginning of the twenty-first, opera has begun to function in new ways within film. She does so empirically and hermeneutically, through archival research coupled with analysis. *Opera as Soundtrack* addresses this still largely unexplored topic in a manner accessible to and significant for both opera studies and film studies.

Roberta Montemorra Marvin

Acknowledgments

Opera as Soundtrack was conceived when I was teaching at the University of Nevada in Reno, which propelled the project by awarding me a fellowship for junior faculty's research (the working title of the book at that time was "What Can Opera Do in Film?"). Two grants I received from the University Research Council of my current university have also contributed to the advancement of the project.

This book would not have come to fruition without the intellectual and artistic stimulation and moral support from some special people in my professional and personal circles. I am immensely indebted to the reader Ashgate engaged for the review of my book manuscript. His or her feedback was indispensible for the completion of the project and the enrichment of my argument: I have particularly benefited from such virtuosic studies the reader recommended to me as Jennifer Fleeger's dissertation "Opera, Jazz, and Hollywood's Conversion to Sound" and Britta Sjogren's book, *Into the Vortex: Female Voice and Paradox in Film*. I was fortunate to work with Ashgate's extraordinary staff—first of all Heidi Bishop, Publisher, Emma Gallon, and her colleagues, Laura Macy, and Barbara Pretty. Sara Peacock also deserves a word of thanks, as her thoughtful and meticulous copyediting improved the conceptual clarity and stylistic refinement of my book.

The work of many scholars in the fields of opera-cinema studies and film music was the essential foundation for my project. To mention a few of them, I am grateful to Marcia Citron and Michal Grover-Friedlander, whose specialty is closest to mine, for their inspiring studies, especially Marcia's *When Opera Meets Film* and Michal's *Vocal Apparitions: The Attraction of Cinema to Opera*. My gratitude to William H. Rosar is immeasurable, as he is the person who opened an entirely new world for me as a film-music scholar by introducing me to people engaged in the film industry who helped my archival studies in the Hollywood areas. He also considerably enhanced my work and methodology through his extensive knowledge in the field and his ruthless yet constructive criticism (as I mention in the Epilogue, the most memorable is my conversation with him over lunch at Musso & Frank Grill, a historic restaurant in Los Angeles frequented by many Hollywood celebrities since its foundation in 1919). I am also grateful to Warren M. Sherk, Database Archivist and Music Specialist at the Academy of Motion Picture Arts and Sciences' Margaret Herrick Library. His help was indispensible for the expansion and enrichment of my knowledge through my archival research.

Roger Hillman's intellectual and moral support for me was invaluable for the completion of this book: throughout a long period of time while the project was evolving, he patiently set me back on track when I was derailed. Also invaluable were Lawrence Kramer's brilliant comments on select chapters, especially Chapter 4: "Is Cinema's Anxiety Opera's Envy?" (I am aware that he would still not be convinced by my main argument in this chapter.) His encouragement when I was skeptical about my methodology was invigorating: "If you do not have a dilemma about your methodology, then the quality of your work would be suspicious."

Chan-wook Park's stimulation for my work has been truly special, extending beyond this project. I first met him in 1988 when he was a struggling film director at Choong-Moo-Ro, a street in downtown Seoul, the name of which had served for a long time as a metonym for the Korean film industry. At that time, I was taking a gap year back in Korea, skeptical about pursuing a doctoral degree in musicology. It was in Chicago in 1993, a year after Chan-wook's debut feature film was released, that we had the first serious and long (around five hours) conversation about film music, more specifically, about Claudia Gorbman's pioneering study in the field, *Unheard Melodies: Narrative Film Music*. Since then, he has tremendously enriched my scholarly work by providing me with a film director's perspectives on the use of music and also with the opportunity to observe and participate in filmmaking: I was particularly fortunate to be able to do my "field work" during the shooting of his most recent, and his first Hollywood, film *Stoker*, premiered at the Sundance Film Festival in 2013.

Thomas Kernan, who served as my research assistant at my university in the academic year of 2006–2007, deserves a special acknowledgment: his administrative and intellectual assistance was at the level of a colleague rather than a graduate assistant. I am also indebted to some other graduate students at my university, especially Leah Branstetter and a few students in the "Crossover" class I offered in the fall semester of 2012: Leah's master's thesis I advised, "Angels and Arctic Monkeys: A Study of Pop-Opera Crossover," stimulated my work, especially for situating "opera as soundtrack" in the wider context of the popera phenomenon; and the "Crossover" students provided me with some critical information about opera's most up-to-date engagement with popular culture, such as the TV show "Popstar to Operastar" in the UK, launched in 2010, and its copycat in Korea, "Opera Star," a brief discussion of which I was able to add to the Epilogue while I was working on the final revision of the book.

As I mentioned in the Introduction to my collection *Wagner and Cinema*, one of the exhilarating joys for a film-music scholar is that a variety of people can be your informants and supporters, as film is such a prevalent and powerful popular entertainment that permeates everybody's everyday life. In this context, my special thanks go to all of my informants—too many to be acknowledged— who have significantly broadened my knowledge about the repertoire of operas used in film. I do not even know the names of some of those people, as they were strangers whom I met purely at unexpected moments and I have not had, and probably will not have, the chance to see them again after my first encounters with them. Those stranger informants include the woman who was sitting next to me on my flight to the IMS conference in Rome in 2012, who first informed me of the use of "Casta diva" in Phyllida Lloyd's film *The Iron Lady* (2011). Another unnamable informant is the nurse whom I met in Portsmouth in the UK, in 2006 when I went to an emergency room for urgent treatment for a rash: she asked me what brought me to Portsmouth and when I answered that it was my conference presentation about the use of opera excerpts in Wong Kar Wai's film *2046*, her eyes sparkled for a couple of seconds and said, "Oh, I heard opera in another film": it was "Nessun dorma" in Phil Alden Robinson's film *The Sum of All Fears* (2002).

Last but not least, my special thanks go to Tamino and Gustav, my four-legged children—a schnauzer and a cocker spaniel; an opera character and an opera conductor. Even their mere existence and presence have given me the greatest support, imbuing me with iron strength and heavenly consolation—heavenly, indeed, for a dog is God's retrograde (but I don't mean it in the context of Christianity). I dedicate *Opera as Soundtrack* to Tamino and Gustav.

Prologue: Tracing Opera as Soundtrack

It may sound far-fetched to compare a dramatic talkie with opera, but there is something in common.

(Alfred Hitchcock)[1]

Opera is full of vengeance, death, excess, obsession, and violence. Because my film *Oldboy* is already full of such operatic traits, using opera on its soundtrack would be redundant. In a way, *Oldboy is* an opera.

(Chan-wook Park)[2]

What happened to opera as an institution is that it transformed itself into film, that film is, or was, our opera.

(Stanley Cavell)[3]

Marc Forster's recent James Bond film *Quantum of Solace* (2008) contains an interesting opera scene, or an "opera visit," to borrow Marcia Citron's expression.[4] The setting is an outdoor performance of Puccini's *Tosca* at Lake Constance in Austria. The members of Quantum, a terrorist organization, are meeting there, sitting scattered in the auditorium and communicating with each other through a wireless network and earphones. By stealing one of their earpieces, James Bond has gained access to Quantum's meeting and announces through their network, "Can I offer an opinion? I really think you people should find a better place to meet." Finding out their meeting has been infiltrated, Quantum members leave the auditorium one by one, and Mr. White, the leader of Quantum, whispers to the woman sitting next to him, "Well, *Tosca* isn't for everyone," and she nods.

Obviously, *Tosca* is not for everyone, at least not for Joseph Kerman:

---

[1]   Quoted in David Schroeder, *Cinema's Illusions, Opera's Allure: The Operatic Impulse in Film* (New York: Continuum, 2002), p. 3.

[2]   Chan-wook Park, personal e-mail to me dated August 23, 2002; translation mine. He did use opera excerpts for the first time in his most recent film *Stoker* (2013), starring Nicole Kidman, Mia Wasikowska, and Matthew Goode. For more details about this film and Park's notion of using opera in cinematic death, see Chapter 2 and the Epilogue.

[3]   Stanley Cavell, *A Pitch of Philosophy* (Cambridge, MA: Harvard University Press, 1984), p. 136.

[4]   Marcia J. Citron, "The Operatics of Detachment: *Tosca* in the James Bond Film *Quantum of Solace*," *19th-Century Music* 34, no. 3 (2011): 317.

Tosca, that shabby little shocker, is no doubt admired nowadays mostly in the gallery. In the parterre it is agreed that *Turandot* is Puccini's finest work. But if *Turandot* is more suave than *Tosca* musically, dramatically it is a good deal more depraved ...[5]

In the revised edition of his book *Opera as Drama*, published thirty-two years after the original, Kerman modified his initial assessment of *Tosca*, admitting that "it was silly to have written about *Tosca* as though it were, indeed, a chain-saw movie."[6] However, Kerman's association of *Tosca* and *Turandot* with popular cultural entertainment was prophetic, for these two operas have become among the most frequently used operas on film soundtracks.[7] Because of its frequent appearance in film and reinforced by the Three Tenors' stadium concerts, "Nessun Dorma" from *Turandot* gained the status of a pop song; and in the United Kingdom, it is officially classified as pop music.[8] Its appearance as soundtrack encompasses diverse genres of film, ranging from war film (e.g., *The Killing Fields*, 1984) and romance (e.g., *New York Stories*, 1989) to science-fiction film (e.g., *The Island*, 2005), thrillers (e.g., *The Sum of All Fears*, 2002), and serial-killer film (e.g., the lesser-known *Boxing Helena* [1993]).[9] It isn't only Puccini's operas that have featured so heavily in film soundtracks, but also many others,

[5]   Joseph Kerman, *Opera as Drama*, new and revised ed. (Berkeley: University of California Press, 1988), p. 205.

[6]   Ibid., p. xii.

[7]   Based on the information at www.bohemianopera.com/classicmovhome.htm, a website about the use of classical music in film (accessed 14 September 2006). This website has been discontinued.

[8]   The origin of the stadium concert of the three tenors, Luciano Pavarotti, Plácido Domingo, and José Carreras, was at the football World Cup in Rome in 1990. The three tenors' concert was repeated in the next World Cup, which took place in Los Angeles in 1994. For the discussion of "Nessun Dorma" as a popera (pop-opera), see Leah Branstetter, "Angels and Arctic Monkeys: A Study of Pop-Opera Crossover" (MM thesis, University of Cincinnati, 2006). I served as Branstetter's thesis advisor.

[9]   The popularity of Puccini's "Nessun Dorma" is not limited to cinema but has been manifested in diverse domains of popular culture. For instance, it was a winning song for two singers in the television show *Britain's Got Talent*: Paul Potts in 2007 and Greg Pritchard in 2009, the latter of whom impressed the judges and the audience with his castrato-like rendition in falsetto voice. For their YouTubes clips, see www.youtube.com/watch?v=1k08yxu57NA&NR=1 (accessed 22 May 2012) and www.youtube.com/watch?v=MuIX3JYq_Z4 (accessed 22 May 2012). The popular status of Puccini's aria was further amplified by numerous pop celebrity singers' rendition of it, including Aretha Franklin's at the 1998 Grammy Award Ceremony (for its YouTube clip, see www.youtube.com/watch?v=_6WW6TXPdPw (accessed 22 May 2012). "Nessun Dorma" was also used in the BBC's title sequence for coverage of the 1990 FIFA World Cup. See http://news.bbc.co.uk/sol/ukfs_sport/hi/av/newsid_4760000/newsid_4766500/nb_wm_4766509.stm (accessed 22 May 2012).

including those that Kerman counts as serious "dramas," such as Wagner's music dramas.[10] Commercial recognition of the increasing use of opera excerpts in film since the 1980s onwards is demonstrated by numerous opera soundtrack CDs: *The Movies Go to the Opera* (EMI, 1988), *My Favorite Opera in the Movies* (London, 1994), and *Opera Goes to the Movies: The Opera CD for the Opera Illiterate* (RAC, 2001), to name only a few. As an inherently multi-media art form—which requires not only music but also poetry (libretto) and such theatrical arts as lighting, staging, and acting—opera has multifarious "faces," according to Peter Symcox.[11] For Marjorie Garber, opera is already a crossover form, "the third thing," which is too elusive to fit into any single genre. She contends that opera performs a kind of "aesthetic transvestitism," embodying aesthetic vestments of other art forms.[12] It was in 1956 that Joseph Kerman examined opera as drama, and almost exactly two decades later, John Storey considered opera as popular culture.[13] In this book, I explore another "face" of opera—namely, opera as soundtrack. What I mean by soundtrack (or soundtrack music or film music) covers a wider scope than in some scholars' usage. For William H. Rosar, it refers to nondiegetic music newly composed for a particular film (i.e., original score), while such scholars as Marcia J. Citron and Michal Grover-Friedlander use the term for any nondiegetic music.[14] In this book, the soundtrack denotes any music accompanying a film, whether diegetic or nondiegetic, pre-existing or original.

Cinema's engagement with opera has a long history, dating back to the very beginning of the motion picture. In 1904, Georges Méliès produced *La Damnation du Docteur Faust*, a thirteen-minute silent film based on Gounod's opera. In May 1908 alone, Pathé, a French film company founded in 1896, produced scenes from numerous operas, including *Pagliacci, Otello, Die Meistersinger, La traviata, Lohengrin, Manon Lescaut, Rigoletto, Don Giovanni*, and *Lucia de Lammermoor*.[15] Pathé's opera films were not limited to popular titles but also included such lesser-known operas as Leo Fall's operetta *Die Dollarprinzessin*, Friedrich von Flotow's *Martha, oder Der Markt zu Richmond*, and Bedřich Smetana's *The Bartered Bride*.

---

[10] For the use of Wagner's music as soundtrack, see the filmography in *Wagner and Cinema*, ed. Jeongwon Joe and Sander L. Gilman (Bloomington: Indiana University Press, 2010), pp. 421–35.

[11] Peter Symcox, "The Four Faces of Opera," *Opera Quarterly* 3 (1985): 1–18.

[12] Marjorie Garber, *Vested Interests: Cross-Dressing and Cultural Anxiety* (New York: Harper Collins, 1993), p. 33.

[13] Kerman, *Opera as Drama*, and John Storey, "Expecting Rain: Opera as Popular Culture," in *Popular Culture and High Culture: An Analysis and Evaluation of Taste*, ed. Herbert J. Gans (New York: Basic Books, 1975).

[14] William H. Rosar, "Film Music—What's in a Name?" *The Journal of Film Music* 1 (2002): 15; Marcia J. Citron, *When Opera Meets Film* (Cambridge: Cambridge University Press, 2010), p. 166; and Michal Grover-Friedlander, *Vocal Apparitions: The Attraction of Opera to Cinema* (Princeton, NJ: Princeton University Press, 2005), p. 27.

[15] Pathé became the largest film company in the world before World War I.

These works can be called "opera shorts" or "opera singles," as they featured a single or a few opera arias, the length of which ranges from five to twenty minutes.

When Thomas Edison (1847–1931) declared in an interview with the *New York Times* in 1910 that "We'll be ready for the moving picture shows in a couple of months, but I'm not satisfied with that. I want to give grand opera,"[16] he was prophetic about the opera–cinema encounter in the American film industry. During the late 1920s and early 1930s, Warner Bros. produced abundant opera shorts using the Vitaphone technique, many of which were directed by Edwin B. Dupar.[17] Vitaphone was a sound film process used on features and during the brief period from 1926 to 1932, it was used for nearly 2,000 titles predominantly produced by Warner Bros.[18] Vitaphone was the most successful of the sound-on-disc processes before the emergence of the sound-on-film. The earlier sound technology did not allow the soundtrack to be printed on the actual film; instead, it was issued on a separate 12- to 16-inch phonograph record. The discs were separately played while the film was being projected. Many early talkies, including *The Jazz Singer* (1927), used the Vitaphone technique.

Jennifer Lynn Fleeger's dissertation "Opera, Jazz, and Hollywood's Conversion to Sound" is a pioneering study of Vitaphone's opera shorts and, to the best of my knowledge, the most extensive of existing studies.[19] Her two main criteria for defining "opera shorts" are the genre, whether a short is an excerpt from the work commonly classified as opera, and vocal quality, whether the performer in a short is an opera singer: thus, she includes the short of "The Star Spangled Banner" (Vitaphone Catalogue No. 451, produced in 1927) sung by Frances Alda (1879–1952), a New Zealand-born soprano, who studied with the legendary vocal pedagogue Mathilde Marchesi in Paris and appeared at many prestigious opera theaters, including the Metropolitan Opera, where her career reached its peak through her performances with such celebrated opera singers as Enrico Caruso. According to Fleeger's criteria, sixty-five opera shorts were released by Warner Bros., five by MGM, two by Fox, twp by Paramount, and one by De Forest during the 1926–32 period. While Warner used the Vitaphone technique—i.e., a sound-*on-disc* method—for opera shorts, the other studios used a sound-*on-film* method, such

---

[16]   Quoted in Schroeder, *Cinema's Illusions, Opera's Allure*, p. 3.

[17]   The name "Vitaphone" derives from the Latin and Greek words ("vita" and "phone"), respectively, for "living" and "sound." For recently reconstructed Vitaphone films, see www.picking.com/vitaphone42.html (accessed 22 May 2012).

[18]   Jennifer Lynn Fleeger, "Opera, Jazz, and Hollywood's Conversion to Sound" (PhD diss., University of Iowa, 2009), p. 49.

[19]   Fleeger, "Opera, Jazz, and Hollywood's Conversion to Sound." For early sound shorts, see also, Edwin M. Bradley's *The First Hollywood Sound Shorts, 1926–1931* (Jefferson, NC and London: McFarland, 2005); Roy Liebman's *Vitaphone Films: A Catalogue of the Features and Shorts* (Jefferson, NC and London: McFarland, 2003); and William Shaman, "The Operatic Vitaphone Shorts," *ARSC Journal* 22, no. 1 (Spring 1991): 35–94. ARSC is the acronym for Association for Recorded Sound Collections.

as Movietone and Phonofilm. But the Vitaphone technology was more appropriate for opera shorts because of its better sound quality for music as opposed to spoken dialogue.[20]

Giovanni Martinelli (1885–1969) was the singer who was the most frequently filmed in Vitaphone's opera shorts: in 15 shorts out of Warner Bros.' 65, including the ones in which he sings with other singers.[21] Famous for Martinelli's adamant refusal to wear Pagliacci's hat,[22] his "Vesti la giubba" from Leoncavallo's opera *Pagliacci* (Vitaphone Catalogue No. 198, produced in 1926) paved the way for the blossoming of opera shorts (Figure 0.1). It was one of the eight short films shown before the premier of Alan Crosland's film *Don Juan*, which was screened at the Warner Theater in New York City's Times Square on August 6, 1926. Produced by Warner Bros., Crosland's film was the first feature-length film with *synchronized* music created by the Vitaphone technique. But since it has no spoken dialogue, it is not a "talkie": Crosland's *The Jazz Singer* (1927) is the first talkie in the sense that it is the first film with *synchronized spoken dialogue*. Other short films shown at the premier of *Don Juan* include Marion Talley's "Caro nome" from Verdi's *Rigoletto* and the overture of Wagner's *Tannhäuser*, performed by the New York Philharmonic under the baton of Henry Hadley.

In some of the Vitaphone opera shorts, Martinelli performs with other singers; one is a collection from Friedrich von Flotow's nineteenth-century comic opera *Martha*—Lyonel's aria "Ach! So fromm, ach! So taut" and "Letzte Rose," a duet between Lyonel and Martha—in which Livia Marracci sings the role of the opera's

---

[20]   Fleeger, "Opera, Jazz, and Hollywood's Conversion to Sound," pp. 106–8. The complete list of the sixty-five Vitaphone opera shorts is provided as an appendix (see pp. 291–6). The majority of the Vitaphone opera shorts were filmed at the Manhattan Opera House; other recording locations were Vitaphone's Burbank studio and the Brooklyn studio (see pp. 111–13). Vitaphone catalogue numbers I cite in the Prologue are based on Fleeger's appendix.

[21]   *The Voice that Thrilled the World* is a documentary short about Martinelli, directed by Jean Negulesco in 1943. It is known that Martinelli's popularity was exceeded only by that of Enrico Caruso. In Mario Ranza's film *Serenade*, directed by Anthony Mann in 1956, the protagonist was modeled after Martinelli. The censorship memo dated January 23, 1952 regarding this film reads: "Also on this page, we establish the fact that Giovanni Martinelli is a singer for a concert given on November 11, 1918 at which Grace Moore is to make her initial appearance as a guest soloist. We hear him singing and subsequently see him introducing Grace Moore to the audience. Martinelli is, of course, still living and might take serious exception both to his personification and to the 'voice' which is ascribed to him. His permission must certainly be obtained. In obtaining his permission, we should remember that although her appearance with Martinelli is factual, it did not happen on November 11, 1918" (p. 3, USC Warner Bros. Archives, School of Cinema-Television, University of Southern California).

[22]   This short is available as a YouTube clip: www.youtube.com/watch?v=ad3fWkTJ U_E&feature=related (accessed 22 May 2012).

Figure 0.1   Giovanni Martinelli as Canio in "Vesti la giubba" from *Pagliacci* (1926), Vitaphone Production No. 198 directed by Edwin B. DuPar

heroine (Catalogue No. 932, produced in 1929). The following is a quote from the letter written by Martinelli's personal representative, dated November 9. 1929.

> Mr. Martinelli and myself saw today the reproduction of Martha made at your studio last Monday. We approve of same and we understand from your studio people that they also like it very much.
>
> Enclosed you will find bill for services rendered by Mr. Giovanni Martinelli in recording "Martha." This is in accordance with your letter of November 4th and my letter of October 28th.
>
> I also enclose bill for five hundred dollars ($500.00) which is in accordance with an agreement between Mr. A.C. Thomas, Mr. Rich and myself.[23]

Other operas employed in the Vitaphone opera shorts, the production records of which I examined at the USC Warner Bros. Archives, include Bizet's *Carmen* and *Pearl Fishers*, Donizetti's *Lucia di Lammermoor*, Gounod's *Faust* and *Romeo and Juliet*, Mascagni's *Cavalleria Rusticana*, Massenet's *Manon*, Offenbach's *Tales of Hoffman*, Ponchielli's *La Gioconda*, and Verdi's *Aida*, *Otello*, and *Rigoletto*. The opera singers who appear in more than one Vitaphone opera short, in addition to the ones mentioned above, include Anna Case, Giuseppe De Luca, Beniamino Gigli, Jeanne Gordon, Charles Hackett, Mary Lewis, and John Charles Thomas. While some of the Vitaphone opera shorts are identified with the aria title, such

---

[23]   Letter to Giovanni Martinelli, 1929, USC Warner Bros. Archives, School of Cinema-Television, University of Southern California.

as "Vesti la giubba" (Catalogue No. 198, in which Martinelli sings the aria) and "Céleste Aïda" (Catalogue No. 204, which also features Martinelli), the titles of some opera shorts only indicate the singer's name: for instance, "Mary Lewis" (Catalogue No. 432, in which she sings excerpts from *Romeo and Juliet* and *Tales of Hoffman*), "Giovanni Martinelli" (Catalogue No. 474, in which Martinelli, along with Jeanne Gordon, sings excerpts from *Carmen*), and "Beniamino Gigli, Tenor of The Metropolitan Opera" (Catalogue No. 517, in which Gigli sings excerpts from *La Gioconda*).[24] The Vitaphone opera shorts, as classified by Jennifer Fleeger, also include a parody of opera, such as "Between the Acts at the Opera" (Catalogue No. 349, produced in 1926), in which the two famous vaudeville singers known as "The Howard Brothers"—Willie and Eugene Howard—act out a story about the two friends who step out on stage between the acts of an opera, discuss a variety of silly topics in spoken dialogue, and sing operatic songs in a mocking way.[25] The increasing popularity of opera around the conversion era—that is, the conversion from silent film to talkies—can be considered to be a strong motivation for the production of the first sound film of an entire opera, *Pagliacci*, directed by Joe W. Coffman in 1931. The credits of Coffman's opera-film declare it as the "world's first sound picture of a grand opera."[26] Like a much-later opera-film, Ingmar Bergman's *Magic Flute* (1975), Coffman's 1931 *Pagliacci* was filmed as a stage production of Leoncavallo's opera. The singers who perform the main characters in this opera-film are Fernando Bertini (Canio), Alba Novella (Nedda), and Mario Valle (Tonio), and the orchestra employed is San Carlo Symphony Orchestra, conducted by Carlo Peroni.

Friedrich Feher's film *The Robber Symphony* (1937) is another manifestation of the opera–cinema encounter, as it was composed specifically for the cinematic screen. Its title is misleading because it is not a symphony but an opera in light musical style, similar to a musical, with some spoken dialogues.[27] What is known

---

[24]   For more comprehensive information about the titles, contents, and other aspects of Vitaphone opera shorts, see the Appendix of Jennifer Fleeger's dissertation, "Opera, Jazz, and Hollywood's Conversion to Sound," pp. 291–6.

[25]   This short is available as a YouTube clip: www.youtube.com/watch?v=6V0uHdgQSpk (accessed 22 May 2012).

[26]   Ken Wlaschin, *Encyclopedia of Opera on Screen: A Guide to More Than 100 Years of Opera Films, Videos, and DVDs* (New Haven, CT: Yale University Press, 2004), p. 526.

[27]   Alexander Thomas Simpson, Jr., "Opera on Film: A Study of the History and the Aesthetic Principles and Conflicts of a Hybrid Genre" (PhD diss., University of Kentucky, 1990), pp. 21–2. If one includes operas composed for TV screens, examples are abundant, including Gian Carlo Menotti's *Amahl and the Night Visitors* (NBC, 1951) and *Labyrinth* (NBC, 1963), Bohuslav Martinů's *What Men Live By* (NBC 1953) and *The Marriage* (NBC 1953), Lukas Foss's *Griffelkin* (NBC, 1955), Arthur Benjamin's *Mañana* (BBC 1956), Benjamin Britten's *Owen Wingrave* (BBC, 1971), Stravinsky's *The Flood* (CBS, 1962), and John Eaton's *Myshkin* (1972). One of the best studies of television opera is Jennifer Barnes, *Television Opera: The Fall of Opera Commissioned for Television* (Oxford: The Boydell Press, 2003).

as "film operettas"—that is, operettas specially composed for film during the silent era—also exemplifies opera's engagement with cinema. Although its circulation was not wide, this genre served as a mediation between live opera and film and also as a transition from silent film to talkies. In his interview with Warren Sherk in 1987, Hans J. Salter (1896–1994)[28] described the film operetta that he conducted in Berlin in 1922 as follows:

> It was silent film. Only at certain spots in the action they stopped, they faced the audience, and started to sing. And this was, in my opinion, the first attempt of a sound film. I don't remember anything like it anywhere else. So in order to create the illusion of these people on the screen singing, there were four singers standing in the pit before me and after maybe a two-bar introduction, they started to sing. The melodic line plus the lyric ran at the bottom of the film, moving from left to right. When they reached about the middle of the screen, there was a bar and at that point they are supposed to be in sync with the character in the film. So by creating the synchronization, the conductor could create the illusion that these people were actually singing until the song ended, and then it continued like any other silent film, just with titles.
>
> …
>
> And the quality of the orchestras was very different. In some of these movie houses they had good-sized orchestras, twenty-eight, thirty, thirty-two men. In others there were only a quartet or just violin and piano. We played only for one or two days in one movie house, then we had to travel to the next one. So I had to go to these houses ahead of time and rehearse the existing orchestra and then my singers just came to the performances. There were three or four performances every day. And this lasted for the whole summer of 1922. And the pay was phenomenal! I think I made in one week more than I made in a whole month conducting operettas.[29]

In addition to "opera shorts" (or "opera singles") and film operettas, many full-length silent films were based on operas: Bizet's *Carmen* alone inspired more than

---

[28] Salter was an American film composer who studied at the Vienna Academy of Music and took private lessons with such composers as Alban Berg and Franz Schreker. Salter composed mainly for Universal, most famously for horror and science-fiction films. His most celebrated scores include *The Wolf Man* (1941), *Creature from the Black Lagoon* (1954), and *The Incredible Shrinking Man* (1957). Salter was nominated for a number of Academy Awards.

[29] Hans J. Salter, an interview with Warren Sherk, an archivist and music specialist at the Margaret Herrick Library of the Academy of Motion Pictures Arts and Sciences, typewritten manuscript, pp. 13–14. The manuscript is housed at the Margaret Herrick Library.

30 silent films, including Cecil B. DeMille's *Carmen* (1915), Charlie Chaplin's *Burlesque on Carmen* (1915), and Ernst Lubitsch's *Gypsy Blood* (1918).

The popularity of *Carmen* continued during the sound era, ranging from Otto Preminger's all-black-cast opera-film *Carmen Jones* (1954) to Robert Townsend's *Carmen: A Hip Hopera* (2001), starring Beyoncé as the title role.[30] Right after the success of Preminger's film, MGM attempted at another Carmen film with Ava Gardner and Arthur M. Loew Jr., a grandson on the maternal side of Adolph Zukor, the founder of Paramount Pictures. MGM asked George Cukor to direct the film, but MGM's plan was aborted mainly because of Loew Jr.'s skepticism about another Carmen film. His letter to Cukor, dated May 18, 1956, reads:

Dear Mr. Cukor:

I talked to my father and Dore about CARMEN and much as they like the idea of doing a picture with you and Ava in Spain, they felt that this story had been done too many times before to make it palatable at the box office again.

I explained your ideas on the production and that this would not be a hip-swinging CARMEN, but after checking with Howard Dietz and Reagan, in sales, they still came back with a turndown. I am sorry about this but I feel that I did everything possible to sell the idea. Hope we can come up with a property soon that will get the nod.[31]

Opera's attraction to cinema during the early stage of the motion picture was not limited to Western cultures. In China, for instance, the first dramatic feature films were films of Peking Opera performances. As Teri Silvio has shown, Chinese opera has served as "an ambivalent parent-figure" within the history of Chinese-languages cinema. The opera-film has demarcated several phases in Chinese cinema history and it has also been "a reviled object against which the Chinese cinema defines itself as modern." Furthermore, Silvio notes:

The dialect cinemas of Taiwan and Hong Kong were also inaugurated by the opera-film genre in the 1940s. And in the People's Republic of China during the Great Proletarian Cultural Revolution (1966–76), films of the twelve "model operas"—a genre that combined Peking Opera with Russian ballet and socialist heroic narratives—were among the few approved for public consumption, defining a generation's experience of the cinema.[32]

---

[30] One of the most recent and comprehensive studies on cinematic *Carmen* is Chris Perriam and Ann Davies, eds, *Carmen: From Silent Film to MTV* (New York: Rodopi, 2005).

[31] Arthur M. Loew Jr's letter to George Cukor, 1956, USC Warner Bros. Archives, School of Cinema-Television, University of Southern California.

[32] Teri Silvio, "Chinese Opera, Global Cinema, and the Ontology of the Person: Chen Kaige's *Farewll My Concubine*," in *Between Opera and Cinema*, ed. Jeongwon Joe and Rose M. Theresa (New York: Routledge, 2002), p. 177.

Some Peking Opera actors inspired Western film directors, the most famous case of which is Charlie Chaplin's fascination with Mei Lanfang (1894–1961), one of the most prominent Peking opera actors in the twentieth century. His role was exclusively *dan*—the female impersonator.[33] As it can be posited that the Wagnerian *Gesamtkunstwerk* anticipated cinematic art, although not without controversy and simplified arguments, we can claim that Peking Opera, too, contains some cinematic elements. In Peking Opera, there are two instrumental ensembles, whose functions are sharply differentiated from each other. *Wuchang* is an instrumental ensemble consisting of percussion instruments and its function is an onomatopoetic imitation of natural sounds, while *Wenchang* has a standard role as an instrumental ensemble, accompanying songs and dances. Considering its peculiar non-musical function, *Wuchang* can be regarded as a prototypical pre-cinematic sound-effects system.

In Japan, too, traditional theatrical genres, such as Kabuki, Noh, and Bunraku, strongly imposed their artistic conventions on early Japanese cinema during the first decade of the twentieth century, and as a result, the development of cinematic idioms and techniques were considerably delayed. As Keiko McDonald has indicated, the first attempt to make a film dates back to the summer of 1897, and the very first cinematic attempt was the filming of two Kabuki *shosagoto* (dance) plays. This film was a failed attempt and a successful first Kabuki-film was produced near the end of the same year.[34] Film directors of early Japanese cinema adopted many elements of Kabuki, including such an antiquarian Kabuki tradition as *onnagata*—the female impersonator (Figure 0.2). They employed not

Figure 0.2   Kazuo Hasegawa as the *onnagata* character Yukinojo Nakamura in Kon Ichikawa's film *An Actor's Revenge* (1963)

---

[33]   Bertolt Brecht was among the Western artists inspired by Mei Lanfang. Peking Opera was an inspiration for Brecht's epic theater and alienation effect. See Bertolt Brecht, "Alienation Effects in Chinese Acting," in *Brecht on Theatre: The Development of an Aesthetic*, ed. and trans. John Willett (New York: Hill and Wang, 1964), pp. 91–100.

[34]   Keiko McDonald, *Japanese Classical Theater in Film* (London and Toronto: Associate University Presses, 1994), p. 23.

only Kabuki female impersonators but also new *onnagata* who were especially trained for the screen at acting schools. *Onnagata* played female roles not only in Kabuki-based films but also in those films that have modern settings: for instance, in Kiyomatsu Hosoyama's *Katyusha*, (a.k.a. *Fukkatsu*, 1914), based on Tolstoy's novel *Resurrection* (1899), multiple *onnagata*s appear in Western dress. During the early stage of the Japanese cinema, both filmmakers and the audience generally welcomed female impersonators, but there was also a strong resistance to utilizing the old theatrical tradition in the new realistic art form of film. The drama critic Kitaro Oka notes:

> I dislike Japanese films, especially those featuring female impersonators in wigs. The female character herself is realistic while her impersonator is a fake. A wig like those worn in the West might possibly pass, but the ones our impersonators use are made of artificial hair which only serves to emphasize the masquerade.[35]

In 1928 it became a studio "policy" to employ female actresses, but even after that, such studios as Nikkatsu Company—Japan's oldest major movie studio, founded in 1912—continued to hire *onnagata*. Nakkatsu's rival company Shochiku Company used real actresses from the very beginning of its foundation in 1920, but even that company occasionally employed female impersonators because of the continuing popularity of *onnagata* among the general audience.

As I will discuss in detail in Chapter 6, the attraction between opera and cinema has been mutual, as a number of prominent classical composers have shown a great interest in film scoring since the emergence of the motion picture. In a letter to Arnold Schoenberg dated May 18, 1930, Alban Berg wrote, "I have long been absolutely convinced of a great future for the talking film (also in connection with our music). Speaking of which, have you seen the latest Jannings film *The Blue Angel*? If not, be sure to go see it!" Exactly three and a half years later (November 18, 1933), Berg wrote another letter to Schoenberg in which he expressed his wish to compose for film: "I'm tremendously interested in the 'sound film' and I hope that my next work will be one. Perhaps it is possible [that] somewhere there is a fool who will want to make [one] with me, to be precise, as *I* want it."[36] Schoenberg, too, demonstrated his interest in film scoring in his orchestral piece *Accompaniment to a Cinematographic Scene* (Op. 34, 1930), written for three imagined, but never realized, cinematic images: danger, fear, and catastrophe.

George Antheil is another classical composer who wrote for film. The following excerpt from his interview with Lawrence Morton in 1950 touches on some issues concerning the intersection between opera and film scoring:

---

[35]   Quoted in ibid., p. 25.

[36]   Quoted in Melissa Ursula Dawn Goldsmith, "Alban Berg's Filmic Music: Intentions and Extensions of the Film Music Interlude in the Opera *Lulu*" (PhD diss., Louisiana State University, 2002), pp. 10–11.

Morton: When you are working simultaneously on opera and film music, Mr. Antheil, do you find yourself leading a kind of Jekyll and Hyde existence? Do you have to keep your operatic right hand ignorant of what your left hand is doing in the studio?

Antheil: No, not at all. I write all my music with my right hand, whether it's a film score or a symphony. Opera and film music, as a matter of fact, are very closely related, both being in the same category of theater music. They are far less separated from each other than they are from another large category— music for the concert hall. Of course all these categories intertwine, and their techniques and styles are transferable.

Morton: Are there any specific film techniques that you can carry over into the field of opera?

Antheil: Yes, there are several. One is the technique of underscoring. In the old operas the voice and the orchestra always go together, and even when they are musically "counterpointed" they are still, in a dramatic sense, presenting different aspects of the same pattern. This is not so in the films. The characters in a film drama never know what is going to happen to them, but the music always knows. Hence an orchestral commentary is possible, but it can comment on the action without necessarily illustrating it. Film music can go against the voice— that is, against the dialogue—and also against the action. I did this in my early operas, and I was interested to notice that Menotti does it in THE CONSUL, which I saw in New York recently. Much of Menotti's music is underscoring and consequently it sounds a great deal like film music.[37]

The kinship between opera and cinema can be found in several other aspects of their interaction. Silent film directors' attraction to opera divas is one of them. Geraldine Farrar (1882–1967) played the role of Carmen in Cecil B. DeMille's *Carmen* (Figure 0.3)[38] and she appeared in numerous silent films that are not based on opera: for instance, DeMille's *Temptation* (1915), a story about fictitious opera singer Renee Dupree's love for an ailing composer Julian (Pedro de Cordoba); another film directed by DeMille, *Joan the Woman* (1916), a liberal biopic of Joan of Arc; and *The Bonds That Tie* (1918) produced by Goldwyn Pictures Corporation,[39] a fund-raising short produced to promote the selling of the United

---

[37]   George Antheil, "An Interview with George Antheil," *Film Music Notes* 10, no. 2 (November–December 1950): 4–5.

[38]   As an exercise in preparation for *Carmen*, which was her first major picture, Farrar played in DeMille's film adaptation of a Spanish play, *Maria Rosa*.

[39]   Goldwyn Pictures Corporation was founded in 1917 and merged with Metro Pictures Corporation and Louis B. Mayer Pictures in 1924. The studio's official name became MGM (Metro-Goldwyn-Mayer) in 1925.

Figure 0.3   Geraldine Farrar as Carmen in Cecil B. DeMille's *Carmen* (1915)

States Fourth Liberty Bond during World War I, in which Farrar plays the role of Miss Columbia, the winner at a beauty pageant. In her autobiography, Farrar expressed how she enjoyed her collaboration with DeMille: he "understood my enthusiasm and left me free to express natural impulses wherever my feeling prompted them." And DeMille, too, highly praised the diva's talent in acting.[40] However, Farrar's *reversed* "importation of movie technique into the high art of opera" became a problem for some opera conservatives, as they complained about her "vulgar" acting style in her performance in *Carmen* during the 1916 season at the Met.[41]

Silent film's fascination with opera divas can be traced to the prominence of "spectacle" during the era of what Tom Gunning calls "cinema of attractions." The cinema of attractions was the stage in the development of cinematic style that preceded the narrative cinema, the transition to which occurred roughly around the 1910s. During the time of the cinema of attractions, spectacle was privileged over narrative elements, and the operatic spectacle—its extravagant theatrical ritual— provided a strong inspiration for the cinema of attraction.[42] The operatic spectacle includes the vocal spectacle; that is, the excessive vocality—an irony considering that silent films do not have any voice. Michal Grover-Friedlander provides one of the explanations for this irony when she draws an analogy between silent

---

[40]   Quoted in Susan J. Leonardi and Rebecca A. Pope, "Divas Do the Movies," in *The Diva's Mouth: Body, Voice, Prima Donna Politics* (New Brunswick, NJ: Rutgers University Press, 1996), p. 175.

[41]   Ibid., p. 176.

[42]   For the concept of the cinema of attractions, see Tom Gunning, "The Cinema of Attractions: Early Film, Its Spectator and the Avant-Garde," in *Early Film*, ed. Thomas Elsaesser and Adam Barker (London: British Film Institute, 1989).

film's "quest for the voice" and opera's aspiration for transcending the voice.[43] Pier Paolo Passolini's film *Medea* (1969) serves as an intriguing dramatization of Grover-Friedlander's argument. In this film, Maria Callas plays a non-singing role as Medea, but one still hears her operatic voice through her powerful visual presence—a kind of "surrogate voice," according to David Schroeder,[44] or an instance of "I Hear You with My Eyes" for Slavoj Žižek.[45]

Cinema's engagement with opera singers was not limited to female divas. Enrico Caruso (1873–1921), "the world's first blockbuster recording artist,"[46] is famous for his strong engagement with cinema. In 1911, he appeared in Thomas Edison's experimental "opera short" as Edgardo in Donizetti's *Lucia di Lammermoor*, and in two commercial silent films directed by Edward José, *My Cousin* (1918) and *The Splendid Romance* (1919), both of which were produced by Paramount.[47] Giovanni Martinelli, as discussed above, was the most popular operatic icon in film during the conversion period, and his popularity is much indebted to Enrico Caruso, who, through Victor's Red Seal Records, had become the most prominent opera star recognized in the domain of popular culture. Since Caruso, who died in 1921, did not survive the birth of the sound film, his legendary voice remained a disembodied entity except in live theater and Edison's experimental opera short mentioned above: people heard his voice on phonograph without seeing his body and they saw his body in the silent films that featured him without hearing his voice. It was in Vitaphone's opera shorts that people first experienced the marvelous operatic voice synchronized with the singer's body. Considering Martinelli's status as Caruso's scion—Caruso himself called

---

[43]   Michal Grover-Friedlander, "*Phantom of the Opera*: The Lost Voice of Opera in Silent Film," *Cambridge Opera Journal* 11, no. 2 (July 1999): 179–92.

[44]   David Schroeder, "Surrogate Voice: Maria Callas as Medea," in *Cinema's Illusions, Opera's Allure*, pp. 296–306.

[45]   Slavoj Žižek, "'I Hear You with My Eyes'; or The Invisible Master," in Renata Salecl and Slavoj Žižek, eds, *Gaze and Voice as Love Objects* (Durham, NC: Duke University Press, 1996).

[46]   Charalampos Goyios, "Living Life as an Opera Lover: On the Uses of Opera as Musical Accompaniment in Woody Allen's *Match Point*," *Senses of Cinema* 40, 2006. http://archive.sensesofcinema.com/contents/06/40/match-point.html (accessed August 19, 2010).

[47]   Caruso's second son, Enrico Caruso, Jr., too, had a career as a singer and actor. He played the title role in *El cantante de Napoles* (1935), directed by Howard Bretherton and Moreno Cuyar and produced by Warner Bros. The soundtrack of this film was consulted for Warner's later film *Serenade* (1956), starring Mario Lanza. The letter from Warner Bros.'s representative, dated January 31, 1955, reads: "In 1934 Warner Bros. or Vitaphone made a picture entitled "SINGER OF NAPLES". This title may have been changed. I believe it starred Enrico Caruso Jr. I am unable to locate a Cue Sheet out here to cover this picture. Will you please check and if you have one please send me a copy. This is in connection with the forthcoming pictre [sic] SERENADE." (USC Warner Bros. Archives, School of Cinema-Television, University of Southern California.)

Martinelli his crown prince[48]—one can claim that through his Vitaphone opera shorts Martinelli satisfied what the public had wished for Caruso.

Cinema's attraction to opera stars was reversed when screen actresses were imported to the domain of opera-films during the silent era. In Ugo Falena's *Tristano e Isotta* (1911), for instance, Francesca Bertini (1892–1985), who was one of the most celebrated silent film stars in the first quarter of the twentieth century, played Isolde. Bertini's popularity continued during the sound era. After the end of World War II, the Fox Film Corporation offered a contract to her but she declined. She made her last appearance in Bernardo Bertolucci's *Novecento* (1976), a film about the rise of fascism in Italy and the peasants' reaction, which opens with the announcement of Verdi's death. Although screen actresses were welcomed to the realm of opera in the movie theater, the operatic stage was not friendly to screen celebrities. Jeanette MacDonald (1903–65) provides an interesting example. While MacDonald was filming *Maytime* (1937), a picture that had more operatic music than any Hollywood movie before it, Edward Johnson, who was the general manager of the Metropolitan Opera House at that time, was considering a contract for her. But MacDonald's status as a movie star was an obstacle, because the Met's board of directors had no wish to compromise their institution's elitism through association with an icon of mass culture.[49]

Jeremy Tambling argues that cinema's frequent employment of opera divas can be read as cinema's aspiration to acquire the high cultural status of opera through the presence of opera divas on screen.[50] By importing Farrar, a singer from the Metropolitan Opera House, to Hollywood, cinema aspires "to the condition of the 'Met'" in order "to advance the dignity of the motion picture": in other words, to elevate the cultural status of cinema by associating it with "operatic glamour" and elitism.[51] It is true that opera in our time and especially in the United States is regarded as an elitist high art to the extent that Herbert Lindenberger described opera as a "bastion of high art,"[52] but its cultural status has been elusive and mutated ever since its birth at the cradle of the Florentine Camerata. As Leah Branstetter

---

[48]   Fleeger, "Opera, Jazz, and Hollywood's Conversion to Sound," p. 149.

[49]   Edward Baron Turk, "Deriding the Voice of Jeanette MacDonald: Notes on Psychoanalysis and the American Film Musical," in *Embodied Voices: Representing Female Vocality in Western Culture*, ed. Leslie C. Dunn and Nancy A. Jones (Cambridge: Cambridge University Press, 1997), pp. 104–5. Another reason for the Met's adamant rejection of MacDonald was her lack of European training. According to Turk, two decades after Rosa Ponselle's debut, no other American soprano had "successfully exorcised the Metropolitan's bias against singers who had not trained abroad" (p. 104).

[50]   Jeremy Tambling, "Film Aspiring to the Condition of Opera," in *Opera, Ideology and Film* (Basingstoke: Palgrave Macmillan, 1987), pp. 41–67.

[51]   Ibid., p. 17 and p. 25.

[52]   Herbert Lindenberger, "From Opera to Postmodernity: On Genre, Style, Institutions," in *Postmodern Genres*, ed. Marjorie Perloff (Norman: University of Oklahoma Press, 1989), p. 41.

has illuminated, from the beginning, opera has existed on two planes: as popular entertainment and as high art. She argues that "although the inventors of opera—coteries of intellectuals, musicians, and theorists who gathered in Florence in the last quarter of the sixteenth century—aspired to the lofty goal of moving souls as the ancient Greeks had done in their dramas, they were also influenced by the popular music of their time."[53] Claude V. Palisca notes that, for Vincenzo Galilei, popular musical styles such as the villanella were the ideal model for opera, and according to Howard Mayer Brown, the popular musical style of Neapolitan songs were an inspiration for Giulio Caccini's operatic aesthetics.[54] Susan McClary supports Palisca's and Brown's view on the hybrid quality of opera when it was born and nurtured in the Florentine Camerata by indicating that the Camerata's members based their operatic singing style on "the improvisatory practices of contemporary popular music."[55] Similarly, Joseph Horowitz has argued that opera was not "a fundamentally aristocratic diversion. But it was not fundamentally egalitarian, either. It was exclusive and it was democratic. It was elevated art and it was cheap popular entertainment."[56]

Since the films I examine in detail are mostly American (i.e., Hollywood) products, the mutability of opera's cultural status in this country requires special attention. In his seminal study, *Highbrow/Lowbrow: The Emergence of Cultural Hierarchy in America*, Lawrence W. Levine explores the path opera had undergone before it was settled as high art in America. His study elucidates that, during much of the nineteenth century, opera was a part of shared popular culture that was widely appreciated by different types of audiences.[57] What determines the cultural hierarchy of certain artistic genres is not those genres themselves, but the social process that governs and institutionalizes the cultural high and low. In John Storey's view, "Opera as 'high culture' is not a universal given, ... Rather, it is an historically specific category institutionalized."[58] From a sociological point of view, Paul DiMaggio argues that the establishment of the cultural status of a certain art

---

[53]   Branstetter, "Angels and Arctic Monkeys: A Study of Pop-Opera Crossover," p. 4.

[54]   Ibid. For the original sources, see Claude V. Palisca, "Vincenzo Galilei and Some Links between 'Pseudo-Monody' and Monody," *Musical Quarterly* 46, no. 3 (1960): 348; and Howard Mayer Brown, "The Geography of Florentine Monody: Caccini at Home and Abroad," *Early Music* 9, no. 2 (1981): 152.

[55]   Susan McClary, Afterword to Jacques Attali, *Noise: The Political Economy of Music*, trans. Fredric Jameson (Minneapolis: University of Minnesota Press, 1985), pp. 154–5; quoted in Branstetter, "Angels and Arctic Monkeys," p. 4.

[56]   Joseph Horowitz, *Classical Music in America: A History of Its Rise and Fall* (New York: W.W. Norton, 2005), p. 122; quoted in Branstetter, "Angels and Arctic Monkeys," p. 9.

[57]   Lawrence W. Levine, *Highbrow/Lowbrow: The Emergence of Cultural Hierarchy in America* (Cambridge, MA: Harvard University Press, 1988), pp. 6–7.

[58]   Storey, "Expecting Rain: Opera as Popular Culture," p. 36.

form is a social process,[59] and it is from the same perspective that Levine contends that the cultural status of a certain art is not fixed but unstable, mutating between high and low according to social and ideological situations. Like Shakespearean drama, Levine notes, "opera was an art form that was *simultaneously* popular and elite" in nineteenth-century America.[60]

As a number of scholars have indicated, the heterogeneity of opera audience, in terms of their class, and the nature of the concerts given by opera singers, which qualified opera as a popular entertainment, are best exemplified by American concerts of Jenny Lind, called "the Swedish Nightingale," in the early 1850s. During her US tour, she did not perform in operas but gave concerts, in which she sang a collection of opera arias often along with popular songs, including Stephen Foster's folk tunes. Her concerts were immensely successful, bringing a great fortune to P.T. Barnum, Lind's manager and the most prominent impresario in America at that time. Furthermore, her fandom endowed her with the status of one of the most renowned celebrities in mid-nineteenth-century America, to the extent that Jenny Lind souvenirs were sold in association with her concerts. Her status, then, was just like that of the pop celebrities of our time, such as the Beatles: "Lindomania" and "Beatlemania," indeed.[61] The mixture of opera arias with popular tunes in the same program was not limited to Jenny Lind's concerts but prevalent at that time on the American stage for opera performed by touring European opera companies, as they were normally not expected to perform an opera in its entirety but instead regularly included popular tunes in the same program. Furthermore, opera was often presented along with a variety of popular entertainment, such as farce, circus, and even dog show.[62] It was also common on the nineteenth-century American operatic stage that the performance of an opera was interspersed with a portion of a different opera. Among the examples that Lawrence Levine cites are the performance of Rossini's *La donna del lago* at the Italian Opera House in 1833, in which the overture to Spontini's *Fernand Cortez* was played between acts of Rossini's opera; and the mixture of Act IV of Verdi's *Rigoletto*, the final act of Vaccai's *Giulietta e Romeo*, and Acts II and

---

[59]   Paul DiMaggio, "Cultural Boundaries and Structural Change: The Extension of the High Culture Model to Theater, Opera, and the Dance, 1900–1940," in *Cultivating Differences: Symbolic Boundaries and the Making of Inequity*, ed. Michèle Lamont and Marcel Fournier (Chicago: University of Chicago Press, 1992), p. 21.

[60]   Levine, *Highbrow/Lowbrow*, p. 86.

[61]   For more detailed study of the social construction of Jenny Lind's cultural status, see George Biddlecombe's "The Construction of a Cultural Icon: The Case of Jenny Lind," in *Nineteenth-Century British Music Studies* 3, ed. Bennett Zon (Aldershot: Ashgate, 2003), pp. 45–64; and Lowell Gallagher, "Jenny Lind and the Voice of America," in *En Travesti: Women, Gender Subversion, Opera*, ed. Corinne E. Blackmer and Patricia Juliana Smith (New York: Columbia University, 1995), pp. 190–215.

[62]   Fleeger, "Opera, Jazz, and Hollywood's Conversion to Sound," p. 100.

IV of Verdi's *Il trovatore*.[63] This tradition, then, follows the eighteenth-century practice of *pasticcio*, an opera consisting of works by multiple composers, the most recent example of which is Jeremy Sams's *The Enchanted Island*, premiered by the Metropolitan Opera on December 11, 2011. With its libretto loosely based on Shakespeare's *The Tempest* and *A Midsummer Night's Dream*, Sams's opera includes the music by various Baroque composers, such as Handel, Rameau, and Vivaldi.

The cultural and artistic kinship between opera and popular music in nineteenth-century America was further solidified, as operatic arias were the basis for numerous popular songs, the lyrics of some of which were English translations of the original language, often Italian. As early as the 1790s, Levine indicates, the popular tune "Away with Melancholy" was derived from Papageno's entrance aria, "Der Vogelfänger bin ich ja," in Mozart's *The Magic Flute*. Popular opera arias, or, "opera singles," sung in English were ubiquitous: for instance, "La ci darem la mano" from *Don Giovanni*, Bellini's "Casta diva" from *Norma*, and "Di tanti palpiti" from Rossini's *Tancredi* (the aria was introduced to America and became popular before the opera was performed in its entirety).[64]

It can be argued, then, that the opera shorts produced during cinema's conversion period are a scion of the operatic tradition in nineteenth-century America in that they focus on individual arias, disregarding the integrity of an opera as it was composed (for instance, in the short titled "Mary Lewis"— Catalogue No. 432—Lewis sings excerpts from multiple operas) and that popular tunes were sung by opera stars as in the last five Vitaphone shorts of Martinelli (Catalogue Nos. 1162, 1174, 1213, 1226, and 1245) and many others.[65] Indicating that by 1929 the Vitaphone shorts were collectively called "Vitaphone Varieties," Jennifer Fleeger contends that this collective title was pertinent to the acknowledgement of the fragmentary and heterogeneous materials of the opera shorts.[66] The title is also reminiscent of the variety nature of Jenny Lind's concerts and other operatic performances by touring opera companies in America at that time. Viewed from a historical perspective, it is valid to claim that the operatic phenomenon of the mixture between high and low in nineteenth-century and early twentieth-century America was revived in the poperatic crossover that emerged in the late twentieth century, represented by the Three Tenors' stadium concerts and opera singers'

---

[63]   Levine, *Highbrow/Lowbrow*, p. 91.

[64]   Ibid., p. 96. For the score of "Away with Melancholy," see www.musicofyesterday. com/sheetmusic/A/Away_With_Melancholy-Mozart.php (accessed February 7, 2012), in which Mozart is credited as its composer. In a YouTube clip of this tune played by the piano, Mozart is identified as its composer, as the title of the YouTube clip is "Althea Plays Away With Melancholy by Mozart": see www.youtube.com/watch?v=6z9XEy7sXFk (accessed February 7, 2012).

[65]   Fleeger, "Opera, Jazz, and Hollywood's Conversion to Sound," p. 295.

[66]   Ibid., p. 97.

collaboration with pop singers, such as Pavarotti and Friends, and Monserrat Caballé and Freddie Mercury's Barcelona concerts.[67]

Ralph P. Locke argues that it was near the end of the nineteenth century that opera in the United States underwent the process of "sacralization"— that is, the process of converting cultural products into high art, according to Lawrence Levine.[68] The social and financial upper class in the US had been under development during the early nineteenth century, but it was not until the 1870s that its aristocratic status was firmly established. And promoting opera and alienating it from the middle class was one of the means by which the "new rich" (*nouveaux riches*) tried to solidify their privileged social and cultural status.[69] The foundation of the Metropolitan Opera Company in 1880 was an outcome: as the "old" elites who ruled the Academy of Music were reluctant to admit the *nouveaux riches* in New York and refused to build more private boxes in the Academy's opera house to accommodate the growing number of the newer members, the *nouveaux riches* founded a new opera company and built their own opera house at the junction of Broadway and 39th Street, which was replaced in 1966 by the current Metropolitan Opera House at Lincoln Center.[70] The first Met subscribers included members of such financially prominent families as the Morgan, Roosevelt, and Vanderbilt families. The Met's inaugural season, 1883–84, opened with Gounod's *Faust* on October 22, 1883. Gounod's opera was sung in Italian, and so were all other operas performed in the first season, including the ones originally written in other languages. The first season was largely a failure and all of the operas staged at the Met between 1884 and 1891 were performed in German, including the ones originally written in Italian. Lawrence Levine notes that in the first twenty years after the inaugural season, more than a third of the operas included in the

---

[67] Each of the three tenors collaborated with various pop artists. For example: Carerras and fado singer Dulce Pontes's "New 7 Wonders" (www.youtube.com/ watch?v=OJT0LrFSt2s), his collaboration with Sarah Brightman (www.youtube.com/ watch?v=y3VNZFCZlbM), Pavarotti and U2's "Miss Sarajevo" (www.youtube.com/watc h?v=wX6c5als1lk&feature=related), Pavarotti and Lucio Calla's "Caruso" (www.youtube. com/watch?v=tRGuFM4DR2Y), and Domingo's collaboration with Sarah Brightman (www.youtube.com/watch?v=aGwevGxYw4M&feature=related). East Village Opera Company should also be mentioned in the context of the popera, as it produced a number of popular cultural "redux" of operatic arias: for instance, "La donna è mobile" (www. youtube.com/watch?v=hxoNqFWQGqE) (all accessed on February 7, 2009).

[68] Ralph P. Locke, "Music Lovers, Patrons, and the 'Sacralization' of Culture in America," *19th-Century Music* 17, no. 2 (Fall 1993): 151–3. For "sacralization," see Levine, Chapter 2: "The Sacralization of Culture," in *Highbrow Lowbrow*, pp. 83–168.

[69] John Ogasapian and N. Lee Orr, *Music of the Gilded Age* (Westport, CT: Greenwood Press, 2007), p. 31.

[70] Rona M. Wilk, "'Vox populi': Popularization and Americanization of Opera, 1931– 1966" (PhD diss., New York University, 2006), p. 5. The Metropolitan Opera Company was founded in 1880 but their new opera house opened in 1883 (i.e., their inaugural season was 1883–84).

Met's programs were Wagner's work.[71] Jennifer Fleeger relates the Met's turning away from Italian opera to "elite New Yorker's resentment of the city's Italian immigrant explosion in the late nineteenth century."[72] Consequently, the Met's new focus contributed to the alienation of opera from the middle class and the sacralization of opera's cultural status, the latter of which was complete, according to Levine, by the beginning of the twentieth century.[73] As discussed earlier, the Met adamantly rejected Jeanette MacDonald when there was a consideration of employing her for its stage around the late 1930s. The Met's high-cultural elitism against MacDonald's popular cultural association with cinema can better be explained in the historical context of the solidification of opera's sacralized status at the beginning of the twentieth century.[74]

In spite of opera's high-cultural arrogance of keeping a distance from cinema, many opera houses were converted into movie theaters around World War I,[75] and movies were often shown at opera houses as late as the 1960s. The following is a quote from Milton Goldstein's letter to Alfred Hitchcock, dated February 8, 1961, about the screening of *Psycho* in Latin America.

> The first engagement of PSYCHO in the Latin American territory took place in the Opera Theatre, Mar del Plate, Argentina, February 6, and I am most happy to be able to quote below the cable that was received from our manager in Argentina in regard to this opening:
> "PSYCHO OPENED MONDAY OPERA MPLATA BREAKING ALL HOUSE RECORDS FOR ANY PICTURE OF ANY COMPANY OUTGROSSING COMMANDMENTS AND TEMPEST AT SAME INCREASED ADMISSION FIFTY PESOS AND TAKING 131341 PESOS WITH THOUSANDS TICKET BUYERS TURNED AWAY STOP PUBLIC REACTION EXCITING AND IMPRESSIVE STOP EXPLOITATION POLICY NOT LETTING IN AFTER START WORKED PERFECTLY STOP HITCHCOCK AND PSYCHO IS TALK OF THE TOWN IN MPLATA FOR FIRST TIME IN HISTORY WE SELLING TICKETS IN ADVANCE WITH CROWDS LINING UP CONGRATULATIONS AND REGARDS."[76]

---

[71] Levine, *Highbrow/Lowbrow*, p. 220.

[72] Fleeger, "Opera, Jazz, and Hollywood's Conversion to Sound," p. 103.

[73] Levine, *Highbrow/Lowbrow*, pp. 100–101.

[74] In light of Levine's theory of the sacralization of culture, the Mother's Day special concert at the Met in 1980, where Plácido Domingo sang a duet, "Perhaps Love," with the country singer John Denver, is indeed an intriguing event, which can signify another stage in the mutation of opera's cultural status—de-sacralization of opera, perhaps. The "Perhaps Love" concert is available as a YouTube clip: see www.youtube.com/watch?v=0TMAGYK dnqM&feature=related (accessed March 15, 2011).

[75] Branstetter, "Angels and Arctic Monkeys: A Study of Pop-Opera Crossover," p. 33.

[76] Milton Goldstein's letter, 1961, USC Warner Bros. Archives, School of Cinema-Television, University of Southern California.

Hitchcock was immensely concerned with soundtrack music and exceptionally meticulous about the instructions for the synchronization between visuals and music. The following are some of his instructions for *Vertigo*, included in the production document entitled, "Additional Music Notes," dated February 4, 1958:

> Reel 1:
> Midge's Apartment. An important factor in the contrast between the dramatic music over the Roof-tops and the soft totally different quality of the background music in Midge's Apartment. Remember that the Roof-tops is background music and Midge's Apartment music is coming from the phonograph and is, therefore, quite small and reduced in volume: It is small, concentrated music coming out of a box.
>
> Reel 6:
> The car ride from Exterior Brocklebank down to Exterior Scottie's Apartment. This music should start off quite dramatically and, by degree, get more comic— developing when Scottie starts to throw up this hands.
>
> Reel 14:
> We should not have crescendo music in the Tower so that we have to take the music down in order to hear the dialogue.[77]

Another piece of evidence that shows Hitchcock's strong interest in the function of music is Frank Caffey's letter dated May 10, 1957. Hitchcock saw J.M. Barrie's play *Mary Rose* at the Haymarket Theatre in London in April 1920, and he wanted to use the incidental music he heard in the play as a guide for Bernard Herrmann for his film scoring for *Vertigo*, the working title of which at that time was *From Amongst the Dead*.

> In April 1920 at the Haymarket Theatre in London, J.M. Barrie's play "Mary Rose" was presented and in the play there was used very effectively a background sound effect, probably a record offstage, or eerie music, angels singing and low moaning wind. The music was written and conducted by Norman O'Neill and the portion that we will be interested in was probably the background music for a scene in the second act that took place on a small island. Mr. Hitchcock is most anxious to obtain a recording of this. The original if possible, to be used for a guide to the composer here for his new picture FROM AMONGST THE DEAD.[78]

---

[77] "Additional Music Notes," 1958, *Vertigo* music file in the Alfred Hitchcock Papers, Margaret Herrick Library of the Academy of Motion Picture Arts and Sciences.

[78] Frank Caffey's letter, 1957, *Vertigo* music file in the Alfred Hitchcock Papers, Margaret Herrick Library of the Academy of Motion Picture Arts and Sciences.

The first epigraph of this Prologue testifies to Hitchcock's recognition of a strong affinity between opera and film: "It may sound far-fetched to compare a dramatic talkie with opera, but there is something in common."[79] Bernard Herrmann's score for *Vertigo* is replete with allusions to Wagner's operas (especially, Herrmann's nondiegetic music that accompanies the "Beauty Parlor" scene is a strong evocation of the Prelude to the second act of *Tristan und Isolde*). Furthermore, it seems that Hitchcock did consider using Wagner's music in *Vertigo*, as suggested by an intriguing memo concerning a San Francisco Opera performance of *Die Walkuere* (*sic*).[80] Hitchcock did not employ any opera excerpt in any of his most popular films, but in his earlier and lesser-known film *Murder!* (1930) the prelude to Wagner's *Tristan und Isolde* is used as a soundtrack to one of the key moments in the film, the "Mirror Scene." This film is notable for the extensive use of opera—almost five minutes—and remains one of the earliest talkies that employed operatic music prominently. In so doing, Hitchcock's 1930 thriller paved the way for the flourish of "opera as soundtrack," which culminated in Woody Allen's *Match Point* (2005)—culminated in the sense that its soundtrack consists *entirely* of opera excerpts with the exception of a cameo appearance of one piano waltz and a thirty-second excerpt from Andrew Lloyd Webber's Broadway musical *The Woman in White*.

Despite the long—more than a century—history of mutual attraction between opera and cinema, it was not until the late 1980s that critical inquiries into the intersection of opera and cinema began to emerge. Since then, the field of opera-cinema studies has been steadily growing, explored by scholars in various disciplines of the humanities and demonstrating a diversity of approaches. There were just a handful of book-length studies produced before the turn of the twenty-first century: Jeremy Tambling's pioneering monograph *Opera, Ideology and Film* (St. Martin, 1986); Alexander Thomas Simpson Jr.'s dissertation "Opera on Film: A Study of the History and the Aesthetic Principles and Conflicts of a Hybrid Genre" (1990); and Tambling's collection *A Night in at the Opera: Media Representations of Opera* (John Libby, 1994). Since the dawn of the new millennium, however, the growth of opera-cinema studies has been expedited. Among the major book-length studies are Marcia Citron's *Opera on Screen* (Yale University Press, 2000); David Levin's *Richard Wagner, Fritz Lang and the Niebelungen* (Princeton University Press, 2000); David Schroeder's *Cinema's Illusions, Opera's Allure* (Continuum, 2002); the essay collection *Between Opera and Cinema* (Routledge, 2002), which I co-edited with Rose M. Theresa; Michal Grover-Friedlander's *Vocal Apparitions: The Attraction of Cinema to Opera* (Princeton University Press, 2005); Jennifer Lynn Fleeger's dissertation, "Opera, Jazz, and Hollywood's Conversion to Sound"

---

[79]   Quoted in Schroeder, *Cinema's Illusions, Opera's Allure*, p. 3.
[80]   A memo in the "*Vertigo* Music File in the Alfred Hitchcock Papers," the Margaret Herrick Library of the Academy of Motion Picture Arts and Sciences. This memo is undated. See also Warren Sherk, "Looking for Richard: An Archival Search for Wagner ," in *Wagner and Cinema*, p. 413.

(2009); Marcia Citron's *When Opera Meets Film* (Cambridge University Press, 2010); and the collection *Wagner and Cinema* that I co-edited with Sander L. Gilman (Indiana University Press, 2010). Growing attention to the opera–cinema encounter is evident not only in scholarly disciplines but also in popular domains. An increasing number of journalistic essays are being published; for instance, Alex Ross's *New York Times* article entitled "Opera and Film" (1995), and his *New Yorker* article "The *Ring* and the *Rings*" on the relationship between Wagner's *Ring* cycle and Peter Jackson's *Lord of the Rings* series (2003).[81]

This book explores a particular aspect of the opera–cinema encounter: the use of opera excerpts on the soundtrack of blockbuster films intended for the general audience: that is, those films which are not blatantly artsy or esoteric but popular enough to be found in the Netflix collection.[82] In my case study analyses, I focus on films from the post-1970s time period. After the silent film era, opera had fallen out of favor in mainstream cinema, but, as many scholars have recognized, the time period my book focuses on is distinguished by the resurgence of opera excerpts on soundtracks of mainstream commercial titles.[83] Unlike pre-1970s talkies, in which opera is heard *mostly* in those films whose plots and/or characters highly motivate the employment of opera or operatic singing, such as the films starring Mario Lanza or Deanna Durbin,[84] opera excerpts are employed in diverse genres of film in the post-1970s, ranging from thriller, drama, comedy, and crime movies (for example, *The Shawshank Redemption* [1994], *Foul Play* [1978], *Death to Smoochy* [2002], and *The Departed* [2006]) to science-fiction, mystery, and horror films (such as *The Fifth Element* [1997], *Birth* [2004], and Werner Herzog's *Nosferatu* [1979]),

---

[81]   Alex Ross, "The *Ring* and the *Rings*—Wagner vs. Tolkien," *The New Yorker* 79, no. 40 (December 2003): 161–2 and 164–5; and "Opera and Film," *The New York Times*, March 12, 1995.

[82]   Later in the book, I sometimes call this type of blockbuster or Netflix films "mainstream" films.

[83]   For instance, see Tambling, *Opera, Ideology and Film*, p. 44; and Marc A. Weiner, "Why Does Hollywood Like Opera?" in *Between Opera and Cinema*, ed. Jeongwon Joe and Rose M. Theresa (New York: Routledge, 2002), p. 77.

[84]   In addition to Hitchcock's *Murder!* (1930) discussed earlier, the following are among the few examples of the pre-1970s talkies whose use of opera excerpts is not motivated by the film's plot or characters: Howard Hawks's gangster film *Scarface* (1932), in which the protagonist Tony whistles "Chi mi frena in tal momento" from Act II of Donizetti's *Lucia di Lammermoor* before he executes a murder; Franz Borzage's romantic drama *A Farewell to Arms* (1932), the last few sequences of which are accompanied by the orchestral arrangement of Wagner's "Liebestod"; and Fritz Lang's film noir *The Blue Gardenia* (1953), on the soundtrack of which we hear the prelude and the "Liebestod" from Wagner's *Tristan*. At the 2012 MaMI (Music and the Moving Image) conference at New York University, Candida Billie Mantica presented an illuminating paper which explored the use of the same aria, "Chi mi frena in tal momento" from Donizetti's *Lucia*, in two different gangster films separated by seventy-four years—Hawks's *Scarface* and Martin Scorcese's *The Departed* (2006).

and non-musician biopics, such as Michael Hoffman's *The Last Station* (2009), a biographical film of Leo Tolstoy, in which "Contessa, perdono" from *The Marriage of Figaro* is used as nondiegetic music in the scene where Tolstoy is apologetic to his wife—a reminiscence of the situation when this aria is sung in Mozart's opera. It is my observation that, since I embarked on this book, the phenomenon of opera-as-soundtrack has been continuously prominent and getting more prominent toward the time I was completing the book: one can think of the examples from the last quarter of 2011, such as Bellini's "Casta diva" in Phyllida Lloyd's *The Iron Lady*, a biopic about Margaret Thatcher; *Don Giovanni* excerpts in Guy Ritchie's *Sherlock Homes: A Game of Shadows*; and, most indelibly, the *Tristan* prelude in Lars von Trier's sci-fi *Melancholia*, the opening of which is an eight-minute music video of the *Tristan* prelude.[85]

I cannot emphasize enough that my book does not attempt to provide a definitive theory of the opera–cinema encounter but rather is intended to propose some possible ways of interpreting multifarious aspects of such an encounter— whether aesthetic, historical, ideological, technological, or others—drawing on recent theories related to opera studies and cinema studies. When analyzing individual films as case studies, my analyses are not drawn from the filmmakers' intentionality but my reading of the interplay of sonic and visual signifiers. In other words, I treat the films I examine in this book as a "text" rather than a "work," as the "readerly" rather than the "writerly."[86]

In the first chapter, "Opera as Geno-Song," I consider the increased use of opera excerpts on soundtracks since the 1970s within the historical context of film music. Given that vocal music containing lyrics is generally avoided in order to prevent potential interference with a film's dialogue,[87] the resurgence of opera excerpts as film music is a thought-provoking phenomenon. In this chapter I propose a possible reason for this resurgence by analyzing how opera excerpts are treated differently from other types of vocal music in films. Based on my case studies, I argue that the operatic voice tends to be represented as a "geno-song"—in other words, voice as a pure sound—with its verbal dimension undermined.[88] This treatment of the operatic voice also accounts for cinema's promotion of what David Levin calls "neo-lyricism," a recent trend in opera criticism, characterized by its "explicitly lyrical, intensely personal" and "logophobic" style, as represented by the works

---

[85]   *Melancholia* was first screened at the Cannes Film Festival on May 18, 2011, but its first release in the US was at the New York Film Festival on October 3, 2011.

[86]   Roland Barthes, "From Work to Text," in *Image, Music, Text*, trans. Stephen Heath (New York: Hill and Wang, 1977), pp. 155–64.

[87]   Claudia Gorbman, *Unheard Melodies: Narrative Film Music* (Bloomington: Indiana University Press, 1987), p. 27.

[88]   The quality of a "geno-song" is not limited to opera arias but "operatic" singing style, as I clarify in the Epilogue. See pp. 185–6.

of such scholars as Sam Abel, Wayne Koestenbaum, and Paul Robinson.[89] What I argue is not an absolute *consistency* but a *tendency*, based on an analysis of selected blockbuster titles, including Luc Besson's *The Fifth Element*, Frank Darabont's *The Shawshank Redemption*, and Wong Kar-Wai's *2046* (2004).

Chapter 2, "Opera in Cinematic Death," examines how opera contributes to the enhancement of the dramatic tension and climactic intensity of cinematic death, especially murders. To show opera's strong resonance with death, I draw on theories developed by such scholars as Michal Grover-Friedlander, Linda and Michael Hutcheon, and Slavoj Žižek. As these scholars have shown, opera's obsession with death was manifested at the very birth of the genre, as the earliest two extant operas, Jacopo Peri's *Euridice* (1600) and Claudio Monteverdi's *L'Orfeo* (1607), are both based on the Orphic myth that centers on Euridice's death. In the original myth, music—Orpheus's song—has the power of redeeming death, and it is the gaze that brings Euridice's life back to her second death. Engaging with existing studies that examine the use of opera in cinematic death—for instance, Marcia Citron's analysis of Francis Coppola's *Godfather: Part III* (1990), Claude Chabrol's *La Cérémonie* (1995), and Marc Foster's *007* film *Quantum of Solace* (2008)[90]— and analyzing the role of opera excerpts in Colin Higgins's *Foul Play* (1978) and Danny DeVito's *Death to Smoochy* (2002), both of which, to the best of my knowledge, have not yet drawn serious scholarly attention, this chapter serves as a prelude to the next chapter.

In Chapter 3, I focus on Woody Allen's *Match Point* and show how the use of opera in the climatic murder sequence of Allen's film is distinctive, compared to those in other films discussed in the previous chapter. For the analysis of Allen's murder scene, I have found particularly compelling Jerrold Levinson's and Claudia Gorbman's theories of the functions of film music, both of which focus on narratological issues.[91] In his article "Film Music and Narrative Agency," Jerrold Levinson theorizes "narrative" versus "additive" nondiegetic music; that is, the music that contributes to the storytelling of the film by providing additional information beyond the film's script versus the music that stands outside the story and its narration. According to Levinson, the narrative music comes from

---

[89]   David J. Levin, "Is There a Text in This Libido?" in *Between Opera and Cinema*, ed. Jeongwon Joe and Rose M. Theresa (New York: Routledge, 2002), p. 123.

[90]   Citron, "Operatic Style in Coppola's *Godfather Trilogy*" and "*Don Giovanni* and subjectivity in Claude Charbrol's *La Cérémonie*," in *When Opera Meets Film*, pp. 19–57 and 136–70; and "The Operatics of Detachment: *Tosca* in the James Bond Film *Quantum of Solace*," *19th-Century Music* 34, no. 3 (2011): 316–40. For *Godfather: Part III*, see also Lars Franke, "*The Godfather Part III*: Film, Opera, and the Generation of Meaning," in *Changing Tunes: The Use of Pre-existing Music in Film*, ed. by Phil Powrie and Robynn Stilwell (Aldershot, England, and Burlington, VT: Ashgate, 2006), 31–45.

[91]   Jerrold Levinson, "Film Music and Narrative Agency," in *Post-Theory: Reconstructing Film Studies*, ed. David Bordwell and Noël Carroll (Madison: University of Wisconsin Press, 1996), pp. 248–82; and Gorbman, *Unheard Melodies*.

"the cinematic narrator," who is a component of the fiction, residing on the same fictional plane of the film as a presenter of the story, but who is not automatically the same as the film's voiceover narrator, whereas the additive music is the voice of "the implied filmmaker," the inventor of the fiction and the discourse—"implied" because he or she should be distinguished from the actual film director.[92] Among the eleven nondiegetic musical cues in *Match Point*, the *Otello* excerpt, which accompanies the murder sequence, is the only one that does not use Caruso's recording. I argue that despite their apparent nondiegetic status, all of the Caruso recordings function as the voice of the cinematic narrator, originating from the internal fictional world of the film, while the *Otello* excerpt is an external voice, emanating from the implied filmmaker, for whom the film's story is acknowledged as fictional, as it is for the film viewer. In other words, the *Otello* excerpt belongs to the domain of filmmaking rather than the storytelling of the film.

Chapter 4, "Is Cinema's Anxiety Opera's Envy?" considers a recent trend in operatic theater, which exploits cinema's "castration anxiety"—that is, the separation of voice and body. I examine how the mediatized unity between voice and body of the cinematic apparatus has changed the embodied-ness of the operatic voice in live theatre. In light of the psychoanalytically oriented film theories that interpret cinema's castration anxiety as the origin of cinema's envy of a live medium where the voice is naturally embodied,[93] the voice–body separation in operatic theatre can be read as opera's *reversed* envy. I trace opera's envy of cinema's anxiety to cinema's ironic privileging of the voice/sound in spite of the seeming dominance of the visual in the cinematic medium, as Slavoj Žižek argues.[94] I support my argument by demonstrating a parallelism between what Žižek calls an "uncanny autonomization of the voice" in sound film[95] and "the

---

[92]   In his paper, "Realistic Song in the Movies," presented at the 2012 MaMI (Music and the Moving Image) conference, Peter Kivy provided a narratologically classified taxonomy of film music similar to that of Levinson's—ornamental song, embedded song, integrated song, and music-track song. Kivy's taxonomy is drawn on Edward T. Cone's study, "The World of Opera and Its Inhabitants," and developed from his earlier article, "Music in the Movies: A Philosophical Inquiry," in *Film Theory and Philosophy*, ed. Richard Allen and Murray Smith (Oxford: Oxford University Press, 1997), pp. 308–28; reprinted in *Music, Language, and Cognition* (Oxford: Oxford University Press, 2007), pp. 62–87. For Cone, see Robert P. Morgan, ed., *Music, A View from Delft: Selected Essays* (Chicago: University of Chicago Press, 1989), pp. 125–38.

[93]   For instance, Kaja Silverman's *Acoustic Mirror: The Female Voice in Psychoanalysis and Cinema* (Bloomington: Indiana University Press, 1988). Psychoanalytically oriented film theories have been criticized by such scholars as David Bordwell and Noël Carroll in part because such theories do not consider the audience and the spectatorship. But those theories are cogent for my argument in this essay, as I focus on "the apparatus" of cinema rather than its audience. See David Bordwell and Noël Carroll, eds, *Post-Theory: Reconstructing Film Studies* (Madison: University of Wisconsin Press, 1996).

[94]   Žižek, "I Hear You with My Eyes," pp. 90–128.

[95]   Ibid., p. 92.

uncanny aspects" of operatic performance: namely, the notion of the performer as a lifeless musical instrument, an automaton, animated by the force of music, as Carolyn Abbate argues in her book *In Search of Opera*.[96] The operas I examine in detail are Harrison Birtwistle's *The Mask of Orpheus* (1986), two works from Alexander Goehr's triptych—*Naboth's Vineyard* (1968), and *Sonata about Jerusalem* (1970)—and Philip Glass's *La Belle et la bête* (1994).

In Chapter 5, "Film Divas: The Problem and the Power of the Singing Women," I address gender issues in several different layers by examining the privileged status of operatic diva heroines in comparison to instrumentalist heroines in cinema. In the films I examine in this chapter, the performances of instrumentalist heroines are confined to domestic and private arenas, such as a recording studio or a practice room, whereas diva heroines are immune from such domestic restrictions. I contextualize this seemingly privileged status of diva heroines in the gendered biology of Western classical music, which has territorialized, if not stigmatized, vocal music as a feminine prerogative and which has demanded the embodied presentation of the female voice. On the surface, film divas are more privileged than instrumental heroines given the flamboyant display of their vocal virtuosity in public arenas. In light of the theories of the cinematic voice developed by such scholars as Kaja Silverman, Amy Lawrence, and Mary Ann Doane, however, the embodied representation of film divas' voice is problematic, for it endorses the cinematic tendency that places female characters in the inferior position in the diegetic hierarchy—inferior in the sense that the female voice is contained in diegetic interiority.[97] To put it in Amy Lawrence's words, this "strategy" is one that tries to confine the female voice to a "recessed area of the diegesis," positioning female characters as a "sign rather than as signifying subject."[98] Yet Britta Sjogren's recent study provides an alternative theoretical perspective from which one can approach the question of film divas' embodied voice. In her book, *Into the Vortex: Female Voice and Paradox in Film*, Sjogren challenges Silverman's theory, particularly its ontological and essentializing perspective, according to which the cinematic apparatus does not allow for any possibility for the articulation of female subjectivity.[99] By offering alternative readings of the four films chosen from Hollywood's classical period—the same period that Silverman's and Lawrence's studies focus on—Sjogren demonstrates how female

---

[96] Carolyn Abbate, *In Search of Opera* (Princeton, NJ: Princeton University Press, 2001), pp. 5–7.

[97] Silverman, *Acoustic Mirror*; Amy Lawrence, *Echo and Narcissus: Women's Voices in Classical Hollywood Cinema* (Berkeley: University of California Press, 1991); and Mary Ann Doane, *The Desire to Desire: The Woman's Film of the 1940s* (Bloomington: Indiana University Press, 1987) and "The Voice in Cinema: The Articulation of Body and Space," *Yale French Studes*, no. 60 (1980): 33–50.

[98] Lawrence, *Echo and Narcissus*, p. 149.

[99] Britta Sjogren, *Into the Vortex: Female Voice and Paradox in Film* (Urbana and Chicago: University of Illinois Press, 2006).

characters can enunciate their subjectivity and discourse through their voice-off, when viewed from the "vortexical" perspective that privileges the vertical (or spiral) rather than linear narrative structure and the aural- rather than vision-based interpretation of a film. Both Silverman's ontological and Sjogren's vortexical theories are illuminating for my inquiry into the embodied-ness of the film divas. The films discussed in this chapter include Frank Borzage's *I've Always Loved You* (1946), Ingmar Bergman's *Autumn Sonata* (1978), Joel Oliansky's *The Competition* (1980), Jean-Jacques Beineix's *Diva* (1981), Claude Sautet's 1992 film, *A Heart in Winter* (*Un Cœur en Hiver*), Claude Miller's *The Accompanist* (1992), and David Cronenberg's *M. Butterfly* (1993).

The final chapter, "Behind the Discourse on the Opera-Cinema Encounter," focuses on the tension between opera (and classical music in general) and film as expressed by composers and scholars, and contextualizes it in different positions regarding two major issues in current film music criticism. First, I discuss the controversy among film music composers and scholars concerning the original score vs. the compilation score, the latter of which includes pre-existing music, such as opera excerpts. I contextualize the artistic and scholarly skepticism about the compilation score in the modernist vs. postmodernist debate about originality and musical autonomy. The second issue I consider is the historical inaccuracy frequently addressed in musicological studies of the biopics about musicians, including opera singers and composers. Problematizing the polarity between hypercritical reactions to historical inaccuracy in film and the generous condoning of such inaccuracy in operas based on historical events or figures, I argue that these dualistic reactions reveal the modernists' disdain for a popular medium and mistrust of its consumers and filmmakers.

In his most recent book on opera, *Situating Opera: Period, Genre, Reception*, Herbert Lindenberger described opera studies as a disciplinary "orphan":

> It's ironic, isn't it, that whereas opera has been an ongoing institution for over
> 400 years, opera studies is in effect an orphan that cannot claim a natural home
> in any one of the existing humanities disciplines.[100]

The phenomenon of opera-as-soundtrack, then, further complicates the orphan-like status of opera studies because of its invitation and openness to more interdisciplinary inquiries. By William Rosar's standards, which I discuss in detail in the final chapter, this book might not be a musicological work, since, according to him, it cannot be musicology if it at the same time occupies a "site" or "space" outside musicology.[101] But I believe that "when opera studies meets film studies" (and other disciplines)—to paraphrase Marcia Citron's book title *When Opera*

---

        [100]   Herbert Lindenberger, *Situating Opera: Period, Genre, Reception* (Cambridge: Cambridge University Press, 2010), p. 264.
        [101]   William H. Rosar, "Film Studies in Musicology: Disciplinarity vs. Interdisciplinarity," *The Journal of Film Music* 2 (Winter 2009): 100.

Meets Film—the encounter between the two can provide more than each can offer for opera lovers, film lovers, and both, whether academic or not. Situating opera-as-soundtrack in the broader realm of film music, my conviction in the promising future of film music and film music studies is as strong as Wagner's faith in his music drama as the artwork of the future. Even if a soundtrack does not contain any music, as in Hitchcock's *The Birds* (except for one diegetic singing by young girls), the future of film music, both as an artistic field and a scholarly subject, would still be prosperous, for silence has been celebrated as an essential part of music even before and beyond John Cage. If "heard melodies are sweet, but those unheard melodies are sweeter" for John Keats, Thomas Mann expressed that "it was music's deepest desire not to be heard at all, not even seen, not even felt, but if that were possible, to be perceived and viewed in some intellectually pure fashion."[102] And film music, too, sonorously glorifies the sounds of silence, as Simon and Garfunkel sing on the soundtrack of *The Graduate* (1967): "And the sign said, 'The words of the prophets are written on subway walls / And tenement halls / And whisper'd in the sound of silence.'"

Unlike film, every sound is silent in such printed media as a book or a photograph, as it cannot convey the auditory sense: sound can only be verbally described or visually implied. The cover image of this book—a still from Jonathan Glazer's film *Birth* (2004)—impresses me as one of the best silent representations of opera as soundtrack: Anna (Nicole Kidman) is at the opera house, listening to the Prelude to the first act of Wagner's *Die Walküre*. It is the crucial moment of the film, in which the heroine Anna becomes convinced by the ten-year-old boy she has just left behind, who claims that he is the reincarnation of her dead husband, Sean. It is a legendary long take—2 minutes and 27 seconds—that is accompanied by Wagner's entire Prelude played by the unseen (i.e., voice-off) orchestra. Anna's gaze, like the face of the genderless figure in Edvard Munch's painting *The Scream* (1895), represents an instance of what Slavoj Žižek claims as "I Hear You with My Eyes."[103] And through Anna's gaze, we, the readers, hear the silent sound of opera as soundtrack.

---

[102]   For Keats, see his poem "Ode on a Grecian Urn"; for Mann, see *Doctor Faustus*, trans. John E. Woods (New York: A.A. Knopf, 1997), p. 68.

[103]   Žižek, "I Hear You with My Eyes."

Chapter 1
Opera as Geno-Song

There is a story which goes like this: In the middle of a battle there is a company of Italian soldiers in the trenches, and an Italian commander who issues the command "Soldiers, attack!" He cries out in a loud and clear voice to make himself heard in the midst of the tumult, but nothing happens, nobody moves. So the commander gets angry and shouts louder: "Soldiers, attack!" Still nobody moves. And since in jokes thing have to happen three times for something to stir, he yells even louder: "Soldiers, attack!" At which point there is a response, a tiny voice rising from the trenches, saying appreciatively "*Che bella voce!*" "What a beautiful voice!"

(Mladen Dolar)[1]

For many film music composers and scholars, Dimitri Tiomkin's title song, "Do Not Forsake Me O My Darling," in *High Noon* (1952) was an undesirable hit, since it fostered the pop-song score based on theme songs. Tiomkin's hit anticipated a major shift in film scoring that would come in the 1960s: a shift from the dominance of the classical symphonic score to vocal score of theme songs, represented by Henri Mancini's "Moon River" scored for *Breakfast at Tiffany's* (1961), the Beatles' songs in *A Hard Day's Night* (1964), and Simon and Garfunkel's soundtrack to *The Graduate* (1967). For its opponents, the pop-song score was a cardinal sin because it was primarily motivated by the film industry's commercial considerations and overlooked serious artistic problems.[2] The formal integrity of a song, for instance, makes it unsuitable for motivic changes required for such standard functions of film music as narrative signification and the synchronization of music and image. The strong emotional and narrative identity of a theme song was also a problem in that instead of *supporting* the story and mood of a film, the song *was* the story and mood.[3] Against the detractors of the theme score, Jeff Smith argues that theme songs can serve "all of the classical score's paradigmatic functions" and demonstrates that such functions are achieved less through purely musical qualities, as with the classical symphonic score, than through extra-musical allusions and associations evoked by the songs.[4] In this

---

[1]　Mladen Dolar, *A Voice and Nothing More* (Cambridge, MA: The MIT Press, 2006), p. 3.

[2]　See Jeff Smith, *The Sounds of Commerce: Marketing Popular Film Music* (New York: Columbia University Press, 1998), p. 163.

[3]　Ibid.

[4]　Ibid., pp. 155 and 184.

chapter, I discuss opera excerpts on soundtrack in the context of the vocal score, focusing on how opera is treated differently from other types of vocal music, which I consider a cinematic "tendency" rather than "consistency," based on the films I examine as case studies. Drawing on the theories of voice in general and the operatic voice in particular, I trace the differences to the peculiar quality of the operatic voice.

Although opera excerpts frequently accompanied silent films, their use dwindled with the early talkies, being largely limited to opera-themed movies. The resurgence of opera excerpts in compilation scores coincided with the shift from the hegemony of the classical symphonic score to the vocal theme score in the 1960s and continued after the classical symphonic score regained its popularity in the 1980s. Woody Allen's *Match Point* (2005) can be regarded as the culmination of this resurgence, as its soundtrack—sixteen musical cues—consists *entirely* of opera excerpts with the exception of a cameo appearance of one piano piece and one Broadway musical piece. According to a comprehensive online source that indexes classical music used in film,[5] Puccini excerpts were used in 21 talkies before 1960 and 104 films between 1960 and 2005. Verdi excerpts, too, are conspicuous by their increase over the same time frame: 43 films prior to 1960 versus 136 after. What draws our attention is that during the post-1960 period, opera is employed in those films intended for a general audience whose themes have little or nothing to do with musicians.

Even if theme songs can achieve the same functions as standard film music, as Jeff Smith demonstrates, it is true that the vocal soundtrack presents problems that the symphonic score does not; for instance, the potential for song lyrics to interfere with the film's dialogue. Claudia Gorbman notes that vocal music, be it diegetic or nondiegetic, requires "narrative to cede to spectacle" and that action usually freezes during a song. "Song lyrics," she continues, "threaten to offset the aesthetic balance between music and narrative cinematic representation."[6] Gorbman compares the function of theme songs to that of a chorus in ancient Greek drama in that a theme song often serves as a voiceover commentary on a character's action or emotional state without participating in the action. In Samuel Fuller's Western *Forty Guns* (1957), for instance, Jidge Carroll's "High Ridin' Woman" functions as a sung description of the heroine, Jessica Drummond (Barbara Stanwyck), riding across the countryside. Jeff Smith notes many other examples in which song lyrics function as a voiceover commentary.

When operatic songs are employed in film, their length is usually not as extensive as that of popular songs; yet their placement, often associated with crucial moments in the film, is prominent and powerful in spite of the excerpts' brevity. In Luc Besson's *The Fifth Element* (1997), for instance, an alien diva

[5]   www.bohemianopera.com/classicmovhome.htm (accessed March 27, 2006). This website has been discontinued.

[6]   Claudia Gorbman, *Unheard Melodies: Narrative Film Music* (Bloomington: Indiana University Press, 1987), p. 20.

performs an excerpt of Donizetti's *Lucia di Lammermoor* at the climax of the plot, when the "fifth element" is discovered. Unlike popular songs, opera excerpts usually do not function as a voiceover commentary through association with their text. In *The Fifth Element*, the verbal and narrative content of the Donizetti excerpt, Lucia's longing for Edgardo, does not reveal an apparent connection to Besson's scene in which it is heard. At the hermeneutic level, one might be able to extract narrative or emotive connections, but compared to popular songs, operatic numbers are more indirect and remote for such connections. A major obstacle to using opera arias as a voiceover commentary is the language, since the opera excerpts frequently used on soundtracks are predominantly sung in Italian. Then what could be the function of opera lyrics? Opera excerpts can support a certain mood and evoke properties commonly associated with opera, such as love, passion, death, gayness, and high culture. But how does the verbal content of a particular opera excerpt contribute to a film? I argue that the *specific* meaning of an opera excerpt *usually* does not have a referential function, although some films show a *general* thematic parallelism between the film narrative and the source opera(s).[7] In the celebrated opera scene of Jonathan Demme's *Philadelphia* (1993), Andrew Beckett (Tom Hanks) provides the narrative context of Umberto Giordano's aria "La mamma morta" to his attorney Joe Miller (Denzel Washington), but the locus of the effect and power of the aria resides not in its semantic meaning but in what opera evokes as a signifier of gayness and in opera's function as a phantasmagoria, as discussed by Marc A. Weiner.[8] Jeff Smith shows that in some films, the lyrics of popular songs are "immaterial to the narrative," as in the Beatles' *A Hard Day's Night*,[9] but the degree of immateriality is significantly higher in opera excerpts.

The opera scene in Frank Darabont's *The Shawshank Redemption* (1994) is illuminating in this context. Prisoner Andy Dufresne (Tim Robbins), the protagonist, picks up a recording of Mozart's *Marriage of Figaro* at the prison library and drops the needle. As the "Letter Duet" between the Countess and Susanna from Act III (sung by Edith Mathis and Gundula Janowitz) issues from

---

[7]   For instance, the heroine Alex Forrest (Glenn Close) of Adrian Lyne's *Fatal Attraction* (1987) is connected to Puccini's Madam Butterfly through the theme of an abandoned woman. Garry Marshall's *Pretty Woman* (1990) is another example. While watching a live performance of Verdi's *La traviata*, the film's heroine Vivian Ward (Julia Roberts) identifies herself with the operatic heroine Violetta because of the problem of their class—a courtesan and a prostitute—which is an obstacle for their love with upper-class men.

[8]   Marc A. Weiner, "Why Does Hollywood Like Opera?" in *Between Opera and Cinema*, ed. Jeongwon Joe and Rose M. Theresa (New York: Routledge, 2002), pp. 77–95. Weiner briefly mentions that in this scene Beckett identifies himself with the operatic heroine Maddalena, who sings this aria (p. 78), but the identificatory function of the aria is far weaker, if not totally ignorable, than the general role of opera as a signifier of gayness at the simplest level, and as phantasmagoria that serves to transcend the social differences between the two protagonists.

[9]   Smith, *The Sounds of Commerce*, p. 160.

the archaic speakers, the prisoners stand speechless and motionless, stunned by the beauty of the music.[10] In the middle of the camera's panning over the prisoners' faces, we hear the voiceover commentary of Andy's prison buddy, Red (Morgan Freeman).

> I have no idea to this day what those two Italian ladies were singing about. Truth is, I don't want to know—some things are best left unsaid ... It was like some beautiful bird flapped into our drab little cage and made those walls dissolve away. And for the briefest of moments every last man at Shawshank felt free.

Like the opera scene in *Philadelphia*, the "Letter Duet" impresses many viewers, whether musically informed or not, as the most powerful and memorable scene of the film. Yet there are only a handful of scholarly writings about this scene. In one of the few studies substantially dedicated to it, Mary Hunter asks why the music chosen for this poignant scene is opera, since opera is the most alien musical genre to the general filmgoers, especially in the United States. In addition to two reasons she provides that I will return to later, Hunter traces the power of the *Figaro* excerpt to the "meaningfulness" of the operatic aria. As a texted genre, opera sings about something definite and the onscreen listeners know that, although they cannot understand its meaning. Hunter locates the power of the opera excerpt in the paradoxical gap between the meaningfulness of the aria and the audience's— both the onscreen prison audience's and the film viewers'—inaccessibility to its meaning. She notes, "The relative meaninglessness (in eighteenth-century terms) of a symphony would presumably not have compelled the listeners' attention in the same way."[11] Slavoj Žižek's interpretation of the opera scene is similar to Hunter's. For him, what makes the opera scene "sublime" is the distance between the beauty of Mozart's duet and the prisoners' unawareness of its "trifling content"—trifling compared to the "divine" nature of Mozart's music, because the duet is about the Countess's mundane concerns about her unfaithful husband.[12] In Hunter's view, "a Beethoven symphony" would not produce the same effect as Mozart's "Letter Duet."[13] Then what would she say about the Choral Symphony, which has verbal

---

[10]   In Stephen King's novella *Rita Hayworth and Shawshank Redemption* (1982), on which the film is based, there is no reference to opera.

[11]   Mary Hunter, "Opera *In* Film: Sentiment and Wit, Feeling and Knowing," in Joe and Theresa (eds), *Between Opera and Cinema*, p. 98.

[12]   Slavoj Žižek, *The Fragile Absolute* (London and New York: Verso, 2000), p. 159.

[13]   Mary Hunter, "Opera *In* Film," p. 99. Focusing on the opera scene in *The Shawshank Redemption*, Daniel Chua explores the role of technology—i.e., reproduction, as Mozart's duet is transmitted from the loudspeakers—in conveying and transforming the redemptive power of music, the power of evoking freedom. Chua's comparison of Beethoven's symphonies to Mozart's duet is different from Hunter's, as he argues that it is the technology that endowed a "seemingly trivial aria" of Mozart with the "communal power of a Beethoven symphony." See Daniel K.L. Chua, "Listening to the Self: *The*

content like opera?[14] Wagner's comments on this symphony may seem extraneous, but they shed light on the issue I explore in this chapter.

In his famous essay on Beethoven, Wagner describes the interplay between Schiller's text and Beethoven's music as follows:

> It is not the meaning of the words that really takes us with the entry of the human voice, but the human character of that voice. Neither is it the thought expressed in Schiller's verses that occupies our minds thereafter, but the familiar sound of the choral chant in which we feel bidden to join and thus take part in an ideal Divine Service.[15]

Wagner's opposition between "the meaning of the words" and "the human character" of the voice can be contextualized in the two dimensions of the voice theorized by such poststructuralists as Julia Kristeva and Roland Barthes. They propose the concept of the "pheno-song" and the "geno-song," referring to the linguistic dimension of the voice and the physicality of the voice as pure sound, respectively. In his essay "The Grain of the Voice," Barthes compares Dietrich Fischer-Dieskau (1925–2012) to Charles Panzera (1896–1976), a Swiss-French baritone who was his music teacher for a brief time. For Barthes, Fischer-Dieskau's singing exemplifies the pheno-song and Panzera's, the geno-song:

> From the point of view of the pheno-song, Fischer-Dieskau is assuredly an artist beyond reproach: everything in the (semantic and lyrical) structure is respected and yet nothing seduces, nothing sways us to *jouissance*. His art is inordinately expressive (the diction is dramatic, the pauses, the checkings and releasings of breath, occur like shudders of passion) and hence never exceeds culture: here it is the soul which accompanies the song, not the body ... The lung, a stupid organ, swells but gets no erection; it is in the throat, place where the phonic metal hardens and is segmented, in the mask that *signifiance* explodes, bringing not the soul but *jouissance* ... With FD, I seem only to hear the lungs, never the tongue, the glottis, the teeth, the mucous membranes, the nose. All of Panzera's art, on the contrary, was in the letters, not in the bellows.[16]

Shawshank Redemption and the Technology of Music," *19th-Century Music* 34, no. 3 (Spring 2011): 354.

[14] For Žižek, the effect of the finale of Beethoven's Choral Symphony would "undoubtedly be pathetic in an extremely vulgar way," because of the "overtly" sublime quality of the text as well as the music. See Žižek, *The Fragile Absolute*, p. 159.

[15] Quoted in Lydia Goehr, *The Quest for Voice: Music, Politics, and the Limits of Philosophy* (Berkeley and Los Angeles: University of California Press, 1998), p. 111.

[16] Roland Barthes, "The Grain of the Voice," in *Music, Image, Text*, trans. Stephen Heath (New York: Hill and Wang, 1977), p. 183.

One might not agree with Barthes's description of Fischer-Dieskau's voice or Panzera's, or neither. One objection could be the fact that Fischer-Dieskau's voice in the 1980s or the early 1990s was significantly different from the voice Barthes had known around the time he was writing the essay, which was the early 1970s: one hears not much of the "lung" in Fischer-Dieskau's singing in his sixties but more of the throat and the "mucous membranes," as in Panzera. No matter whose voices they may be, Barthes's description of the geno-song and the pheno-song elucidates his concept of the two dimensions of the voice: the bodily and sonorous materiality in the geno-song, which takes us to an ecstasy of pure voice or *jouissance*, where the signifying function of the pheno-song "explodes." Guy Rosolato's theory of the voice also focuses on the two realms of the voice that he calls "body" and "language"—that is, the pure sonic materiality and the system of signification, respectively.[17] To put it in Kaja Silverman's words, the voice is the vehicle of "both the cry and the word."[18] As Caryl Flinn points out, Rosolato locates the pleasure of hearing in the voice's oscillation between body and language.[19] I argue that the celebration of the physicality of the voice, while undermining its verbal dimension, is a cinematic tendency when opera excerpts are employed in mainstream film titles, as epitomized by Morgan Freeman's voiceover in *The Shawshank Redemption*: "I have no idea to this day what those two Italian ladies were singing about … Some things are best left unsaid." The opera excerpts in Wong Kar-Wai's *2046* can be illuminated in this context.

2046

I started hearing a strange voice through the wall.
I thought someone had moved in.
But it was the daughter of the hotel owner, Mr. Wang.
I had no idea what she was saying…

(Chow Mo-wan, *2046*)

China-born Hong Kong-based Wong Kar-Wai is one of the most prominent Asian film directors, having gained much international recognition through his visibility at numerous prestigious film festivals, including the Cannes Film Festival.[20] He was the first Asian film director to be appointed as the jury president for the Festival in 2006, and four of his nine feature films have been nominated for

---

[17] Guy Rosolato, "La Voix: entre corps et langage," *Revue Française de psychanalyse* 38, no. 1 (January 1974): 75–94.

[18] Kaja Silverman, *The Acoustic Mirror: The Female Voice in Psychoanalysis and Cinema* (Bloomington: Indiana University Press, 1988), p. 86.

[19] Caryl Flinn, *Strains of Utopia: Gender, Nostalgia, and Hollywood Film Music* (Princeton, NJ: Princeton University Press, 1992), p. 54.

[20] I thank Thomas Kernan, who was my research assistant while I was working on this chapter, for his bibliographical research on this film and other help that was indispensable for writing the chapter.

the Palme d'Or: *Happy Together* (1997), *In the Mood for Love* (2000), *2046* (2004), and most recently, *My Blueberry Nights*, starring Norah Jones, which was selected as the opening film for the sixtieth anniversary of the Cannes Film Festival in 2007.[21] *2046* completes a trilogy with two of Wong's previous films: *Days of Being Wild* (1991), often described as the Chinese *Rebel without a Cause*, and *In the Mood for Love* (2000). The temporal setting of the trilogy is continuous: the first film takes place between 1960 and 1962, while the second begins in 1962 and ends in 1966; *2046* unfolds over the period from 1966 to 1970. There is no obvious narrative continuity, although some characters, or simply their names, are repeated. The hero of *2046*, Chow Mo-Wan, is first glimpsed in the final scene of *Days of Being Wild*, where he briefly appears as an unidentified new character named Smirk with no dramatic relationship to any other characters in the film, although his gesture of combing his hair with a grin in front of the mirror suggests that he could be the double of the murdered hero, Yuddy (Leslie Cheng).[22]

2046 is commonly identified as a science-fiction film, Wong's first work in this genre. Some critics regard it as the culmination of Wong's feature films,[23] while for others it represents "more a beautiful failure than a genuine masterpiece."[24] The protagonist, Chow Mo-Wan, is carried over from the second work of the trilogy, *In the Mood for Love*, and is played by the same actor, Tony Leung Chiu Wai. The previous film centers on his unconsummated love for a married woman, Su Li Zhen (also the heroine's name in *Days of Being Wild*), which Peter Brunette describes as "one of the most powerful renditions of mutually unrequited love in cinema history."[25] In *2046*, Chow is a pulp-fiction writer and pursues a playboy lifestyle, trying to flee from his wounded memory of love yet endlessly longing for the ever-lost, unattainable love. He is writing a science fiction novel entitled "2046," which is about the passengers of a train who travel to 2046 to restore their lost memories. The film takes the form of the story-within-a-story, as the "2046"

---

[21] Although none of them received the Palme d'Or, Wong won Best Director Award for *Happy Together*, and *In the Mood for Love* brought the Best Actor Award to Tony Leung Chiu Wai, who also played the title role in *2046*.

[22] Film critic Nathan Lee describes this mysterious introduction of a new character at the very end of the film as the "queer coda." See Nathan Lee, "Bleeding Men and the Women Who Love Them," *New York Sun*, August 5, 2005.

[23] Stephen Teo, *Wong Kar-Wai* (London: BFI Publishing, 2005), p. 149.

[24] Philip Martin, "Perplexing Beauty is the Lure to 2046," *Arkansas Democrat Gazette*, October 7, 2005.

[25] Peter Brunette, *Wong Kar-Wai* (Urbana Champaign: University of Illinois Press, 2005), p. 89. At the Cannes press conference, Tony Leung said that *2046* is a "film about a man who is trying to get rid of his past. Wong told me that it was the same character as before. But that I should treat him as a completely new character. This was quite different and challenging to do, so I asked Wong if I could at least have a moustache to represent this change in the same character for me." Quoted in ibid., pp. 102–3.

passengers are parallel to the film characters. The following voiceover opens the film:

> In the year 2046, a vast rail network spans the globe. A mysterious train leaves for 2046 every once in a while. Every passenger going to 2046 has the same intention: They want to recapture lost memories, because nothing ever changes in 2046. Nobody really knows if that's true because nobody's ever come back except me.

This narration is spoken by Tak, a character in both the film and the novel and also Chow's alter ego, played by Takuya Kimura, a Japanese pop-music celebrity. As the opening voiceover suggests, the film title *2046* has several different layers of meaning: it is both time and place, as well as the title of the novel Chow is writing. As a place, 2046 is not only the destination of the train but also a hotel room number, which itself has layered meanings as the room associated with Chow's lovers: it is the room where Lulu, also known as Mimi (Carina Lau), is murdered; where Bai Ling (Zhang Ziyi) lives for an extended time; and where the hotel owner's daughter Wang Jing-Wen (Faye Wong), the only female character who does not have a sexual relationship with Chow, briefly resides. This unconsummated love in *2046* is a reminiscence, or even a continuation, of Chow's unrequited love for Su Li-Zhen in *In the Mood for Love*.[26]

The year 2046 is an important political demarcation for Hong Kong. When the sovereignty over Hong Kong was returned to China in 1997 after 156 years of British colonial rule, Hong Kong was promised a high degree of autonomy for 50 years, making 2046 the last year before Hong Kong's full absorption into China. Although Wong has said that he did not intend any political content in *2046*, he conceived the film in 1997, the year of Hong Kong's handover, and admitted that the film was inspired by the political promises made at the time. "The number 2046 represents the last year of that promise. We wanted to make a film about promises, and whether anything remains unchanged for that long in life," said Wong in his interview with the *New York Times*.[27] And it was the theme of promise that motivated him to use opera excerpts, which I will discuss in detail after elucidating the general aspects of Wong's use of music.

Music in Wong's Films

Unlike other internationally famed Asian directors such as Chen Kaige, Zhang Yimou, and Kwon-taek Im, Wong Kar-Wai has avoided exotic settings and epic themes related to the culture of his origin and instead has focused on those themes

---

[26]   2046 is the room number of a hotel where Chow and Su Li-Zhen attempt to consummate their love in *In the Mood for Love*.

[27]   Quoted in *New York Times*, January 28, 2001.

that deal with more primordial, universal human conditions—loneliness and isolation, for instance—set in highly cosmopolitan cities such as Hong Kong. His soundtracks, too, are characterized by multicultural diversity. The soundtrack of *Happy Together* is dominated by Astor Piazzolla's "Tango Apasionado" and Brazilian singer Caetano Veloso's "Cucurrucucu Paloma," along with Frank Zappa's instrumental music, while Hawaiian guitar is the most prominent music in *Days of Being Wild* (1991). In *Chunking Express* (1994), The Mamas and the Papas' "California Dreamin'" serves as the main theme song.

As acclaimed by many film critics and scholars, a brilliant handling of music is one of the distinguished trademarks of Wong's films. Steve Murray calls *2046* a "visual tone poem," and for Peter Brunette, the effect of Wong's "striking visuals" is always reinforced by music, in which he locates the greatest expressive intensity in Wong's films.[28] Some of his films evoke music videos because of the dialogue-free images accompanied by music for an extended time and the visual editing synchronized with the musical rhythm, rather than the other way around, as is standard in narrative films. Wong acknowledges that he borrowed the format made popular by music videos in his first feature film, *As Tears Go By* (1988), but beyond that, he denies a close affinity between his films and music video: "Well, there's a lot of music in my films, and my editing's fast. But that's it, and I don't think my films are really like MTV."[29]

The significance of music in Wong's films goes beyond its mere prominence in his soundtracks. He often uses a musical metaphor when he describes his films, calling *Fallen Angels* a "rock opera" and *In the Mood for Love* "chamber music."[30] Musical inspiration for Wong extends to the *making* of a film, especially its temporal elements. Before shooting a film, he usually looks for music that can serve as a reference point for the rhythm of the film, and plays it to the cast and crew before he showing them the script. While the script has no inherent tempo, states Wong,

> music creates the rhythms. So if I want to explain to [director of photography] Chris Doyle the rhythm of the film, then I would play the CDs, play the music instead of showing him the script, because he wouldn't read the script anyway. It's very effective in a way, and also it helps me because I think the rhythm of the film is very important. So you have to get the rhythm, and then everything comes out slowly after that.[31]

---

[28] Steve Murray, "Between Past and Future and Memory and Regret," *Atlanta Journal-Constitution*, September 2, 2005; and Brunette, *Wong Kar-Wai*, p. 94.

[29] Interview with Peter Brunette at the 2005 Toronto International Film Festival, quoted in Brunette, *Wong Kar-Wai*, p. 119.

[30] Ibid., pp. 100 and 120.

[31] Unpublished interview with Wong (n.d.), housed at the Margaret Herrick Library (MHL) of the Academy of Motion Picture Arts and Sciences in Beverly Hills.

In terms of specific roles of music in a film, Wong has avoided using music as an emotional or narrative underscoring. Instead, music often serves as the structural division and expression of particular time periods, and for the latter purpose, Wong has employed pre-existing popular music extensively. This is because, compared to an original score or pre-existing classical music, popular music has much more specific historical and social associations.[32] In *2046*, Latin American music such as the song "Siboney," written by Cuban composer Ernesto Lecuona, functions as an aural historical setting of the 1960s, since at that time Latin American music was very popular in Hong Kong. Also prominent is Nat "King" Cole's rendition of "The Christmas Song." It serves as a structural refrain, returning at the opening of each "chapter" of the film, which begins on Christmas Eve for three consecutive years, from 1966 to 1968.[33] Nat "King" Cole's voice also creates a sonic continuity between the second and third work of the trilogy, for his songs, such as "Aquellos ojos verdes" and "Quizás, quizás, quizás," permeate the soundtrack of *In the Mood for Love*. As recognized by both specialists and the general audience, the musical culmination of *2046* is "Casta diva" from Bellini's *Norma*, sung by Angela Gheorghiu. In the bonus track of the film's DVD, this song is chosen to accompany the music video rendition of the film synopsis, a testimony to the special status of this aria. Wong has used pre-existing music and vocal music extensively, but *2046* is his first film to employ opera excerpts. What motivated him to explore opera in this science fiction film? How is the function and effect of "Casta diva" different from those of other soundtrack songs?

Opera in *2046*

As noted above, *2046* was inspired by the Chinese government's promise that Hong Kong would not change for fifty years after its handover in 1997. Wong's film, however, is not about this specific political promise but a philosophical skepticism about whether anything can remain unchanged, through which his recurring themes of lost memories and nostalgia are underscored. Wong finds a special relevance for opera to the theme of promise in *2046*, because for him, "Opera is about promises, betrayals and myths, ... The form has been here for hundreds of years—much longer than 50. And these topics never change."[34] He also relates the chapter division of *2046* to operatic structure. According to

---

[32]   Smith, *The Sounds of Commerce*, pp. 164–5.

[33]   About his choice of Christmas Eve as a structural demarcation, Wong said, "The film is more like a diary of this writer [Chow Mo-Wan], and I wanted to have each chapter related to a certain day. I read a newspaper story that said we have the highest suicide rate every year on Christmas Eve. For some people, it's the loneliest moment in their life, so I put Christmas Eve in each chapter in the story." Unpublished interview, housed at MHL. See n. 31.

[34]   Wong Kar-Wai, interview by Leslie Camhi, *New York Times*, January 28, 2001, Section 2, p. 11.

some interviews, opera had a more substantial role in Wong's initial conception of *2046*, as he planned to use excerpts from three operas—*Madama Butterfly*, *Carmen*, and *Tannhäuser*—to provide a three-part structure for the film.[35] In addition to "Casta diva," the final film released on DVD contains one more opera excerpt, "Oh! S'io potessi dissipar le nubi," from another Bellini opera, *Il pirata*, and sung by Maria Callas.[36]

In Wong's film, the *Pirata* excerpt is associated with the female character Lulu, played by Carina Lau. She is the character carried over from the first film in the trilogy, *Days of Being Wild*, and as in the previous film, she is also called Mimi. Both of her names are an obvious reference to the operatic heroines (Lulu in Berg's *Lulu* and Mimi in Puccini's *La bohème*), but without making a narrative parallelism with either of the operas, except that like Berg's heroine, Wong's cinematic Lulu is also murdered, although in a different dramatic context: her ex-boyfriend stabs her out of jealousy over her new lover. The *Pirata* excerpt accompanies the murder scene, which is visualized like a music video without any spoken dialogue. There is no apparent narrative connection between the opera excerpt and the scene it accompanies beyond the general theme of a love triangle and impending death: in Bellini's opera, the heroine Imogene sings this aria in the state of mental derangement just before her beloved is executed by her husband.

"Casta diva" functions as a leitmotif for another female character, Wang Jing-Wen (Faye Wong), a new character who does not appear in either of the earlier films of the trilogy. She is one of the women associated with the hero Chow but the only woman who does not have a sexual relationship with him, and in this respect, she evokes Su Li-zhen, "the elegantly forbidden lover" in *In the Mood for Love*.[37] Like the *Pirata* excerpt, the signifying function of the lyrics of "Casta diva" is only minimal to the film narrative: at the broadest level of the film, the "chaste goddess" can be related to Chow's pure unconsummated love for Miss Wang, as opposed to his physical love with other women. To examine the possibility of more specific functions of Bellini's aria, one needs to know the narrative context

---

[35]   Ibid., and Wong Kar-Wai, interview by Geoff Andres, *Time Out*, January 5, 2005, pp. 22–3.

[36]   The bonus track of the DVD includes the following commentary on the choice of the recordings: "'Casta Diva' ... has captivated countless hearts for almost two centuries from operatic stage to MP3 player. While recording technology of past decades captured Maria Callas at the height of her powers [in the 1950s] Wong Kar-Wai chose a new diva Angela Gheorghiu and her 2000 rendition. But he also used Maria Callas's voice in her interpretation of another Bellini opera, *Il Pirata*. Recording technology has captured time for all of us, and has also frozen in time those beautiful voices in their prime."

[37]   Ty Burr, "Wong's *2046* is a Mind-Altering Cocktail, Perfectly Blended," *Boston Globe*, August 19, 2005. In *2046*, the presentation of the character Su Li-zhen is threefold: in addition to Wang Jing-Wen, one character has the actual name Su Li-Zhen, played by Gong Li, and Maggie Cheng, who plays the same character in *In the Mood for Love*, briefly appears when she is recalled in Chow's memory in a flashback shot.

in which this aria is employed. Miss Wang has a Japanese boyfriend, Tak (Takuya Kimura), but because of his different cultural background, her father does not approve of their marriage, which motivates him to go back to Japan. After Tak leaves her, she momentarily loses her speech out of despair and talks to herself, uttering fragmentary words in Japanese. "I had no idea what she was saying," Chow's voiceover narrates. The next scene shows Miss Wang's wordless and exaggerated bodily gestures as in a pantomime or a silent film on the top of her father's hotel (Figure 1.1). This is the scene in which "Casta diva" is used for the first time in the film.

Figure 1.1   Miss Wong, accompanied by "Casta diva" in *2046*

As I discussed at the beginning of this chapter, non-operatic popular songs often function as a chorus-like commentary on what is being seen. "Casta diva," too, comments on the heroine's state of mind, but not through its verbal content as a popular song typically does, but by serving as a sonic image of her loss of speech. Here I find a parallelism between the opera scene in *2046* and that of *The Shawshank Redemption*, for both suggest that the verbal content of the respective opera excerpts is irrelevant. In *2046*, this suggestion is subtle and indirect, because it is not through a film character's direct comment on the opera excerpt, as in *The Shawshank Redemption*, but through opera's role as nondiegetic music to represent the heroine's loss of speech; in other words, her linguistic impotence. When "Casta diva" is used diegetically later in *2046*, it shows the undermining of the verbal in a different realm of the voice—not the operatic but the cinematic voice—and in a more literal way, as the opera excerpt is employed to silence the dialogue within the film. Chow hears the recording coming out of Mr. Wang's room and is about to ask him to reduce the volume. He assumes that Mr. Wang plays it so loudly because he loves the opera, but finds out that he was having a brawl with his daughter about her Japanese boyfriend and was playing the opera so that people would not overhear the family row. When the *Pirata* excerpt appears later in the film, it is used for the same purpose of masking Mr. Wang's and his daughter's voices. Put another way, the linguistic dimension of their (cinematic) voices, the pheno-song, is silenced by the physicality of the operatic voice, the geno-song. While in *The Shawshank Redemption*, the registering of opera as a geno-song happens at only one level within the diegesis of the film (Red's voiceover commentary), it operates on three levels in *2046*: when the verbal meanings of the opera excerpts are indifferent to the scenes they accompany, when "Casta diva" represents Miss Wang's linguistic impotence, and when the opera excerpts are used to cover up the conversation between her and her father.

"Casta diva" returns in two more scenes later in the film, and in both cases it accompanies Chow's voiceover narration as nondiegetic music, a departure from the standard practice of not using vocal music as nondiegetic music, particularly for voiceovers. Drawing on Susanne Langer's thesis that music is an "unconsummated symbol," Royal Brown locates the effect of nondiegetic music in a "dialectical opposition between the unconsummatedness of the musical symbol and the consummatedness of the cinematic object-events."[38] And he explains that the reason nondiegetic film score has remained "almost totally" free of lyrics is that they disrupt the "consummated/unconsummated balance of the cine/musical relationship." When the human voice is employed as nondiegetic music, continues Brown, it is usually vocalized without lyrics in order to produce a "quasi-instrumental effect," as exemplified by the vocalized chorus of György Ligeti's *Lux aeterna* used in Stanley Kubrick's *2001: A Space Odyssey* (1968), and in many vocal scores by Ennio Morricone.[39] If this is the case, do the last two appearances of "Casta diva" in *2046* produce a quasi-instrumental effect? If so, how? One possible answer is that in spite of the presence of its text, opera can still function as an unconsummated symbol like textless instrumental music, because in opera the "body" of the voice à la Rosolato (i.e., the pure sonic materiality of the voice) is more prominent than its linguistic dimension: in other words, opera as a geno-song rather than a pheno-song.

It is pertinent to contextualize David Levin's essay on Jean-Jacques Beineix's film *Diva* (1981) within the cinematic tendency of privileging the geno-song over the pheno-song when opera is used as soundtrack. Levin reads Beineix's film in light of what he calls "neo-lyricism," a recent trend in opera criticism characterized by its "explicitly lyrical, intensely personal" style and represented by the works of such scholars as Sam Abel, Wayne Koestenbaum, and Paul Robinson. Levin quotes Robinson as saying: "I found myself listening to the performance [of Gounod's *Roméo et Juliette*] over and over. I listened without a libretto; nor did I consult a synopsis of the opera. I simply indulged myself in the thing itself."[40] For Levin, this extremely autobiographical, "logophobic" style of opera criticism is

---

[38] Royal S. Brown, *Overtones and Undertones: Reading Film Music* (Berkeley and Los Angeles: University of California Press, 1994), pp. 27 and 40.

[39] Ibid., pp. 40–41.

[40] David J. Levin, "Is There a Text in This Libido?" in Joe and Theresa (eds), *Between Opera and Cinema*, p, 123. Later in his essay, Levin sarcastically states that "more than ten years later, I still don't know what 'the thing itself' is" (p. 129).

highly problematic because it privileges a "libidinal, masturbatory, and privatized pleasure" over textual analysis. Levin contends that Beineix's film promotes a neo-lyricist approach in several ways, one of which is the absence of translation (that is, subtitles) for the film's title aria, "Ebben? ... Ne andrò lontana," from Alfredo Catalani's opera *La Wally*. This encourages the audience to indulge in "musical *jouissance*" without any textual mediation, the kind of listening mode celebrated by neo-lyricism.[41] Furthermore, Catalini's aria remains a "floating signifier": since it is performed as an individual song at the singer's recital rather than shown within in a staged opera, the context of the aria is not just absent but has been "absented."[42]

In Gérard Corbiau's *Farinelli, Il castrato* (1994), too, all of the opera excerpts are presented in concert format and none are translated. For Ellen Harris and Katherine Bergeron, the most problematic scene in terms of the absence of subtitles is Farinelli's performance of "Lascia ch'io pianga," Almirena's aria from Handel's opera *Rinaldo*—a scene that cross-cuts, as parallel editing, with a flashback to Farinelli's castration. Harris and Bergeron criticize this scene, arguing that knowing the words of Handel's aria, "Let me lament my cruel fate / and sigh for my liberty," would help the film viewer recognize the emotional and psychological parallelism between the operatic heroine and the film's hero. "The sophisticated fantasy sequence from *Rinaldo*," notes Bergeron, "has to be understood, then, as some sort of private musical joke, made more for Corbiau's amusement than for that of his audience."[43] Although Bergeron's discussion focuses on a single film, as does Levin's, *Farinelli* and *Diva* are not exceptional cases but are among many examples that testify to mainstream cinema's "logophobic" representation of opera excerpts.[44]

Logophobia and the Maternal Voice

Theories of the maternal voice can illuminate the logophobic employment of opera excerpts as floating signifiers, as shown in the films discussed above. In the

---

[41]   Mary Hunter finds the promotion of the same type of listening in *The Shawshank Redemption*, which she describes as "emotionally engaged but intellectually decontextualized." See Hunter, "Opera *In* Film," p. 99.

[42]   Levin, "Is There a Text in This Libido?," p. 127.

[43]   Katherine Bergeron, "The Castrato as History," *Cambridge Opera Journal* 8, no. 2 (July 1996): 182; and Ellen Harris, "Twentieth-Century Farinelli," *The Musical Quarterly* 81, no. 2 (Summer 1997): 182.

[44]   Examples abound, both Western and Asian: to cite only a few, Bernardo Bertolucci's *La Luna* (1978); Sae-Jung Kim's *The Glory of Death* (1990), a film based on the life of an early twentieth-century Korean soprano; Istvan Szabo's *Meeting Venus* (1991); Yan Cui's *The Chinese Chocolate* (1995); Don Boyd's *Lucia* (1999); and, more recently, Franco Zeffirelli's *Callas Forever* (2002).

Lacanian psycho-analysis, sound in general and voice in particular take a special position in the formation of the subject, because aural experience is anterior to visual and other sensorial experiences in that the prenatal infant hears its mother's voice and her non-vocal sounds while within her body.[45] Michel Chion states:

> In the beginning, in the uterine darkness, was the voice, the Mother's voice. For the child once born, the mother is more an olfactory and vocal continuum than an image. Her voice originates in all points of space, while her form enters and leaves the visual field. We can imagine the voice of the Mother weaving around the child a network of connections it's tempting to call the *umbilical web*.[46]

For Guy Rosolato, the maternal voice provides the first auditory pleasure and the sense of the blissful plenitude, where he locates the roots of musical pleasure and our nostalgic yearning for the return to the "sonorous womb, a murmuring house—or *music of the spheres*."[47] The prenatal infantile plenitude evoked by the maternal voice represents the preverbal stage in the development of the subject, anterior to the paternal linguistic condition, and in this respect, Chion's biblical reference to the opening of Gospel of John ("In the beginning was the Word, and the Word was with God, and the Word was God") in the passage quoted above is ironic. As Kaja Silverman points out, "In the beginning" also alludes to the book of Genesis, and thus the anteriority of the maternal voice is associated with the chaotic state, "primitiveness rather than privilege," especially in terms of discursive power.[48] Slavoj Žižek's opposition of the voice to the Word is also evocative of, and can be contextualized in, the gendered tension between the maternal voice and the paternal word. For he associates the singing voice with the feminine *jouis-sense*, "a consuming self-enjoyment," not anchored in meaning, and opposes it to "the reliable masculine Word."[49]

In the theories of the voice discussed above, music appears as an emblem of the maternal voice primarily because of music's relative lack of referentiality and its distance from semiotic rigidity when compared to language. As Caryl Flinn points out, Barthes acknowledges language's "inherent polysemy," but his notion of the "Third Meaning" goes further than that, exceeding language. For Barthes, this semiotic excess, which in a way opposes language, is essentially the domain of music.[50] Julia Kristeva's concept of the chora is also related to music

---

[45] Flinn, *Strains of Utopia*, p. 53.

[46] Michel Chion, *The Voice in Cinema*, ed. and trans. Claudia Gorbman (New York: Columbia University Press, 1999), p. 61.

[47] Quoted in Silverman, *The Acoustic Mirror*, p. 85.

[48] Ibid., 75.

[49] Žižek, "'I Hear You with My Eyes'; or The Invisible Master," in *Gaze and Voice as Love Objects*, ed. Renata Saleci and Slavoj Žižek (Durham, NC: Duke University Press, 1996), p. 104.

[50] Flinn, *Strains of Utopia*, p. 56.

in that both are associated with a pre-linguistic condition and thus challenge the paternal symbolic order and visually oriented systems of representation.[51] Music's semiotic flexibility (or excess) and its association with the maternal voice have provided some film scholars with the theoretical framework for exploring the role of film music. Although Royal Brown does not directly draw upon Barthes, Rosolato, or Kristeva, his main source—Susanne Langer's concept of music as an unconsummated symbol—is rooted in the same notion of music's lack of referentiality. For Flinn, music's link to the pre-linguistic state of the maternal voice, and more specifically, the ever-lost plenitude it evokes, is one of the major theoretical perspectives from which she explores the connection between music and utopia, nostalgia, and femininity in Hollywood film. While Brown, Flinn and many other film scholars do not differentiate the degree of the maternal and semiotic flexibility in different types of soundtrack music, I find a distinctive and ironic status for opera—ironic because, as shown in the films I examined above, it is usually employed with the least degree of signifying function (that is, as a floating signifier) despite the fact that as a texted genre, it is the most referential. One of the few scholars to recognize the special status of opera in film is Kaja Silverman. Drawing on Rosolato's theory that opera is the closest "terrestrial equivalent" of the "celestial melody" of the maternal voice, she demonstrates how this "operatic version of the maternal voice fantasy" is cinematically formulated in Orson Welles's *Citizen Kane* (1941), Jean-Jacques Beineix's *Diva* (1981), and Francis Ford Coppola's *The Conversation* (1974).[52] Similarly, Mary Hunter argues that *The Shawshank Redemption* evokes the prenatal infantile unity associated with the maternal voice through two Italian women singing a Mozart duet. She notes, "In *The Shawshank Redemption*, the filmmakers have cleverly tied the universal human yearning for boundless plenitude to the prisoners' more particular yearning for a world with no locks."[53] In the remainder of this chapter, I will analyze the opera scene in Luc Besson's science-fiction film *The Fifth Element* and extend Silverman's and Hunter's work by tracing opera's evocation of the maternal voice to the peculiar qualities of the operatic voice, especially in nineteenth-century opera. My focus will be how the opera scene in Besson's film is self-referential in its celebration of the "body" of the voice, to borrow Rosolato's concept.

---

[51]   For detailed discussion, see ibid., pp. 58–60. The origin of the term "chora" is in Plato's *Timaeus*, which describes it as "an unnameable, improbable, hybrid [receptacle], anterior to naming, to the One, to the father, and consequently, maternally connoted." See Silverman *The Acoustic Mirror*, p. 102.

[52]   Silverman, Chapter 3: "The Fantasy of the Maternal Voice," in *The Acoustic Mirror*, pp. 72–100.

[53]   Hunter, "Opera *IN* Film," p. 99. As Hunter indicates, the lack of a female voice in the sonic world of this film, both diegetically and nondiegetically, makes more conspicuous the women's duet and its evocation of the maternal voice. There are only four female characters in the film and they are almost silent. Furthermore, all other songs on the soundtrack are sung by male voices.

The Fifth Element

The Fifth Element opened the 50th anniversary of the Cannes Film Festival in 1997. The film is set in a futuristic New York City and outer space in the twenty-third century. Evil comes every five thousand years to destroy Earth, which can only be saved by the sacred stones known as "the four elements." While the stones are being transported to Earth on a ship, the Mangalores, an alien race, attack the ship, but the Mondoshawan, a peaceful alien race, intercept the stones, which are partially fragmented by the attack. From the fragmented stones left on the ship, the human race genetically engineers a new being named Leeloo (Milla Jovovich), a symbol of supreme love. Later in the film, she is revealed to be the "fifth element" that can save Earth. The intercepted sacred stones are believed to be in the possession of an alien diva, a human-alien hybrid, who sings for about five minutes every ten years at a hotel called the Phloston Paradise in an outer space resort. Her concert is impending and the protagonist, Korben Dallas (Bruce Willis), an air-cab driver, goes to the resort with Leeloo to retrieve the stones. Jean-Baptiste Emanuel Zorg (Gary Oldman), an incarnation of Evil, is also trying to obtain the stones with the help of the Mangalores, to prevent the protection of Earth. During the battle to find the stones after the concert, the diva is shot and, while dying, she reveals to the Korben that the stones are stored inside her body. He acquires the stones and the universe is saved.

Like the prison house of *The Shawshank Redemption*, the futuristic space of *The Fifth Element* is dominated by male characters: except for the stewardesses and the hotel hostesses, there are only two major female characters, Leeloo and the alien diva.[54] A third female character, the hero's mother, is only present by her voice, through telephone calls to her son. These three female characters are connected to each other by their maternal quality. Korben's mother *is* a mother, not in a figurative or symbolic way, which is the case for the other two characters. The diva's carrying of the stones in her abdomen creates an image of pregnancy, which is intensified when Korben draws the stones out of her abdomen, evoking a Caesarean operation.[55] Leeloo is imbued with a maternal image through her identification with the diva, as though she were her double, which is suggested several times throughout the film. When Leeloo first meets the diva, their silent exchange of a gaze implies a telepathic transfer of information and emotions between the two. During the second half of the concert scene, the parallel editing between the diva's performance and Leeloo's combat with Mangalore warriors in the diva's dressing room visually connects the two characters, which is further strengthened by a music video-like synchronization between visual and musical

---

[54]   Another character who could be regarded as female is Ruby Rhod (Chris Tucker), a kind of drag queen at the Phloston Paradise.

[55]   In Michal Grover-Friedlander's description, the diva delivers the stones "as if giving birth to them." See Grover-Friedlander, *Vocal Apparitions: The Attraction of Cinema to Opera* (Princeton, NJ: Princeton University Press, 2005), p. 54.

rhythms. More importantly, at the moment the diva is shot, Leeloo reacts as though she herself were wounded.

The three female characters are also linked to one another by their linguistic characteristics. Every time Korben's mother calls him, her talk is represented as nagging and babbling rather than a meaningful conversation with her son, which suggests the lack of discursive potency often associated with the infant's or the child's preverbal reception of the maternal voice, as discussed above. The fact that Korben's mother exists only through the telephone adds another layer to her lack of masculine, verbal authority, if we consider the link Kaja Silverman makes between the telephone system and the "umbilical net" in her analysis of Anatole Litvak's 1948 film *Sorry, Wrong Number*.[56] In her chapter "The Problem of the Speaking Woman," Amy Lawrence discusses the same film and reveals the social and commercial registering of the telephone as a woman's instrument, promoted by and reinforcing the cultural "canard" about women "talking too much." She quotes Lana Rakow, who notes that "early commentar[ies] ... extolled the virtue of the telephone in reducing women's loneliness."[57] Leeloo's vocal characteristics suggest the anteriority (and primitiveness, according to Silverman) of the maternal voice more literally. At the time she is born as a cyborg, her linguistic state represents infantile chaos: she does not speak any meaningful human language but just babbles and screams and cannot communicate with Korben, from whom she eventually learns his language.

The operatic voice is evocative of the maternal voice in part because of the primacy of the non-verbal physicality, especially in nineteenth-century coloratura singing. In *The Fifth Element*, the diva's voice is connected to the maternal voice via her operatic singing. At the concert, she sings the opening of the Mad Scene from Donizetti's opera *Lucia di Lammermoor*.[58] The diva's performance is repeatedly called an "opera" and is identified this way on the concert ticket without giving its title, in spite of the fact that the "opera" is her recital of a single aria without staging. The use of *Lucia* as the generic for opera undermines the particularities of an individual opera, which adds validity to the hermeneutic reading of this scene

---

[56]   Silverman, *The Acoustic Mirror*, pp. 78–9.

[57]   Amy Lawrence, *Echo and Narcissus: Women's Voices in Classical Hollywood Cinema* (Berkeley and Los Angeles: University of California Press, 1991), p. 132.

[58]   The diva is played by Maïwenn Le Besco, who is lip-synching to the recording of Inva Mulla Tchako (a.k.a. Inva Mulla), the winner of the first Plácido Domingo International Voice Competition in 1997. In the opera sequence, the end of the Donizetti excerpt is connected to pop-style word-less coloratural song, in which the diva not only sings but also dances. The music for this scene called, "The Diva Dance," was scored by Eric Serra, the composer of the film's original soundtrack music. The vocal virtuosity that Serra's music demands was beyond the capacity of any human singer, so Serra's score required a technological enhancement by the computer which manipulated Inva Mulla Tchako's original singing.

in terms of the general characteristics of opera and the operatic voice.[59] The alien diva's name is Plavalaguna, but onscreen characters always call her "the Diva" or "Ms. Diva," which also suggests that what her singing represents is the voice of a diva, the operatic voice in general (Figure 1.2).

Figure 1.2   The diva's performance of the Mad Scene from Donizetti's *Lucia di Lammermoor* in *The Fifth Element*

The choice of the Mad Scene further enhances the pre-Symbolic (i.e., the pre-linguistic) state of the operatic voice in the film. In this scene, which is celebrated as one of the most exquisite coloratura passages in the operatic repertoire, Lucia's music represents her mental state of delirium—a conspicuous departure from logos.

> Trills, melismas, and high notes suggest hysteria, an unbearable pitch of emotion; they liberate music from text, allow it to escape from the rational, connect it with pre-symbolic modes of communication. In a sense coloratura is free from the confinement of music and of language: a syllable stretched beyond recognition is an escape from signification, the emergence of irrationality and madness.[60]

In *The Fifth Element*, then, the operatic heroine joins the three filmic characters—Korben's mother, Leeloo, and the diva—via her maternal, pre-Symbolic voice;

---

[59]   In this context, it is intriguing that in the cue sheet of Jonathan Demme's *Philadelphia*, which I examined at the music library of the Columbia/Sony studio, the entry of Umberto Giordano's aria, "La Mamma morta," used in the celebrated opera scene, is simply described as "opera enters here," while other vocal numbers, such as Bruce Springsteen's "Streets of Philadelphia" and Neil Young's "Philadelphia" are specified by their titles. This is a testimony to the undermining of the particularities of individual operas. Another testimony is that when Paul Potts sang "Nessun Dorma" in the television programme *Britain's Got Talent* in 1994, he simply introduced the title of his song as an "opera."

[60]   Mary Ann Smart, "The Silencing of Lucia," *Cambridge Opera Journal* 4, no. 2 (July 1992): 128.

and like Korben's mother, Lucia's presence is invisible and only vocal, conveyed through the alien diva's voice.[61]

Michel Poizat locates the empowerment of the operatic voice in the moment it verges on the Lacanian "cry," a pure, non-signifying form of sonorous materiality that transcends verbal meaning. For him, the cry is not the "nemesis of the word" but "father" to the word, and the ultimate condition that opera aspires to become.[62] For Poizat, the cry—the shriek, the scream, fading out into after-echoes and silence—is the "high extreme" of the voice, a sound beyond signification (melos), while the "low extreme" of the voice is logos: "a logical, minimally inflected, and unsung speech."[63] And this argument is extremely pertinent to explain cinema's representation of the "logophobic" dimension of the operatic voice.

A few other scholars have focused on the non-verbal physicality of the operatic voice—or to use Hans Ulrich Gumbrecht's expression, the "presence" of the voice beyond meaning—away from the pheno-centric tradition of the Western concept of the voice.[64] Stanley Cavell is one of such scholars. He contends that the operatic voice is "the sign of abandonment to your words, hence of your mortal immortality."[65] For Mladen Dolar, "The aria could represent the voice beyond

---

[61]   I am indebted to Audrey Walstrom, a diva, who brought this connection to my attention in the term paper she wrote for my film music seminar I taught at the University of Cincinnati (Audrey Walstrom, "The Feminine in *The Fifth Element*: Musical Underpinnings of Spectacle, Hysteria, Sacrifice, Silence, and Androgyny," typewritten manuscript, University of Cincinnati, March 2012).

[62]   Michel Poizat, *The Angel's Cry: Beyond the Pleasure Principle in Opera*, trans. Arthur Denner (Ithaca, NY: Cornell University Press, 1992), p. 62.

[63]   Grover-Friedlander, *Vocal Apparitions*, p. 4.

[64]   Hans Ulrich Gumbrecht, *Production of Presence: What Meaning Cannot Convey* (Stanford, CA: Stanford University Press, 2004).

[65]   Quoted in Michal Grover-Friedlander, *Operatic Afterlives* (New York: Zone Books, 2011), p. 13. A trend in contemporary opera realizes those voice theories that privilege the non-verbal elements of the voice (i.e., the materiality of the singing voice). Meredith Monk's *Atlas* (1991) is an example. For Monk, "too many words get in the way of the language of the voice." So when she uses words, "it's as much for their sound as their meaning": in other words, the *texture* of the voice is privileged over the *text* of the opera. For the quotation of Monk, see Dana Reason, "The New Vocal Utterance: The Music of Meredith Monk," *20th-Century Music* 6, no. 3 (1999): 19. Another good source for Monk's concept of the voice is her own essay, "Notes on the Voice," in *Meredith Monk*, ed. Deborah Jowitt (Baltimore, MD: Johns Hopkins University Press, 1997). John Zorn's newest opera, *La Machine de l'être* (2011), is an extreme example, as it is a *textless* opera written for a soprano (Anu Komsl). Zorn's opera is a musical translation of Antonine Arteau's drawings—a translation without the mediation of language. Its world premiere was performed by New York City Opera in 2011 (March 25 through April 8). Stravinsky's *Oedipus Rex* can be contextualized in the privileging of the materiality of the voice. He wrote: "Much to the contrary of the traditional concept, which submits music to the psychological expressiveness or to the dramatic significance of the word, in my *Oedipus Rex* the word is pure material, functioning

meaning, the object of fascination beyond content; it could aim at enjoyment beyond the signifier."[66] In the epigraph of this chapter, too, Dolar addresses the same issue: "the voice beyond meaning," in other words, the voice as a signifier without a signified, although in this case, voice is not limited to operatic singing voice. As to the failed command "Soldiers, Attack!" when it is heard as a mere sound ("What a beautiful voice!"), Dolar notes, "So the command fails, the addressees do not recognize themselves in the meaning being conveyed, they concentrate instead on the medium, which is the voice."[67]

Gary Tomlinson describes opera's aspiration toward a pure cry in terms of the Kantian metaphysics of the noumenon versus the phenomenon. At the simplest level, Kant's noumenon is defined as "a thing which is not to be thought of as object of the senses but as a thing in itself, solely through a pure understanding."[68] Tomlinson considers the Lacanian cry to be a vocal embodiment of the Kantian noumenon, an idea anticipated by Wagner. In a strong echo of Schopenhauer's philosophy, Wagner described a cry as "the immediate expression of the anguished will," which introduces us to an alternative to phenomenal reality. The moment we step outside of phenomenal reality, according to Tomlinson, we enter into the realm of the Kantian noumenon by being exposed to "the nature of the Thing-in-itself."[69]

As Tomlinson emphasizes, the operatic voice that aspires to reach the state of the cry is not universal but historically specific, a characteristic of nineteenth-century opera. In Western history, the development of vocal music, both sacred and secular, has swung between *prima le parole* and *prima la musica/voce* (in other words, non-linguistic vocality): "Thou shalt sing, but the Word shall be Law: pure singing shall come only after the Word, and not any which way." This was the rule that governed Gregorian chant. For St. Augustine, it was a sin, a "grievous sin," if singing itself was more moving than the text it conveyed.[70]

---

musically like a block of marble or stone in a work of sculpture or architecture ... The text becomes purely phonetic material for the composer ... To kill words were more exhilarating than to find dead syllables." Quoted in Daniel Albright, "Stravinsky's Assault on Language," *Journal of Musicological Research* 8 (March 1989): 271. Schoenberg, too, once stated his interest in non-linguistic use of the singing voice, although this statement does not represent the general aesthetics of his vocal music: "*Let the singer sing!* He is not to declaim but to sing. When he sings, the word ceases. From the moment on, there is only the music and the voice singing it; the word is a mere accompaniment." See Schoenberg, *Style and Idea*, ed. Leonard Stein and trans. Leo Black (Berkeley: University of California Press, 1975), p. 338.

[66] Mladen Dolar, "The Object Voice," in Saleci and Žižek (eds), *Gaze and Voice as Love Objects*, p. 19.

[67] Dolar, *A Voice and Nothing More*, p. 3.

[68] Quoted in Gary Tomlinson, *Metaphysical Song: An Essay on Opera* (Princeton, NJ: Princeton University Press, 1999), p. 76.

[69] Quoted in ibid., p. 86.

[70] Saint Augustine of Hippo, *The Confessions of St. Augustine* (New York: Bartleby. com, 2001), electronic book (accessed March 27, 2011).

Like sacred music, opera also began by privileging textual clarity over musical *jouissance*, as the Florentine Camerata's operatic ideals testify, but both sacred music and opera underwent transgressive developments in their own ways. While the development of the former showed an ironic reversal in the fifteenth-century motet, in which the multiplicity of vocal lines and even texts in different languages eventually dissolved the intelligibility of words, operatic transgression culminated in the nineteenth century, when singing verged on the cry and its vocal excess obscured linguistic intelligibility. The incompatibility between the vocal excess of the operatic singing and textual clarity is a scientific fact, considering that high-pitched singing makes intelligible verbal articulation impossible, for vowel sounds become indistinguishable above 660 hertz (approximately E5).[71]

Nineteenth-century opera's incompatibility with linguistic articulation grants it a closer kinship with the preverbal state of the maternal voice. In this respect, it is intriguing that when the alien diva in *The Fifth Element* moves from the *Lucia* excerpt to rock-style music during the second half of her "opera" (that is, concert), she sings no text but only vocalized syllables. Since the lyrics of popular songs usually have a strong referential function in film, this convention explains why the diva's rock song *should* be devoid of lyrics to be a part of her "opera." For the operatic voice, especially that of the nineteenth century, is associated with a pure signifier (the pure voice), derailed from referential function. The alien-ness of the diva's bodily appearance can also be contextualized in the vocal excess of the nineteenth-century operatic voice: her alien body as a metaphor of the alien-ness (non-naturalness) of the operatic voice. The vocal excess of nineteenth-century opera produces semiotic excess, privileging the physical sound of the voice over its linguistic role. The freedom from verbal and semiotic rigidity makes it possible for opera to function as an "unconsummated symbol," to borrow Susanne Langer's concept once more, in spite of the presence of the text. And it is this freedom, I would argue, that partially explains the popularity of nineteenth-century opera on film soundtrack (or at least on the soundtracks of the films I considered in this chapter). It seems that the recognition of the peculiarity of opera as a geno-song—an entity beyond its verbal meaning—does not require pedantic sophistication; it is something that can be discerned by the general public, as demonstrated in the following fan letter sent to Jack Warner about Mario Lanza's voice in Warner Bros.' 1956 film *Serenade*:

> I am a steady movie goer and enjoy them very much. This week for the third time I saw Mario Lanza's picture Serenade. So I just had to drop you a few lines to congratulate your company on making such a wonderful picture. Mario Lanza

---

[71]   Poizat, *The Angel's Cry*, p. 42. As Poizat indicates on p. 50, the prevalent association with opera singers among general audiences is screaming: "The performers don't sing; they scream!"

just fit the part beautiful and *his voice was something words can't express*. So let us have more of Mario Lanza's beautiful voice.[72] (my emphasis)

I close this chapter by returning to the *Lucia* excerpt in *The Fifth Element*—an ironic return because I now engage its verbal content. The aria is self-referential in that it endorses the film's celebration of the geno-song of the operatic voice. When Lucia recalls Edgardo at the beginning of the Mad Scene, it is not her tactile or visual memory of him but his voice that activates her longing for him; and not the verbal content of his voice but its "sweet sound":

Il dolce suono	The sweet sound
Mi colpi di sua voce! Ah, quella voce	Of his voice I hear! That voice
Mi e qui nel cor discesa!	So deeply embedded in my heart!

---

[72] Typewritten letter from the person identified as Mrs. Angelina Scafidi, 1956, USC Warner Bros. Archives, School of Cinema-Television, University of Southern California. The letter is undated but is filed between the documents dated May 8 and 13, 1956.

Chapter 2
Opera in Cinematic Death

> *Loretta*: That was so awful.
> *Ronny*: Awful?
> *Loretta*: Beautiful ... sad. *She died!*
> *Ronny*: Yes.
> *Loretta*: I was surprised ... You know, I didn't really think she was gonna die.
> I knew she was sick.
> *Ronny*: She had TB.
> *Loretta*: I know! I mean, she was coughing her brains out, and still she had to
> keep *singing!*
>
> (Norman Jewison, *Moonstruck*; my emphasis)

The above dialogue, from Norman Jewison's 1987 film *Moonstruck*, occurs after Loretta Castorini (Cher) and Ronny Cammareri (Nicholas Cage) see a performance of Puccini's *La bohème* at the Metropolitan Opera.[1] Their dialogue humorously reveals the centrality of death in opera and the consequent absurdity of "singing while dying." Linda Hutcheon and Michael Hutcheon describe opera as an art form "obsessed with death,"[2] and even musical dilettantes would not consider the Hutcheons' description to be exaggerated upon considering the innumerable operas that involve death in various forms, regardless of its cultural or temporal associations, such as *Madama Butterfly*, *Tosca*, *Pagliacci*, *Carmen*, *Pelléas et Mélisande*, *Dialogues des Carmélites*, *Salome*, *Tristan und Isolde*, *Wozzeck*, *Lulu*, *Lady Macbeth of Mtsensk*, *Eugene Onegin*, *Katya Kabanova*, *Peter Grimes*, *Death in Venice*, and *The Death of Klinghoffer*. Opera's obsession with death has been manifest from the very birth of the genre, as the earliest two extant operas, Jacopo Peri's *Euridice* (1600) and Claudio Monteverdi's *L'Orfeo* (1607), are both based on the Orphic myth that centers on Euridice's death (although these operatic dramatizations changed the original, tragic story to one with a happy ending because of the festivities they were composed for—Peri's opera for the wedding

---

[1]   To the best of my knowledge, the most substantial study of Jewison's *Moonstruck* is Marcia Citron's article, "'An Honest Contrivance': Opera and Desire in *Moonstruck*," *Music and Letters* 89, no. 1 (2008): 56–83. A later version of this article was included in her monograph *When Opera Meets Film* (Cambridge: Cambridge University Press, 2010), pp. 173–211. Drawing on such interdisciplinary studies as Werner Wolf's theories of "intermediality," Citron's discussion of Jewison's film focuses on how opera serves to fulfil the spectators' desires at several defferent levels of the film.

[2]   Linda Hutcheon and Michael Hutcheon, *Opera: Desire, Disease, Death* (Lincoln and London: University of Nebraska Press, 1996), p. 11.

of Henry IV and Maria de' Medici, and Monteverdi's for the annual carnival in Mantua). Even in Mozart's *The Magic Flute*, the surface story of which is more comical than tragic, the contemplation of death looms behind the comical surface, as shown in the following excerpts of the libretto:

Wenn er des Todes Schrecken überwinden kann,	And when he shall have conquered death's fear
Schwingt er sich aus der Erde himmel an.	Then shall he rise from earth to heaven's sphere.
Wir wandeln durch des Tones Macht,	We tread with music as our shield,
Froh durch des Todes duster Nacht!	Through murky death's darkest field!

The dialogue between Tamino and the chorus of the Voices in Act I, scene 15 also points to the theme of death through Tamino's uncertainty about Pamina's life and through the metaphor of day and night (or light and darkness):

Tamino:	O ewige Nacht!	Oh, eternal night]
	Wann wirst du schwinden?	When will you vanish?
Chorus:	Bald, Jüngling, oder nie!	Soon, Youth, or never!
Tamino:	Lebt den Pamina noch?	Does Pamina still live?
Chorus:	Pamina lebet noch!	Pamina still lives!

Ingmar Bergman regards this scene as the thematic crux of the opera. In his opera-film *The Magic Flute* (1975), the dialogue between Tamino and the chorus of the Voices is staged as the highlight of the opera primarily by visual means through lighting, and in his narrative film *The Hour of the Wolf* (1968), the same scene of Mozart's opera is presented as a fascinating puppet show.[3] Bergman indicates that the theme of the triumph of light/life over darkness/death reflects the composer's own struggling for "the spectre of death."

> When Mozart wrote his opera, he was already ill, the spectre of death touching him. In a moment of impatient despair, he cries: "Oh, dark night! When will you vanish? When shall I find light in the darkness?" The chorus responds ambiguously. "Soon, soon or never more." The mortally sick Mozart cries out a question into the darkness. Out of this darkness, he answers his own questions— or does he receive an answer?[4]

Over the past few decades, the use of operatic music in conjunction with cinematic death, especially ritualized, stylized, and climactic murder scenes, has been notable across diverse genres of popular titles, ranging from comedy, drama,

---

[3] The film is about a lunatic painter, Johan Borg (Max von Sydow). When Johan and his wife Alma (Liv Ullmann) are invited to a mysterious castle, the castle's host, Lindhorst (Georg Rydeberg), presents this scene from *The Magic Flute* in his puppet theater.

[4] Ingmar Bergman, *The Magic Lantern: An Autobiography*, trans. Joan Tate (New York: Viking, 1988), pp. 216–17.

and action to thriller, horror, and science-fiction films: to name a few among many, Colin Higgins's *Foul Play* (1978), Dario Argento's horror film, *Opera* (1987), Francis Ford Coppola's *Godfather III* (1990), Jennifer Chambers Lynch's serial-killer story *Boxing Helena* (1993), Claude Chabrol's *La Cérémonie* (1995), Danny DeVito's comedy *Death to Smoochy* (2002), Phil Alden Robinson's *The Sum of all Fears* (2002), and the James Bond film *Quantum of Solace* (2008), directed by Marc Forster. In this chapter, I will examine cinema's general attraction to opera as a sonic enhancement of its death scenes, drawing on theories about opera's versatile relationship with death as explored by such scholars as Michal Grover-Friedlander, Linda Hutcheon and Michael Hutcheon, and Slavoj Žižek.

Opera and Death

Opera's attraction to death has drawn intense scholarly attention over the past few decades, stimulated in part by "death studies" in biomedical and social sciences and in the humanities, studies such as Philippe Ariès's *Western Attitudes towards Death* (1974) and *The Hour of Our Death* (1981), *The Oxford Book of Death* (1983), and Robert Wilkins's *Fireside Book of Death* (1990).[5] Specialized studies of opera's fascination with death have taken diverse approaches, addressing different dimensions of death in opera. Catherine Clément's *Opera, or the Undoing of Women* (1989) is a classic feminist study, focusing on opera's thematic orientation toward the heroine's death at the level of plot, whether a sacrificial death, especially prevalent among Wagner's heroines (Senta and Brünnhilde), love-related suicide (Madama Butterfly and Tosca), or patriarchal violent murder (Carmen and Lulu).[6] As Michel Poizat indicates, however, diverse kinds of death are also common for male protagonists in opera: not only Isolde but also Tristan dies; if Desdemona and Carmen are stabbed, so is Lucia's husband, Lord Arturo Bucklaw, a homicide by his wife; Scarpia is killed by Tosca and Cavaradossi is executed; after Wozzeck kills his wife Marie, he drowns himself; Peter Grimes also drowns himself even without having killed anybody; Don Giovanni goes to hell at the end of the opera; and many Wagnerian heroes—Siegfried, Wotan, Tannhäuser, Amfortas, to name a few—experience a different sort of death than Tristan's *Liebestod*. Hence Michel Poizat's claim that in a "quick autopsy of the

---

[5] Philippe Ariès, *The Western Attitude towards Death: From the Middle Ages to the Present*, trans. P.M. Ranum (Baltimore, MD: Johns Hopkins University Press, 1976); Ariès, *The Hour of Our Death*, trans. Helen Weaver (New York: Vintage Books, 1981); D.J. Enright, ed., *The Oxford Book of* Death (New York: Oxford University Press, 1983); Robert Wilkins, *Fireside Book of Death* (London: Time Warner Paperbacks, 1992).

[6] Catherine Clément, *Opera, or the Undoing of Women* (Minneapolis: University of Minnesota Press, 1989).

heaps of bodies strewn across the opera stage since the beginning ... male and female graves appear with equal frequency."[7]

Like Poizat, Linda Hutcheon and Michael Hutcheon have expressed strong reservations about Clément's feminist and plot-based interpretation of death in opera,[8] and propose their own theories to explain opera's obsession with death. Focusing on a specific type of operatic death—that caused by illness— the Hutcheons' study, *Opera: Desire, Disease, Death* (1996), explores the representation of certain diseases in opera and their socio-cultural meanings: tuberculosis in *La traviata* and *La bohème*; syphilis in *Parsifal*; the pox and other epidemics in *The Rake's Progress*, *Death in Venice*, and *Lulu*; and AIDS in *Angels in America*. The Hutcheons' second book on death in opera, *Opera: The Art of Dying* (2004), examines the contribution of German Romanticism to positive meanings of death in Western culture. According to Ariès, at the beginning of the eighteenth century it was already the case that dying was understood positively as the individual's plunging into an "irrational" and "violent" but "beautiful" world—a world not "desirable" but "admirable in its beauty."[9] For the Hutcheons, opera is the best "cultural vehicle" to examine artistic representation of death because of its "limited canon" and "historically clear thematic orientation toward death and dying."[10] Arguing that Wagner's music dramas are the crux of the operatic manifestation of Western culture's positive embracing of death—death as redemption, reunion, or transcendence—the Hutcheons exclusively focus on Wagner's work in *Opera: The Art of Dying*.

Opera's Second Death (2002), co-authored by Slavoj Žižek and Mladen Dolar, is a psychoanalytically oriented study of opera's engagement with death.[11] At the outset of their study, Žižek and Dolar point out a paradoxical connection between opera and psycho-analysis, which they find in the historical coincidence between the birth of psycho-analysis at the beginning of the twentieth century and the death

---

[7]   Quoted in Linda and Michael Hutcheon, *Opera: Desire, Disease, Death*, p. 12.

[8]   Abbate's article "Opera, or the Envoicing of Women," in *Musicology and Difference: Gender and Sexuality in Music Scholarship*, ed. Ruth A. Solie (Berkeley: University of California Press, 1993) can also be contextualized in the discourse of opera and death as a rebuttal to Catherine's Clément's claim for the opera as the "undoing of women." Privileging the phenomenal power of singing over a plot-based interpretation of opera, Abbate argues that the "singing-while-dying" heroines (for its cinematic recognition, see the epigraph quoted from Norman Jewison's film *Moonsturck* on the first page of this chapter) survive and transcend their death brought by patriarchal, murderous plots.

[9]   See Linda and Michael Hutcheon, *Opera: Desire, Disease, Death*, p. 3. Christopher Marlowe is credited for the first dramatic—theatrical—use of death, making the manner of speaking and acting at the moment of death relevant to the character's personality. See ibid., p. 9.

[10]   Linda and Michael Hutcheon, *Opera: The Art of Dying* (Cambridge, MA: Harvard University Press, 204), p. 27.

[11]   Slavoj Žižek and Mladen Dolar, *Opera's Second Death* (New York: Routledge, 2002).

of opera, at least in its "traditional" form, with Berg's *Lulu*.[12] Opera's obsession with the death of the heroine, well chronicled in Catherine Clément's study, had made a spectacular death "a diva's main business." But Lulu's demise is the most spectacular death, because it marks a death knell for opera itself, and, if opera is considered a sonic emblem of death, "the death of the death itself."[13] Žižek and Dolar trace opera's engagement with death to its very beginnings, not only because of the Orphic myth, as mentioned above, but also because of the emphatic anachronism of operatic settings in ancient or legendary times and distant mythical places: "from its very beginning, opera was dead, a stillborn child of musical art."[14] Most importantly, Žižek locates the centrality of death in opera in its protagonists' status as the "living dead" and their death wish to end the "horrible fate of being caught in the endless, repetitive cycle of wandering around in guilt and pain."[15] Their longing to die is not simply for their biological death but for the so-called second death: to die in piece with no symbolic debt left. Žižek argues that only this concept of the second death can explain the enigma of Wotan's and the other gods' demise at the end of Wagner's *Ring* cycle—the enigma because they should die even after the ring is finally returned to the Rhine. From this perspective, Wagner's plot change is significant. According to his original plot, Erda warns the gods that they will perish if the gold is not returned to the Rhine; in the final version, they will die anyway. Evidently, this death represents the second death. Between the two deaths, Žižek continues, is "the very undead life" of eternal longing and unfulfilled desire, which are the loving condition for Tristan and Isolde. Paradoxically, the state of being caught between the two deaths is parallel to the desire "to enjoy life in excess," which Žižek identifies as the "ultimate lesson of psychoanalysis."[16]

Like Linda and Michael Hutcheon, and Žižek and Dolar, Michal Grover-Friedlander downplays the "overobvious perspective of the libretto and the plot" in her exploration of a correlation between the (operatic) voice and death. In her book *Vocal Apparitions: The Attraction of Cinema to Opera* (2005), she approaches opera's celebration of death from an abstract angle, namely the immanent mortality of the operatic voice.[17] While the operas examined in Žižek's study and the Hutcheons' *Opera, The Art of Dying* are limited to Wagner's music dramas, the focus of Grover-Friedlander's book is nineteenth-century Italian opera. Of the four premises for her understanding of opera, the first is that the operatic voice

---

[12]   Ibid., pp. vii and 2.

[13]   Mladen Dolar, "If Music Be the Food of Love," in Žižek and Dolar, *Opera's Second Death*, p. 2.

[14]   Žižek and Dolar, *Opera's Second Death*, p. viii.

[15]   Ibid., p. 107.

[16]   Slavoj Žižek, "The Death Drive and the Wagnerian Sublime," in Žižek and Dolar, *Opera's Second Death*, pp. 107–10.

[17]   Michal Grover-Friedlander, *Vocal Apparitions: The Attraction of Cinema to Opera* (Princeton, NJ: Princeton University Press, 2005), p. 4. See also her dissertation, "Voicing Death in Verdi's Operas" (PhD diss., Brandeis University, 1997).

is the aesthetic foundation of opera, which for Grover-Friedlander is the most distinctive characteristic of Italian opera. The Italian notion of song engenders an ecstatic anticipation of "beautiful moments" of singing that are transcendental and superhuman—a state of "operatic immortality."[18] Yet at the same time, this state of immortality is always laden with a sense of loss and mortality because of the evanescence of those beautiful moments when the performance of singing is over. It is here that Grover-Friedlander finds the inherent mortality in the operatic voice.[19] This argument can be supported by Carolyn Abbate's article "Music—Drastic or Gnostic?": privileging the "phenomenal" power of singing that extends her critique of Clément's plot-based approaches to opera heroines' death, Abbate proposes to investigate music as a performed, phenomenal event as opposed to the studies based on scores and librettos, which she calls a "souvenir."[20] What Abbate is arguing for in this article is not only the phenomenal power of performance but also its *ephemerality*, the latter of which warrants the inherent *mortality* of the operatic voice that is an essential point of Grover-Friedlander's theory of opera's kinship with death.

Grover-Friedlander's notion of the operatic voice is significantly informed by Michel Poizat's Lacanian theorization of the operatic voice. Poizat considers the voice the essence of opera, and the highest form of the operatic voice a pure sound beyond its signifying function; the linguistic dimension is only its lowest extreme. The state of pure sound is reached when the operatic voice verges on a cry, which fades out into the abyss of silence. Poizat argues that, in opera, the voice does not express the text; on the contrary, opera's death-driven plots embody "a logic of vocal jouissance"—that is, the logic or fate of the operatic voice destined to the cry and die into silence.[21] Grover-Friedlander, in addition to Poizat's concept of the operatic voice, draws our attention to the Orphic myth to explicate her argument

---

[18]   To support her arguments, Grover-Friedlander contextualizes Carolyn Abbate's *In Search of Opera* (Princeton, NJ: Princeton University Press, 2001) in the scholarship on the relationship between opera and death. Addressing Abbate's discussion of the voice, which is projected by the music independent of the composer's authorial voice, Grover-Friedlander interprets this voice as an agent that allows "a form of operatic immortality" (*Vocal Apparitions*, p. 5). What further supports Grover-Friedlander's thesis of operatic immortality is Abbate's discussion of the autonomy of the voice that transcends the singer's body, as symbolized by Orpheus's post-mortem song from his decapitated head (see *In Search of Opera*, pp. 1–6).

[19]   Grover-Friedlannder, *Vocal Apparitions*, pp. 1–4.

[20]   Carolyn Abbate, "Music—Drastic or Gnostic?" *Critical Inquiry* 30, no. 3 (Spring 2004), pp. 505–36. For a critique of this article, see Lawrence Kramer, "Music, Metaphor and Metaphysics," *The Musical Times* 145 (Autumn 2004): 5–18.

[21]   Michel Poizat, *The Angel's Cry: Beyond the Pleasure Principle in Opera*, trans. Arthur Denner (Ithaca, NY: Cornell University Press, 1992), p. 145. My understanding of Poizat's theory and its contribution to the discourse on opera's attraction to death is slightly different from Grover-Friedlander's. She contends that, for Poizat, opera's murderous narratives "allegorize the tendency of voice to reach for its own high extreme," which she

for the inevitable association between opera and death. What supports her study is not merely the thematic centrality of death in this myth but the tension between the vocal and the visual surrounding Euridice's death: it is Orpheus's song, the vocal, that revives her from death, but it is his gaze, the visual, that returns her to death. This "passage toward death or away from it,"[22] activated by the interplay between voice and gaze, is indeed an intriguing perspective from which one can explore the opera–cinema encounter. Opera is primarily a vocal medium while cinema focuses on visual elements in the sense that voice-less opera is an oxymoron while cinema ceases be a motion picture without moving images. Yet both art forms require various and continuous negotiations between the aural and the visual.

Opera in Cinematic Death

It was my privilege to serve as a personal music consultant to Chan-wook Park, a film director best known for *The Vengeance Trilogy: Sympathy for Mr. Vengeance* (2002), *Oldboy* (2003), and *Sympathy for Lady Vengeance* (2005). Park has received numerous awards at prestigious international film festivals. When Park was shooting *Oldboy*, the winner of the Grand Prix at Cannes in 2004, I suggested that he use opera excerpts for the climactic murder scene near the end of the film. He did not take my suggestion, explaining that "Opera is full of vengeance, death, excess, obsession, and violence. Because my film *Oldboy* is already full of such operatic traits, using opera on its soundtrack would be redundant. In a way, *Oldboy is* an opera." In addition, Park wanted to avoid opera because "it has become almost a cinematic cliché to use opera excerpts in association with murder, especially violent, ritualized, and stylized murders."[23] No matter how clichéd it might be to underscore murder-related violence with opera, I find that the ways opera excerpts are used differ intriguingly from film to film, and that diverse theories of the complex relationship between opera and death have expanded the hermeneutic scope for interpreting the use of opera in cinematic death. Before examining Woody Allen's distinctive use of opera in the murder scene of *Match Point* in the

---

regards as an "unattainable quest" for something that does not exist (see Grover-Friedlander, *Vocal Apparitions*, pp. 4–5).

[22] Grover-Friedlander, *Vocal Apparitions*, p. 7.

[23] Chan-wook Park, personal e-mail to me dated August 23, 2002; translation mine. He did use opera excerpts for the first time in his most recent film *Stoker* (2013), starring Nicole Kidman, Mia Wasikowska, and Matthew Goode. See the Epilogue of this book for details of this film. In *The Ax*, a film currently in development, Park intends to use opera excerpts again, mostly diegetically, in association with the opera-loving character Ricardo Como. *The Ax* is an adaptation of Donald E. Westlake's novel *The Ax* (1998) and a liberal remake of Costa Gavras's 2005 film *Le Couperet*, also based on Westlake's novel. Park's *The Ax* is a collaboration between South Korea (director), Canada (cast), and France (sponsor). Como's obsession with opera is Park's addition to the original novel.

next chapter, I examine in this chapter some other examples of cinematic use of opera in murder scenes in order to make the distinctiveness of *Match Point* clearer.

As Chan-wook Park noted in the interview quoted above, opera would normally be expected in those crime movies or thrillers in which the depiction of murder is highly stylized and ritualized. But comedy has not escaped from the influence of opera's enhancement of death, as can be seen in Colin Higgins's *Foul Play* (1978) and Danny DeVito's *Death to Smoochy* (2002). *Foul Play* is a story about a divorced librarian, Gloria Mundy (Goldie Hawn), who becomes accidentally entangled with an anti-religious crime group, including an albino stranger nicknamed as Whitey Jackson (William Frankfather). Gloria discovers that their final goal is to assassinate the pope, Pius XIII (Cyril Magnin). The male protagonist, Tony Carlson (Chevy Chase), is a policeman who becomes romantically involved with Gloria during their pursuit of the suspects of a series of mysterious murders. The film's climactic scene takes place at the San Francisco Opera House, where the assassination of the pope is planned. The opera being performed is Gilbert and Sullivan's *The Mikado*. The opera performance is intercut with action backstage, where Tony is chasing Whitey Jackson, the assassinator, who has kidnapped Gloria as a hostage and is dragging her up into the catwalks above the stage. Shot by Tony, Whitey falls and gets caught in the huge net of a stage set sailing ship hung from the ceiling. When the set drops down at the end of the opera, the audience is shocked to see two dead men (a policeman shot by Whitey also caught in the stage set) and are stunned into silence. But the pope, who must be thinking that the opera is meant to end this way, starts clapping joyously, and the audience joins him in enthusiastic applause. When the curtain is down, Tony and Gloria find each other and embrace and kiss behind the curtain, without realizing that the curtain is about to be lifted for a curtain call. The film ends with the audience applauding the people on stage, including Tony and Gloria, who bow along with the opera performers.

The final sequence of the opera performance cross-cut with the attempted assassination is quite extensive, lasting about 17 minutes. Operatic music is given prominence not only by its length but also by its rarity, since the *Mikado* excerpts are the only opera on the soundtrack. As I will further illustrate later in this section, opera tends to be reserved for a film's climactic murder scene, making its presence more conspicuous. The use of Gilbert and Sullivan's "operetta" rather than a serious opera seems to be a good choice, considering the comical nature of the film's plot. When opera is used for a murder scene, it is often employed as a diegetic performance. As Michel Chion argues, diegetic performance in general serves to expand the diegetic space of a film into the movie theater by suturing the film's viewers to the onscreen audience.[24] Among diegetic opera performances used in cinematic death scenes I have considered, the *Mikado* sequence in *Foul Play* is distinctive because it presents the film's protagonists, Gloria and Tony,

---

[24]   Michel Chion, *Audio-Vision: Sound On Screen*, trans. Claudia Gorbman (New York: Columbia University Press, 1994), p. 151.

as a part of the stage life of the operetta. When Tony and Gloria bow to the onscreen audience along with the opera performers who are taking a curtain call on stage, it signals both the end of Gilbert and Sullivan's operetta and that of Higgins's film. At this moment the fictionality of the operetta and that of the film converge in a kind of distancing effect, comparable to Brecht's alienation effect (*Verfremdungseffekt*) of epic theater, creating the impression that the cinematic protagonists bow to the audience of the movie theater to inform them of the end of the film as well as the opera. The convergence between operatic and cinematic fictionality is further solidified by the aural dissolve: that is, the overlapping of the last diegetic sound—the onscreen audience's applause that discloses the end of the opera performance—and the nondiegetic music that accompanies the closing credits—Barry Manilow's song "Ready to Take a Chance Again."

The association between opera and cinematic death has even been introduced into the children's domain. Danny DeVito's film *Death to Smoochy* is a comedy whose plot unfolds around Randolph Smiley (Robin Williams), known as Rainbow Randolph, the corrupt host of a children's television show. When he is found accepting bribes from parents who want their children to appear on the show, Randolph is fired and replaced by Sheldon Mopes (Edward Norton), whose character is Smoochy the Rhino, a parody of Barney the Dinosaur. Randolph develops several schemes to bring down Sheldon in order to regain his show, but always fails. Sheldon's villainous agent, Burke Bennett (Danny DeVito), forces him to participate in a Smoochy ice show run by a corrupt charity organization. Sheldon agrees to do the ice show but only on the condition that all the profits go to the children's rehabilitation clinic he used to work at. In retaliation, Burke hires Buggy Ding Dong (Vincent Schiavelli), another former children's show host, to assassinate Sheldon during the ice show. It is during this assassination sequence that opera excerpts are used. As in *Foul Play*, opera is employed diegetically as the music that accompanies the ice show, which is presented intercut with the assassination preparation backstage. When Randolph is informed of the assassination plan, he rushes to the ice show and tackles Buggy just as he is about to fire his rifle from the catwalk above the ice rink. Smoochy's life is saved but Buggy falls to his death. The film has a happy ending: Smoochy and Randolph launch a new children's show together.

The music that accompanies the ice show is an opera collage, beginning with a drastically abbreviated "Liebestod" from Wagner's *Tristan und Isolde* and including Puccini's "Vissi d'arte" from *Tosca*, Wagner's "Ride of the Valkyries," instrumental excerpts from Puccini's *Madama Butterfly*, and the "Intermezzo" from Mascagni's *Cavalleria rusticana*, which is the last piece. The two vocal excerpts in the opera potpourri—the "Liebestod" and "Vissi d'arte"—are lip-synched by the ice princess (Cara Wakelin). Like the *Mikado* excerpts in *Foul Play*, the opera collage in *Death to Smoochy* is distinguished by its uniqueness in the film: all other music on the soundtrack, whether diegetic or background, is non-operatic music. The music used at the climax of the assassination attempt is the "Intermezzo" from *Cavalleria rusticana*, the same music that accompanies the last sequence of Francis Coppola's *Godfather III*.

The murder sequence at the end of *Godfather III* exhibits one of the most celebrated appearances of opera in film. The Corleone family is at Teatro Massimo in Palermo, watching Mascagni's *Cavalleria rusticana*, in which Anthony (Franc D'Ambrosio), the son of Michael Corleone (Al Pacino), is performing the lead role. During the opera performance, multiple brutal murders are executed, having been planned by Michael's nephew Vincent Mancini (Andy Garcia) as a revenge against the Corleone family's enemies: Keinszig (Helmut Berger) is hanged; the "pope" (Raf Vallone) is poisoned, as is Don Altobello (Eli Wallach); Archbishop Gilday (Donal Donnelly) is shot and so are two of Vincent's men; and finally, Don Lucchesi (Enzo Robutti) is stabbed. These brutal murders are shown cross-cut with the opera performance, the entire length of which lasts about 19 minutes.[25] The opera performance ends but the murders continue. Mosca (Mario Donatone), the assassin hired by Don Altobello, shoots Michael when he is stepping down the staircase of the opera house façade. Michael survives but his daughter Mary (Sofia Coppola), who was standing next to Michael, dies when one of the two bullets Mosca fires toward Michael hits her in the chest. And Vincent kills Mosca. As Michael is holding Mary's dead body in his arms, the "Intermezzo" of *Cavalleria rusticana* enters the soundtrack nondiegetically and continues until the end of the film, the final image of which is an aged Michael, slumping out of his chair and falling to the ground—the last death in the *Godfather* trilogy.

In her book *When Opera Meets Film* (2010), Marcia Citron dedicates a chapter to *Godfather III*.[26] Among the issues she considers, Michael Corleone's silent scream at the loss of his daughter is most relevant to the theories about the relationship between opera and death examined above. Holding his daughter's dead body in his arms, Michael screams. The wide opening of his mouth is shown in close-up, but his vocal sound is completely muted. Accompanying Michael's violent cry is the instrumental "Intermezzo" from Mascagni's opera. In other words, his voice is only evoked by the voiceless operatic music. Drawing upon Michel Poizat's theory of the operatic voice, Citron proposes that Michael's scream can be read as a visualization of the ultimate state that the operatic voice aspires to be—the voice before and beyond verbal signification, the voice that resembles a "primal cry," which represents an unattainable quest to return to the origin—that is, the pre-symbolic stage preceding one's acquisition of linguistic and cultural knowledge. Considering Poizat's claim for the paradoxical relationship between the primal

---

[25]   Lars Franke provides a table of the musical cues in the murder sequence. See Franke, "*The Godfather Part III*: Film, Opera, and the Generation of Meaning," in *Changing Tunes: The Use of Pre-existing Music in Film*, ed. Phil Powrie and Robynn Stilwell (Burlington, VT: Ashgate, 2006), p. 36.

[26]   Citron, *When Opera Meets Film*, pp. 19–57. Her chapter on *Godfather III* is a revised version of her article, "Operatic Style and Structure in Coppola's *Godfather Trilogy*," published in *Musical Quarterly* 87, no. 3 (Fall 2004): 423–67.

cry and silence—the death of the cry as the birth of silence—the muteness of Michael's cry is certainly convincing as a "sign that the voice of opera is always related to muteness and silence."[27] Slavoj Žižek describes Michael's voiceless cry as a "scream vocalized with deferral." He argues that, while the scream remains silent, we experience a kind of stasis of time or timeless now.[28] From the viewpoint of opera's affinity for death, the most fascinating aspect of Michael's muted cry is its ability to represent the irony of the immanent mortality of the operatic voice— the irony of the coexistence of sound and silence; that is, the coexistence of life and death, as theorized by Michal Grover-Friedlander. It is fascinating especially in terms of the interplay between sight and sound: Michael's vocal utterance is evoked by a silent image—an instance of the sensorial world where "I hear you with my eyes," to quote Žižek.[29]

Marc Forster's *Quantum of Solace* (2008), the twenty-second James Bond film, is another example of cinema's celebrated use of opera in association with death.[30] All James Bond films involve a myriad deaths, but using opera on the soundtrack seems to be particularly suitable for *Quantum of Solace*, because Forster's James Bond has a special motivation for killing, an "operatic" motivation, according to Chan-wook Park's notion of opera quoted above—"revenge" for his beloved, who died in the previous *007* film *Casino Royale* (2006). Furthermore, the Bond girl, Camille Montes (Olga Kurylenko), also seeks revenge for the murder of her parents by a collaborator of the film's main villain. In the opening of *Quantum of Solace*, Agent 007 (Daniel Craig) is driving in Italy, transporting the captured Mr. White (Jesper Christensen), the villain from *Casino Royale* responsible for the death of Bond's beloved. As Bond interrogates Mr. White about his organization, Quantum, Mr. White manages to escape with the help of a double agent. In the course of searching for Mr. White, Bond uncovers Quantum's scheme for a coup d'état in Bolivia. The leader of this terrorist scheme is Dominic Greene (Mathieu Amalric), the main villain in Forster's sequel, who is the chairman of an ecological organization called Greene Planet, the façade of Quantum. Bond follows Greene to

---

[27]   Citron, *When Opera Meets Film*, p. 53. According to her footnote 87 (p. 262), it was not Coppola but the sound editor of the film, Walter Murch, who came up with the idea of a muted cry.

[28]   Slavoj Žižek, *Enjoy Your Symptom! Jacques Lacan in Hollywood and Out*, 2nd ed. (New York: Routledge, 2001), p. 141.

[29]   Slavoj Žižek, "'I Hear You with My Eyes'; or The Invisible Master," in *Gaze and Voice as Love Objects*, ed. Renata Salecl and Slavoj Žižek (Durhman, NC: Duke University Press, 1996), pp. 90–128.

[30]   It is a direct sequel to the 2006 James Bond film *Casino Royale*, directed by Martin Campbell, in which Daniel Craig first played the 007 role. Citron's article, "The Operatics of Detachment: *Tosca* in the James Bond Film *Quantum of Solace*," *19th-Century Music* 34, no. 3 (2011): 316–40, focuses on how the opera sequence signifies a "detached operatic subjectivity" by visual means, such as montage, and through opera's interaction with the film narrative—for instance, how opera is presented as an "isolating phenomenon" in this film (p. 318).

Austria, where he infiltrates a meeting of Quantum held at the outdoor performance of Puccini's *Tosca* at Lake Constance. Bond infiltrates Quantum's meeting by stealing one of the member's earpieces, through which they are communicating during the opera performance. As Greene and his associates are leaving the opera auditorium after having discovered that their conversation has been intercepted, they bump into Bond on the stairs of the opera house; a gunfight follows and several people are killed. Bond follows Greene to a hotel in the Bolivian desert, where Greene has a meeting with the Bolivian general Medrano (Joaquín Cosio) to finalize their execution of the coup. After interrogating him about Quantum, Bond leaves Greene stranded in the middle of the desert with only a can of motor oil. Bond goes to Russia to find Yusef Kabira (Simon Kassianides), a member of Quantum who was his beloved's former boyfriend and is responsible for her death. Bond does not kill Yusef but allows him to be arrested by a member of the British intelligence service. At the end of the film, Bond hears that Greene was found dead in the middle of the desert, where he was left, with his stomach filled with motor oil.

The opera sequence in *Quantum of Solace* shows several similarities with the opera scenes in the other films examined above. First, opera is used as diegetic music. Second, the opera performance is cross-cut with the action of killing. But unlike the other films, Forster uses an opera scene in the middle of the plot rather than at the dénouement, and those who are killed during the opera performance are not major characters but minor ones. The length of the opera sequence in *Quantum of Solace* (around 5 minutes) is not as lengthy as that of *Foul Play* (around 17 minutes) or *Godfather III* (22 minutes, including the 3 minutes of nondiegetic music, Mascagni's "Intermezzo"). In spite of the brevity of its appearance, opera in *Quantum of Solace* serves as a powerful and effective means to enhance the turbulence of the cinematic death through its parallel onstage action: Tosca's stabbing of Scarpia and Cavaradossi's execution. In order to make a tighter thematic and visual connection between the onscreen killing and the onstage death, the *Tosca* excerpts are radically edited. The opera scene begins with the announcement at the theater: "Tonight's opera *Tosca* will be performed shortly." The first music we hear is the four lines from Scarpia's song, "Palazzo Farnese!" interspersed with the chorus at the end of Act I (italics indicate the portions omitted in the film):

Palazzo Farnese!	*Farnese Palace!*
Va Tosca!	*Go, Tosca!*
Nel tuo cuor s'annida Scarpia! ...	*Now Scarpia digs a nest within your heart!*
Va, Tosca! E Scarpia che scioglie a volo	Go, Tosca! Scarpia now sets loose
Il falco della tua gelosia.	The soaring falcon of your jealousy!
Quanta promesa nel tuo pronto sospetto!	How great a promise in your quick suspicions!
Nel tuo cuor s'annida Scarpia! ...	Now Scarpia digs a nest within your heart!
Va, Tosca!	*Go, Tosca!*

The extra instrumental music is inserted after "s'annida Scarpia!" and before the next vocal entry of the opera in order to avoid the simultaneous sounding of the opera's singing voice and the film's spoken dialogue. It is also during this instrumental interlude that Bond suggests to the Quantum members (through the earpieces he stole) that they should "find a better place to meet." Then the opera excerpt cuts to the middle of Scarpia's next entry, skipping the chorus (italicized lines are cut).

A doppia mira tend oil voler,	*My will takes aim now at a double target,*
Né il capo del ribelle è la piú preziosa ...	*nor is the rebel's head the bigger prize ...*
Ah, di quegli occhi vittoriosi veder la flamma illanguidir	Ah, to see the flame of those imperious eyes,
Con spasimo d'amor fra le mie braccia illanguidir d'amor ...	Grow faint and languid with passion ...
L'uno al capestro,	For him, the rope,
L'altra fra le mie braccia ...	And for her, my arms ...

Following this excerpt is an instrumental interlude, during which Mr. White whispers to the woman sitting next to him, "Well, *Tosca* isn't for everyone," as he sees Greene's associates leaving the auditorium. Once again, the potential for the operatic voice to interfere with the film dialogue is carefully avoided. The opera performance then cuts to the *Te Deum* ("Te aeturum / Patrem omnis terra veneratur!"), sung by the chorus and Scarpia at the very end of Act I. The onscreen action shown during the *Te Deum* is Bond's encounter with Greene and several of his associates on the stairs, as they hurriedly leave the opera house.

The following scene contains a radically liberal editing of Puccini's opera—a cut from the end of Act I to the end of the opera (Act III) and back to the end of Act II, which significantly intensifies the connection between the onstage visuals and the onscreen actions. At the final chord of the *Te Deum*, the opera stage shows a glimpse of Cavaradossi's execution at the end of the opera, which cuts to the onscreen action of the eruption of the gunfire. The beginning of this gunfire scene is silent, as all of the diegetic sounds are momentarily muted.[31] Unlike Michael's silent scream in *Godfather III*, this is a complete silence without any background music. When the soundtrack is restored, we hear the last scene of Act II, in which Tosca kills Scarpia. However, we no longer hear any vocal music for the rest of the opera scene: we see Tosca stabbing Scarpia onstage, but Scarpia's death cry—"Aiuto ... muoio! Soccoroso! Muoio!" ("Help! I am dying! Help! I die!)—and Tosca's declamatory singing—"Ti soffoca il sangue?" (Is your blood choking you?)—are replaced by the instrumental music from the previous scene of the opera, in which Scarpia is writing a letter: the instrumental music containing one of the signature motives of

---

[31] For the use of silence to represent death in film, see Stan Link, "Going Gently: Contemplating Silences and Cinematic Death," in *Silence, Music, Silent Music*, ed. Nicky Losseff and Jenny Doctor (Burlington, VT: Ashgate, 2007), pp. 69–86.

Tosca and which recurs several times later in the opera. With Puccini's vocal sounds silenced, the last part of the gunfight sequence on stage carefully avoids obscuring the cinematic voice. And the rapid parallel editing between the onstage murder and the onscreen gunfight enhances the frantic commotion of the cinematic murders.

Another interesting aspect of the later part of the gunfight sequence is the reversal of the function of operatic music. In many movie scenes that use opera, operatic music tends to serve as an additional sonic content of—or a kind of additional "sound effect" for—the film action. In *Quantum of Solace*, it is the diegetic sounds of the film, such as the roar of gunshots and the frantic footsteps, that become the sound effects for the visuals of the opera performance—the sound effects that compensate for the vocal absence (Scarpia's scream, "Soccorso! Aiuto!"; Tosca's infuriated voice, "Muori damnato! Muori! Muori!" and so on). To put it differently, in *Quantum of Solace*, I argue, the function of opera is more of a visual effect than a sound effect.

Claude Chabrol's *La Cérémonie* (1995) is the last film I examine before moving to the main discussion of the murder scene in *Match Point*. As Marcia Citron indicates, the appearance of opera in Chabrol's film is idiosyncratic: it is presented as a televised opera that the onscreen characters are watching.[32] The opera televised in this film is the 1987 Salzburg Festival production of Mozart's *Don Giovanni*, conducted by Herbert von Karajan and staged by Michael Hampe. Chabrol's film is an adaptation of Ruth Rendell's 1977 crime novel *A Judgment in Stone*. The protagonist of *La Cérémonie* is Sophie (Sandrine Bonnaire), who has just been hired as a live-in maid by the Lelièvres, a wealthy French family. Sophie is a visual dyslexic but she desperately hides her illiteracy from everybody. She becomes friends with Jeanne (Isabelle Huppert), a post office employee. Georges, the father of the Lelièvre family, suspects that Jeanne opens and reads the family's mail, and one day he tells Sophie that Jeanne was charged with the murder of her four-year-old daughter, and that although she was acquitted for lack of evidence, he doesn't believe her innocence. During a conversation with Jeanne, Sophie is also revealed to have been a murder suspect, but whether these two characters are guilty or innocent remains equivocal throughout the film. When Georges asks Sophie not to invite Jeanne to his house any more, the tension between Sophie and the Lelièvre family increases. The tension culminates when the teenage daughter, Mélinda, discovers Sophie's illiteracy and the family hears how Sophie has blackmailed her: if Mélinda discloses Sophie's illiteracy to her family, Sophie will reveal Mélinda's premarital pregnancy, which she has found out from eavesdropping on Mélinda's telephone conversation with her boyfriend. Sophie is fired and given a week to leave her employer's house. Jeanne is furious and asks Sophie to stand up against her arrogant and pretentious bourgeois employers. The murder sequence begins when the Lelièvre family is watching a telecast of *Don Giovanni*, which Mélinda is recording on her boom

---

[32]   Citron, *When Opera Meets Film*, p. 136. Citron's book has a chapter on this film "*Don Giovanni* and Subjectivity in Claude Charbrol's *La Cérémonie*" (pp. 136–70).

box, using an external microphone positioned in front of the television. Sophie and Jeanne each take a shotgun that belongs to the family and shoot everybody in the family. On her way out, Jeanne takes Mélinda's boom box as a kind of a war trophy, and while she is driving back to her house she dies in a car accident. The police find the boom box and play it. The film ends mysteriously: Sophie is shown outside, hearing from afar the playback of the boom box, which recorded not only the opera telecast but also the crime sounds—shootings, screams, and the voices of Sophie and Jeanne.

As in *Foul Play* and *Godfather III*, the length of the opera-murder sequence in Chabrol's film is extensive (about 13 minutes), and as in *Quantum of Solace*, *Death to Smoochy*, and *Foul Play*, the opera-murder scene stands out through parallel editing between the operatic and the cinematic events. As Marcia Citron's brilliant analysis of the film has illuminated, the function of Mozart's opera in *La Cérémonie* is highly complex.[33] At the narrative level, the opera excerpts often provide a parallel to the filmic plot and action. The duet between Don Giovanni and his servant Leporello, "Eh via buffoné," is an example. In this duet, Leporello complains about his boss's mistreatment of him—an evocation of the relationship between Sophie and her employers. Sophie's murder of Georges is another example of a parallelism between the operatic action and that of the film: Georges finds Sophie and Jeanne in the kitchen and asks them to put down the guns, but Sophie, emotionless and merciless, immediately fires her rifle and kills her master. The music heard with this filmic action is Leporello's arguing with his master from the same duet above: "Ed io non burlo, ma voglio andar" ("And I'm not kidding, I want to go") / "Eh via buffone" ("Come on, you fool") / "No no padrone" ("No, no, boss") / "Va' che sei matto!" ("You're mad!"). Sometimes the parallelism between Mozart's opera and Chabrol's film is visually reinforced: for instance, the camera is continuously panning from the pillars of Giovanni's ballroom shown on television to the balcony on which the cinematic characters—Sophie and Jeanne—are standing. As Citron mentions, this visual composition creates the impression that the operatic space shown on television and the cinematic space are fused.[34]

The narrative parallelism between the opera and the film is often presented with ironic distance in *La Cérémonie*.[35] Claudia Gorbman claims that diegetic music has capacity to create irony in a more "natural" way than nondiegetic music does, because diegetic music is supposedly unaware of or even indifferent (or "anempathetic," to put it in Michel Chion's term), or even relentless to the dramatic situation of the film. Gorbman mentions the murder of a man during a

---

[33] Marcia Citron, "*Don Giovanni* and Subjectivity in *La Cérémonie*," in *When Opera Meets Film*, pp. 140–60. See Table 4.1 on pp. 142–3 for Citron's analysis of the shot-by-shot murder sequence with musical numbers excerpted from Mozart's opera, the corresponding action in the film, and their exact timing in the DVD.

[34] Ibid., p. 150.

[35] Ibid., p. 147.

dance party in Hitchcock's *The Man Who Knew Too Much* (1934). If the murder were executed in a different environment and cheerful dance music were used nondiegetically, the musical style, whose affective quality does not conform to the tragic atmosphere of the film event, would puzzle the film viewers, because nondiegetic music is normally expected to "underscore" the film action.[36]

According to Citron's analysis, "Protegga il giusto cielo" ("My righteous Heaven protect"), from the Act I Finale of *Don Giovanni*, presents an instance of ironic distance within the narrative parallelism in Chabrol's film,. In this song, Donna Anna, Don Ottavio, and Donna Elvira are determined to avenge Don Giovanni: Donna Elvira sings, "Véndichi il giusto cielo / Il mio tradito amor" ("May righteous Heaven avenge / my betrayed love"). The revengeful feeling of Mozart's characters mirrors Sophie and Jeanne's rage toward the Lelièvre family and foreshadows their murder as a vengeance. And the procession of the operatic characters' movement from outside to the inside of Giovanni's ballroom is paralleled by Sophie's and Jeanne's entering the Lelièvres' house. However, "Protegga" creates an ironic distance from the film in terms of the class of the characters: Mozart's revengeful characters all belong to the same social station as the person they want to avenge, Don Giovanni, while Sophie and Jeanne are sharply differentiated and alienated from the privileged upper class of the Lelièvre family. In fact, Chabrol's film presents a strong social critique of the cultural and class conflict, to the extent that the director once called it "the last Marxist film."[37] Chabrol had considered using Mozart's *The Marriage of Figaro* for the opera-murder sequence because it addresses social issues, especially class conflict, more strongly than *Don Giovanni* does. But he eventually decided to follow Rendell's choice of opera for his novel, although his selections from *Don Giovanni* are different from Rendell's.[38]

For me, the most fascinating and sophisticated aspect of Citron's approach to *La Cérémonie* is her analysis of the tension between the aural and the visual, drawn an such studies as Michal Grover-Friedlander's *Vocal Apparitions: The Attraction of Cinema to Opera*.[39] This tension is primarily conveyed by the role of the television, through which the Lelièvre family is watching Mozart's opera, and that of the boom box, which records not only the telecast of Mozart's opera but also the crime sounds. Focusing on the fact that it is Mélinda's boom box that contains the final vestige of the televised opera, which we hear as the last

---

[36]   Gorbman, *Unheard Melodies*, pp. 23–4. Gorbman has also demonstrated that in the practice of standard narrative filmmaking, diegetic music, too, is often employed to match the mood and pace of the film scene "with an uncanny consistency." For me, the performance of *Tosca* in *Quantum of Solace* is one of the best examples of this "uncanny consistency."

[37]   Quoted in Citron, *When Opera Meets Film*, p. 139.

[38]   For detailed information about the difference between Chabrol's selection and Rendell's, see Citron, *When Opera Meets Film*, pp. 151–4.

[39]   Michal Grover-Friedlander, *Vocal Apparitions: The Attraction of Cinema to Opera* (Princeton, NJ: Princeton University Press, 2005.

sounds at the end of the film and continues during the closing credits,[40] Citron argues that the aural is privileged over the visual in *La Cérémonie*, as well as in many of Chabrol's other films. In the "aural remains" of the opera recorded in the boom box, the visual element contained in the televised opera is totally effaced: hence Citron's illuminating claim for "the audible as the remains of the visual."[41] She also contextualizes "the triumph of the aural" in the socio-cultural implication of the television apparatus in Chabrol's cinematic oeuvre: in *La Cérémonie*, television functions as a venue for the Lelièvre family's high-cultural pleasure (viewing an opera), and in this respect, Citron continues, the effacement of the visual (television) by the aural (the boom box) signifies the insurrection of the underprivileged class against the privileged, enacted with the murder of the Lelièvre family by Sophie and Jeanne.[42] From this perspective, it is symbolic that, after the murder, Jeanne bluntly turns off the television and takes the boom box: symbolic if one reads the cessation of the television as a metaphor for the termination of the Lelièvres' lives.

Furthermore, Citron suggests another symbolic meaning behind the privileging of the aural over the visual in Chabrol's film, contextualizing it in the redeeming power of music in the Orphic myth. Revising Joël Magny's view that Mozart is "assassinated" in Chabrol's *La Cérémonie*, Citron proposes that in the aural remains of the opera, Mozart's *Don Giovanni* is resurrected, if the taped version recorded in the boom box is considered to be a new opera with the sounds of the murder "composed" onto Mozart's original music.[43] Considering the resurrection—that is, the afterlife of Mozart's opera—it is the sounds as opposed to the images of Chabrol's film that have a redeeming power, like Orpheus's song.

From the perspective of the Orphic myth, I suggest an alternative reading of the murder scene. My reading of the interplay between the aural and the visual in Chabrol's film is more pessimistic than Citron's. I agree with Citron about the implication of the Orphic power of the aural in Chabrol's film, for I too regard the "aural remains" stored in the boom box as a suggestion of the afterlife of Mozart's opera. From an ideological point of view, the power of the aural can be considered redeeming, since "the triumph of the aural" allegorizes the revolt of the socially and culturally underprivileged against the privileged. And this reading might be close to the filmmaker's intention when one considers that the class conflict is emphatically addressed in Chabrol's film through an intense, almost exaggerated, contrast between Sophie's literal illiteracy and the Lelièvre

---

[40]   Citron notes, "It is as if Chabrol creates a new kind of credits-music genre." See Citron, *When Opera Meets Film*, p. 169.

[41]   Ibid., p. 168.

[42]   Ibid., p. 161.

[43]   Ibid., p. 167. In this reading, Citron is drawing on Michal Grover-Friedlander's concept of the aural remains as afterlife.

family's "virtuosic" cultural literacy, according to Citron's characterization.[44] However, when the interplay between sight and sound is applied to the power dynamics between the Lelièvre family and their murderesses, it seems to me that the function of the aural in Chabrol's film becomes pessimistic—more destructive than redemptive. In the interpretation I propose here, the aural in Chabrol's film takes the role of the Orphic *gaze* that brings rather than overcomes death. Sophie's dyslexia is highly allusive in this context: since she is *visually* dyslexic, her linguistic communication is only through *the sounds* of language; for her, *the visual dimension* of language—that is, language represented as written symbols—is simply impotent. From this point of view, Sophie can be interpreted as the embodiment of the aural, and the power of the aural represented by her is not redeeming but destructive like the Orphic gaze, since it engenders death, the death of the Lelièvre family. The aural in Chabrol's film is a deathly voice, unlike Orpheus's song, which brings the dead back to life. "The triumph of the aural"—the aural as the remains of the visual, represented by the recorded sounds in the boom box—may be destructive to Sophie's life, too, since it is clear evidence of her homicide and may lead to her identification as a criminal. In this respect, Jeanne's death at a car accident is also allusive, as thought she were killed because she was carrying the emblem of the triumph of the aural— the boom box, the container of the deathly voice.

---

[44]   Ibid., p. 143. As for Citron, I am also greatly indebted to Michal Grover-Friedlander's insightful and pioneering study of the dynamics between the aural and the visual and the afterlife of the aural, explored in many of her works, including her two books, *Vocal Apparitions: The Attraction of Cinema to Opera* (Princeton, NJ: Princeton University Press, 2005) and *Operatic Afterlives* (New York: Zone Books, 2011).

Chapter 3
Opera in Woody Allen's *Match Point*

"Allen—Woody, that is—manages to be both irreverent and absolutely true to the music and the spirit of the work ... But what is perhaps most surprising about Allen's production, which is brilliantly sung and acted down to the most minor character and walk-on, is how uncinematic it is. He begins with a screen in front of the stage projecting silly film credits, but that only underscores the sheer theatricality of the classic farce that follows." This is how Mark Swed described Woody Allen's staging of Puccini's *Gianni Schicchi* for the Los Angeles Opera in 2008—Allen's first step into opera staging.[1] If Allen's staging of Puccini's opera surprised people because it was "uncinematic," his film *Match Point* (2005) was another surprise for the reverse reason—that is, the dominance of opera on the soundtrack: all of the eleven nondiegetic numbers and three out of the five diegetic numbers are pre-existing opera excerpts. Film critic Stanley Kauffmann wrote,

> The scores for Allen films have often used pop songs of the past—pre-rock. This time the present is left behind in a different way. Near the beginning comes a scene in a box at the opera, and the soundtrack thereafter is laced with bits of Verdi, Donizetti, and others. These excerpts have nothing to do with what we see at the moment; maybe Allen just felt that a film made abroad ought to have a classy score.[2]

Although jazz and popular music are the most frequently used types of music in his films, Allen's use of classical music is not infrequent: to cite a few examples, Prokofiev in *Love and Death* (1975), Gershwin and Mozart in *Manhattan* (1979), J.S. Bach in *Hannah and Her Sisters* (1986), J.S. Bach and Schubert in *Crimes and Misdemeanors* (1989), Mahler in *Husbands and Wives* (1992), and J.S. Bach, Bartók, and Stravinsky in *Melinda and Melinda* (2004). But among classical genres, opera is relatively rare in Allen's films: *Hannah and Her Sisters* and *Love and Death* are among the few, featuring Puccini's *Manon Lescaut* and *Madama Butterfly*, and Mozart's *Magic Flute* and Prokofiev's *Love for Three Oranges*, respectively. Given the rarity of opera in Allen's soundtracks, *Match Point* is

---

[1]   Mark Swed, "'Il Trittico,' the Los Angeles Opera: Filmmaker Woody Allen Helps Deliver Great Comic Puccini," *Los Angles Times*, September 8, 2008, www.latimes.com/entertainment/news/arts/la-et-trittico8-2008sep08,0,7203446.story (accessed February 7, 2012).

[2]   Stanley Kauffmann, "Stanley Kauffmann on Films: Scene Changes," *The New Republic*, January 30, 2006, p. 22.

indeed special.[3] Although Kauffman notes that the opera excerpts "have nothing to do with what you see at the moment," one can draw broad parallels between the theme and/or plot of the film and those of the source operas in many of the scenes accompanied by opera excerpts, a possibility of which Jennifer Fleeger has given us a glimpse.[4]

In this chapter, I will explore the diverse functions of the opera excerpts in *Match Point*, with particular attention to the murder scene. As discussed in the previous chapter, the use of operatic music in death scenes in film has been notable over the past few decades. In the death scenes of the films examined in Chapter 2, opera stands out by its unique presence on the soundtrack; through its singular use, opera contributes to the enhancement of the dramatic tension and climactic intensity of cinematic death, which is often a key moment of a film. In *Match Point*, however, opera is ubiquitous on the soundtrack, yet the excerpt used in the murder sequence—from Verdi's *Otello*—is distinguished from the other opera excerpts and creates special effects for the murder sequence. In what follows I will show how the *Otello* excerpt is distinctive in terms of the idiosyncratic way it evokes death, and the way it interacts with the fictional world, or diegesis, of the film in spite of its apparent extradiegetic status. Among the major studies I use for a close analysis of the murder sequence are Jerrold Levinson's theory of the functions of film music and Claudia Gorbman's work, both of which focus on narratological issues.[5]

The Plot

Set in London, the story of Allen's *Match Point* centers on the catastrophic love affair between Chris Wilton (Jonathan Rhys Meyers) and Nola Rice (Scarlett Johansson), which culminates in Chris's murder of Nola. A former tennis player from an Irish family, Chris works as a tennis teacher. One of his students is Tom

---

[3] A soundtrack CD, which contains all of the opera excerpts in the film, is produced by Milan Records in 2006 as a part of the "Music from the Motion Picture" series.

[4] Jennifer Fleeger, "Opera, Jazz, and Hollywood's Conversion to Sound" (PhD diss., University of Iowa, 2009), p. 1. She notes, "opera enthusiasts could interpret the musical selections as Allen's commentary on the story; for example, the opening aria, 'Una furtiva lagrima' from Gaetano Donizetti's *L'elisir d'amore* (1832), neatly mirrors the relationship of the film's two main characters." But she does not go further than this statement. Instead, her dissertation focuses on what opera and jazz share in their role as the sonic paradigm during cinema's conversion period (ca. 1926–32). Given this, suggests Fleeger, it is not surprising for Woody Allen, a jazz aficionado New Yorker whose earlier films are replete with jazz, to make a transition to opera for the soundtrack of *Match Point*.

[5] Jerrold Levinson, "Film Music and Narrative Agency," in *Post-Theory: Reconstructing Film Studies*, ed. David Bordwell and Noël Carroll (Madison: University of Wisconsin Press, 1996), pp. 248–82; and Claudia Gorbman, *Unheard Melodies: Narrative Film Music* (Bloomington: Indiana University Press, 1987).

Hewett (Matthew Goode), who is from a prominent upper-class family. The beginning of the film unequivocally portrays Chris as an opportunistic social climber; he is an opera fan, but his interest in opera is primarily motivated by his aspiration to approach and socialize with upper-class people. His interest in literature, Dostoyevsky in particular, also serves the same purpose: he is first shown reading *Crime and Punishment*, but he soon abandons the novel and instead moves on to *The Cambridge Companion to Dostoyevsky*. And his opportunistic interest in Dostoyevsky does help him accomplish his purpose, as Tom's father, Alec Hewett (Brian Cox), praises Chris to his family as a "cultured" man—cultured enough to get acquainted with his family. Chris's interest in opera also connects him to the Hewett family and especially his wife-to-be, Chloe (Emily Mortimer): When Tom hears about Chris's interest in opera, he invites his tennis teacher to the family's opera outing to Covent Garden, where Chris first meets Tom's sister, Chloe. Chloe and Chris begin to date. A little later, Chris meets Tom's fiancée, Nola Rice, a sexy American woman and struggling actress. Tom's mother, Eleanor Hewett (Penelope Wilton), is strongly opposed to Nola for the reason that she lacks high cultural tastes and background. At first sight, Chris is fatally drawn in by Nola's sexual charm. They begin an affair but Nola refuses to continue their relationship, so Chris marries Chloe. When he finds out that Tom has broken up with Nola, the affair resumes. Nola becomes pregnant, while Chloe struggles with fertility treatments. Chris requests that Nola get an abortion but she adamantly refuses. As Nola becomes more and more demanding, Chris decides to kill her. He steals a machine gun from his father-in-law's home. To disguise his murder of Nola as an accident, Chris plots a meticulous plan: he first kills Nola's neighbor in the same apartment building, Mrs. Eastby (Margaret Tyzack), to fake it as a drug-related burglary. Then he kills Nola and disguises her death as an accidental murder resulting from the burglar's effort to remove a witness who happened to come back to her apartment as he was leaving the crime site. The detectives discover Nola's relationship with Chris when they discover her diary; he is summoned to the police station and insists on his innocence. Although one of the detectives strongly suspects Chris, he is saved because a drug dealer is found with an item of jewelry, a ring, that Chris took to disguise his murder of Mrs. Eastby as a burglary and later threw away. The image of Chris throwing the ring into the River Thames parallels the opening scene, which shows a tennis ball at the match point (Figure 3.1) heard with Chris's voiceover narration: "There are moments in a match when the ball hits the top of the net, and for a split second it can either go forward or fall back. With a little luck, it goes forward and you win. Or maybe it doesn't, and you lose." Luck was on Chris's side: the ring drops inside a fence rather than falling into the river, and is picked up by a drug addict whom the police identify as the killer of Nola and Mrs. Eastby. The film ends with a sequence celebrating Chris and Chloe's baby.

Figure 3.1   Opening scene of *Match Point*

The Soundtrack and Its Narrative Relationship to the Film

There are 16 musical cues in *Match Point*, among which 11 are nondiegetic and 5 are diegetic. Four out of the five diegetic pieces appear as live performances in the film narrative; three of them are opera excerpts and the fourth is from a musical. The only diegetic number that is not presented as a live *performance* is a piano waltz: it is *suggested* as party music without its sound source being shown on screen. In Table 3.1 I label as nondiegetic all other musical cues whose sound sources are not shown on screen, but some could be regarded as "metadiegetic" (Claudia Gorbman's term) or "psycho-diegetic" (Marcia Citron's preferred term),[6] as I will discuss later in the chapter. All 11 nondiegetic numbers are opera excerpts and all of them are taken from recordings of Enrico Caruso, except for the excerpt from Verdi's *Otello* that accompanies the murder sequence (no. 13). Six of the Caruso recordings have piano accompaniment (nos. 1, 5, 9, 10, 12, and 16), and four are accompanied by chamber ensemble (nos. 3, 4, 8, and 15). Three of the nondiegetic musical cues appear more than once. What follows is a detailed description of the musical cues and their narrative relationship to the film. Excluded from this section is the excerpt from Verdi's *Otello*, which will be discussed in a separate section.

---

[6]   Gorbman, *Unheard Melodies*, pp. 22–3. Marcia Citron explains the origin of the term "psycho-diegetic music" as follows: "The term was coined by Alexis Witt in an unpublished paper for a seminar at Rice University, 'Opera and Film,' spring 2006. I have used it subsequently in published work, especially in 'An Honest Contrivance': Opera and Desire in *Moonstruck*," *Music and Letters* 89, no. 1 (February 2008): 56–83. Psycho-diegetic, which refers to a remembered use of music, falls under the umbrella of "metadiegetic," Claudia Gorbman's term for larger-level functions of film music that go beyond diegetic and nondiegetic. See Citron, "'Soll ich lauschen?': Love-Death in *Humoresque*," in *Wagner and Cinema*, ed. Jeongwon Joe and Sander L. Gilman (Bloomington: Indiana University Press, 2010), p. 184 (n. 17).

Nondiegetic Music

The aria "Una furtiva lagrima" from Donizetti's *Elixir of Love* is the most frequently used opera excerpt (nos. 1, 9, 12, and 16 in Table 3.1).[7] This aria is sung by the opera's male protagonist, Nemorino, in Act II, scene 8, when he finds that the love potion he bought appears to be working on the woman he's in love with, Adina. Since Nemorino's aria is about love, it is loosely related to Chris's passion for Nola. In spite of the difference between Chris's fatalistic and tragic lust for Nola and the opera protagonist's happy-ending love, Donizetti's aria is connected to the story of Allen's film through the word "morir" (to die) in the libretto. Although the opera concludes with a happy ending, Nemorino's aria implies a kind of *Liebestod*, broadly defined as love-related death, when he emphatically and climactically sings, "Si può morir! Si può morir d'amor" ("Yes, I could die! Yes, I could die of love"). The contemplation of *Liebestod* is emphasized by the repetition of the word "morir" in the libretto, which is musically reinforced at each repetition. Given this, it is intriguing that the first stanza of the aria, which does not contain the word or idea of death, is not used on the soundtrack of Allen's film. Every time Donizetti's excerpt is used, only the second stanza is heard, although a different portion is used each time (italics indicate omission on the soundtrack):

Una furtiva lagrima	*A single secret tear*
negli occhi suoi spuntò:	*from her eye did spring:*
Quelle festose giovani	*as if she envied all the youths*
invidiar sembrò.	*that laughingly passed her by.*
Che più cercando io vo?	*What more searching need I do?*
Che più cercando io vo?	*What more searching need I do?*
M'ama! Sì, m'ama, lo vedo. Lo vedo.	*She loves me! Yes, she loves me, I see it. I see it.*
Un solo instante i palpiti	For just an instant the beating
del suo bel cor sentir!	of her beautiful heart I could feel!
I miei sospir, confondere	As if my sighs were hers,
per poco a' suoi sospir!	and her sighs were mine!
I palpiti, i palpiti sentir,	The beating, the beating of her heart I could feel,
confondere i miei coi suoi sospir ... [third entry ends in the middle of "confondere"]	to merge my sighs with hers ...[third entry ends in the middle of "confondere"]
Cielo! Si può morir! [first entry ends here]	Heavens! Yes, I could die! [first entry ends here]
Di più non chiedo, non chiedo. [second entry ends here]	I could ask for nothing more, nothing more. [second entry ends here]
Ah, cielo! Si può! Sì, può morir!	Oh, heavens! Yes, I could, I could die!
Di più non chiedo, non chiedo.	I could ask for nothing more, nothing more.
Si può morire! Si può morir d'amor. [final entry ends here]	Yes, I could die! Yes, I could die of love [final entry ends here]

---

[7] The numbers of the musical cues in this section correspond to those in Table 3.1.

Table 3.1   Musical cues from *Match Point*

Individual song	Source opera	Remarks
1. "Una furtiva lagrima"	Donizetti's *The Elixir of Love*	Nondiegetic. Caruso's recording with piano accompaniment used for the opening credits connected to the opening scene of a tossed tennis ball.
2. "Un di felice, eterea"	Verdi's *La traviata*	Diegetic performance with piano accompaniment at Covent Garden.
3. "Mal reggendo all'aspro assalto?"	Verdi's *Il trovatore*	Nondiegetic. Caruso's recording with chamber ensemble, accompanying Chris's first visit to the Hewetts' estate.
4. "Mia piccirella"	Carlos Gomes's *Salvator Rosa*	Nondiegetic. Caruso's recording with chamber ensemble, accompanying Chris and Chloe's first date, connected to their love-making after a cut during the movie-theater scene.
5. "Mi par d'udir ancora"	Bizet's *Pearl Fishers*	Nondiegetic. Caruso's recording with piano accompaniment, heard while Chris is waiting for Nola in front of the Royal Court during her acting audition.
6. "Caro nome"	Verdi's *Rigoletto*	Diegetic performance with piano accompaniment at Covent Garden.
7. A piano waltz		Implied diegetic (no sound source is shown), accompanying a party at the Hewetts' estate
8. "Mia piccirella"	Gomes's *Salvador Rosa*	Nondiegetic. Caruso's recording with chamber ensemble, accompanying Chris and Chloe's wedding.
9. "Una furtiva lagrima"	Donizetti's *The Elixir of Love*	Nondiegetic. Caruso's recording with piano accompaniment during Chris's encounter with Nola at Tate Modern.
10. "Mi par d'udir ancora"	Bizet's *Pearl Fishers*	Nondiegetic. Caruso's recording with piano accompaniment during Chris's love-making with Nola.

11. "Arresta!"	Rossini's *William Tell*	Unseen diegetic performance with orchestral accompaniment at Covent Garden.
12. "Una furtiva lagrima"	Donizetti's *The Elixir of Love*	Nondiegetic. Caruso's recording with piano accompaniment heard when Chris decides to kill Nola.
13. "Si per ciel"	Verdi's *Otello*	Nondiegetic. Performed by Janez Lotric as Otello and Igor Morozov as Iago, accompanying Chris's double murder of Nola and Mrs. Eastby.
14. "I Believe My Heart"	Andrew Lloyd Webber's *The Woman in White*	Unseen diegetic performance that Chris watches with Chloe right after the murder scene.
15. "O figli, o figli miei!"	Verdi's *Macbeth*	Nondiegetic. Caruso's recording with chamber ensemble heard when Chris throws Mrs. Eastby's ring and other jewelry on his way to the police station.
16. "Una furtiva lagrima"	Donizetti's *The Elixir of Love*	Nondiegetic. Caruso's recording with piano accompaniment, entering near the end of the final scene and connected to the closing credits.

Another aspect of the Donizetti opera that contributes to the narrative parallelism with Allen's film is a reference to the love potion in *Tristan und Isolde* in the earlier part of the opera. In Act I, scene 4, Nemorino sings to Dulcamara, the man who sold him the false potion: "It was Tristan who employed it / To awaken love's desiring." Therefore, *Tristan*'s tragic *Liebestod*, which involves actual death, has a covert presence in Donizetti's comic opera, providing a stronger parallel between Allen's film and Donizetti's opera.

The next nondiegetic opera excerpt is the aria "Mal reggendo all'aspro assalto" from Verdi's *Il trovatore*, which features a love triangle involving Count di Luna, Manrico, and Leonora (no. 3). "Mal reggendo..." is Manrico's aria from Act II, scene 1. In this aria he tells Azucena, his supposed mother, about his duel with the Count, which he won, but in which he did not kill his opponent. Although this particular aria does not bear any immediate relationship to the scene that it accompanies—Chris's first visit to the Hewetts' estate—the general theme of a love triangle in *Il trovatore* is echoed by Chris's inappropriate passion for his brother-in-law's fiancée. Another broad relationship between the plot of *Match Point* and that of Verdi's opera is the death of a principal female character: Leonora's suicide and Nola's homicide.

Mal reggendo all'aspro assalto,	Fighting off poorly my fierce attack,
Ei già tocco il cuolo avea:	He had already fallen to the ground:
Balenava il colpo in alto	The thrust that was to pierce him
Che trafiggerio dovea.	Already flashed in the air,
Quando arresta un moto arcano	When a mysterious feeling
Nel discender questa mano!	Stopped my hand, as it descended!
Le mie fibre acuto gelo	Suddenly a sharp chill
Fa repente abbrividir!	Ran shuddering through my being
Mentre un grido vien dal cielo,	As a cry came down from heaven,
Che mi dice: non ferir!	That said to me: "Don't strike!"

"Mia piccirella" (no. 4) is from a lesser-known opera, *Salvator Rosa* (1874), by the Brazilian composer Antonio Carlos Gomes (1836–96). Set in Naples in 1674, Gomes's opera is a fictionalization of the life of the historical figure Salvator Rosa (1615–73), an Italian painter and poet. The opera's plot mixes the theme of love with the political struggle during the Neapolitan resistance against the Spanish invasion. Rosa is in love with Isabella, the daughter of the Duke of Arco, a villainous character. When Salvator is arrested for a political reason, the Duke promises to free Salvator on the condition that Isabella marries Fernandez, a commander of the Spanish troops. The opera ends with the heart-broken Isabella's suicide. The aria used on the *Match Point* soundtrack is a diegetic song within the opera,[8] sung by a secondary character named Gennariello at the beginning

---

[8]   At the 1997 conference of the International Musicological Society (IMS) in London, Claudia Gorbman informed me in an informal context that she prefers Carolyn Abbate's

of Act I. Gennariello is a musician, and with this Neapolitan song he is trying to inspire the protagonist Rosa in his painting.

Mia piccirella, deh? Vieni allo mare!	My little one, ah! Come to the sea!
Nella barchetta v'e un letto di fior …	In my little boat is a bed of flowers …
La Bianca prora somiglia un altare,	Its white prow looks like an altar,
L'onde e le stele sfavillan d'amor.	Waves and stars glitter with love.
E quando tu vorrai,	And when you want
La vela io scioglierò …	I'll unfurl the sail …
Lontan … lontano assai	Far … over the sea
Pel mar ti porterò.	We'll float away.

This song functions as a kind of leitmotif for Chloe and Chris, since its first entry accompanies their first date, and it returns when the couple are making love and also at their wedding. Like the *Il trovatore* excerpt, there is no immediate connection between the narrative content of Gomes's song and the film scenes it accompanies beyond the general theme of love, but at the larger level of the plot, Gomes's opera relates to Allen's film through the shared theme of a principal female character's love-related death: again a *Liebestod*, as in *Il trovatore*.

The function of the excerpt from Bizet's *Pearl Fishers* (no. 5) is similar to that of Gomes's song in that it also serves as a leitmotif, but for a different couple: Chris and Nola. It is associated with them twice throughout the film: first, when Chris is thinking of Nola while waiting for her during an audition; and second, during their extramarital affair. One can draw a broad thematic connection between Bizet's opera and Allen's film, for the opera, too, features two men's love for the same woman—Nadir and Zurga for Leïla—and the feeling of jealousy, which is echoed by Chris's jealousy of Tom. The aria used in the film, "Je crois entendre encore," is a romance sung by Nadir just before the Act I finale, in which he expresses the longing that Leïla's unexpected appearance has aroused in him. The recording of Caruso used for the soundtrack is his Italian rendition of the song ("Mi par d'udire ancora").

---

terms "phenomenal music" versus "noumenal music" than diegetic and nondiegetic music in the discussion of opera, because opera is a dramatic art, while the term "diegesis" originated as a term for the narrative art (fictional storytelling), as opposed to "mimesis" in dramatic art, when the term was first used in Book III of Plato's *Republic*. Abbate explains phenomenal music as follows: when she discusses the "Bell song" in Delibes' opera *Lakme*, she notes, "The scene involves 'phenomenal' performance, which might be loosely defined as a musical or vocal performance that declares itself openly, singing that is heard by its singer, the auditors on stage, and understood as 'music that they (too) hear' by us, the theater audience." See Abbate, *Unsung Voices: Opera and Musical Narrative in the Nineteenth Century* (Princeton, NJ: Princeton University Press, 1991), p. 5.

Je crois entendre encore,	I think I can still hear,
Caché sous les palmiers,	Hidden under the palm-trees,
Sa voix tendre et sonore	Her tender and sonorous voice
Comme un chant de ramiers.	Singing like a dove's.
Ô nuit enchanteresse,	O bewitching night,
Divin ravissement!	Exquisite rapture,
Ô souvenir charmant,	O delightful memory,
Folle ivresse, doux rêve!	Mad elation, sweet dream!
Aux clartés des étoiles	Under the light of the stars
Je crois encore la voir	I can almost see her
Entr'ouvrir ses longs voiles	Slightly opening her long veils
Aux vents tièdes du soir.	To the tepid evening breeze.
Ô nuit enchanteresse, etc.	O bewitching night, etc.

The thematic parallel between Allen's film and Verdi's *Macbeth*, the last opera on the soundtrack to *Match Point* (no. 15), is even more tenuous than the ones examined above. Only the general themes of the opera, murder and crime, are connected to the main event of the film, and Macbeth's guilty suffering over the murder he has committed mildly hints at the disturbed emotional state of Chris in the scene accompanied by the *Macbeth* excerpt—his trip to the police station. The aria excerpted for the film, "O figli, o figli miei," is Macduff's song from Act IV, scene 1, in which he expresses his determination to avenge the murder of his wife and children by the tyrant Macbeth. The selection of this particular aria from Verdi's opera is ironic, if not puzzling, because of the reversed roles between Chris and Macduff in their dramatic situations: Chris is the person who committed a crime and deserves a punishment, while Macduff is the person who, as a victim of the crime, enacts a punishment on the murderer of his wife and children, Macbeth.

O figli, o figli miei! da quel tiranno	Oh, my children, my children! By that tyrant
Tutti uccisi voi foste, e insieme con voi	You have all been murdered, and along with you
La madre sventurata! … Ah, fra gli artigli	Your unhappy mother! … Alas, in the clutches
Di quel tigre io lasciai la madre e i figli?	Of that tiger did I abandon my children and their
Ah, la paterna mano	Dam? Alack, a father's hand was not by to shield
Non vi fu scudo, o cari,	You, dear ones,
Dai perfidi sicari	From those dastardly cut-throats
Che a morte vi ferir!	Who did put you to death.
E me fuggiasco, occulto,	And fugitive and in hiding as I was,
Voi chiamavate invano,	As the last gasp, with your dying breath,
Coll'ultimo singulto,	You called to me in vain.
Coll'ultimo respir.	Front to front bring Thou this
Trammi al tiranno in faccia,	Fiendish tyrant and myself,
Signore! e s'ei mi sfugge,	Oh, Lord, and if he escape me then,
Possa a colui le braccia	Extend Thou Thine arms to him in pardon.
Del tuo perdono aprir.	

Diegetic Music

Most of the opera excerpts used diegetically in the film's soundtrack also afford some general parallels to the story and/or themes of the film. Verdi's *Rigoletto* shares the trope of the murder of the heroine, and the fact that the song performed onstage is Gilda's Act I signature aria, "Caro nome" (no. 6), accentuates the connectedness of the two heroines (although the two heroines are diametrically different from each other: Gilda is an innocent lady, while Nola is a femme fatale). In this context, it is significant that the title music of the film's DVD is also "Caro nome." Out of all the opera excerpts on the soundtrack of *Match Point*, Gilda's aria is the only one sung by a female character.

Caro nome che il mio cor	Sweet name, you who made my heart
Festi primo palpitar.	throb for the first time,
Le delizie dell'amore	you must always remind me
Mi dei sempre rammentar!	the pleasures of love!
Col pensiero il mio desir	My desire will fly to you
A te sempre volerà	On the wings of thought
E fin l'ultimo sospir.	And my last breath
Caro nome tuo sarà.	Will be yours, my beloved.

The aria "Un dì, felice, eterea" from *La traviata* presents an ironic connection to the dramatic situation of the film during its diegetic performance (no. 2). In this song from Act I, Alfredo is declaring his love for Violetta for the first time in the opera, and it is while viewing this scene at Covent Garden that Chloe falls in love with Chris. The parallelism between the opera and the film is ironic because of the gender reversal: Alfredo's song voices Chloe's unspoken emotion.

Un dì, felice, eterea,	That day I've never forgotten,
Mi balenaste innante,	When I beheld your beauty.
E da quell dì tremante	Since that moment I loved you,
Vissi d'ignoto amor.	Loved and adored from afar.
Di quell'amor ch'e palpito	Hoping for love, love that fills the universe,
Dell'universo, Dell'universo intero,	Love that inspires radiant dreams of life eternal,
Misterioso, altero,	Strangely mysterious,
Croce e delizia cor.	Shining in golden splendor,
Misterioso, Misterioso altero,	Sorrow, sorrow and rapture,
Croce e delizia al cor.	Sorrow and rapture, rapturous joy!

The excerpt from Rossini's *William Tell* constitutes the weakest connection to the plot of *Match Point*. Rossini's opera focuses on a political theme—Switzerland's resistance against Austria—although romantic love is not entirely excluded: Arnold Melchtal's love for Mathilde, a niece of the villain Gesler. The excerpt heard diegetically in the film, "Arresta! Qual dolor" (no. 11), is a duet from Act I between the protagonist, William Tell, and Arnold, in which Arnold confesses his tormented heart, torn between love for his country and love for Mathilde. But their love is not in vain, despite a serious political barrier. Instead, the couple are happily reunited at the end of the opera. The duet is heard as a voice-off (that is, without showing the opera stage) and is cut before Arnold's first entry.

Tell:

Arresta! Auali sguardi!	Stop! How strangely you look at me!
Tu tremi innanzi a me,	You tremble at my presence,
Nè mi vuoi dire ond'ardi?	Yet will not explain what troubles you?
Tremar, tremar perchè?	You are frightened, but why?

Arnold: *No ... no ... no ...*

Among the soundtrack's music cues in *Match Point*, the excerpt from Andrew Lloyd Webber's musical *The Woman in White* is the only non-classical piece.[9] Like Verdi's *Il trovatore* and Bizet's *Pearl Fishers*, Webber's musical, based on Wilkie Collins's 1859 mystery novel, also centers on a love triangle, but with a reversed gender configuration: in this case it is two women, Marian Fairlie and her sister Laura, who love the same man, Walter Hartright. As with *William Tell*, Lloyd's musical is also heard as an unseen performance. The song selected for the film is a love duet between Walter and Laura, "I Believe My Heart" (no. 14), which is sung at the beginning of Act I and returns with the second reprise at the end of the musical. In addition to the theme of a love triangle in both the musical and the film, there is a character similarity between Laura and Chloe, for both are heiresses to a huge estate. Unlike *Match Point*, Webber's musical concludes with a happy ending when Laura and Walter marry and Walter inherits the estate of Laura's family, Limmeridge House. In spite of the miniature (20 seconds) and invisible appearance of Webber's musical—since it is heard as voice-off—its story line foreshadows the dénouement of the film: a happy ending for Chris, who successfully remains in his marriage with Chloe. Like Walter, Chris could inherit Chloe's family estate; at least such potential is suggested at the end of the film. The song excerpt in the film begins with the instrumental prelude to the duet and stops at Walter's first word, "Whenever."

Whenever I look at you
The world disappears.
All in a single glance so revealing.
You smile and I feel as though
I've known you for years.
How do I know to trust what I'm feeling?

---

[9]   Webber's musical premiered in September 2004, less than a year before Allen's film was released.

I believe my heart.
What else can I do?
When ev'ry part of ev'ry thought
Leads me straight to you.
…

The Murder Sequence

Compared to the films examined above, the use of opera in the murder scene of
Match Point is distinctive in several ways. First, it is nondiegetic music. When
opera excerpts are employed as diegetic music, they have the potential to engage
more actively with the filmic action visually and narratively. For instance, the
parallel editing between the onscreen action and the onstage action, if the
opera is presented as a diegetic performance, contributes to the enhancement
of the fervor of the filmic action. Especially when the cross-cuts occur in quick
succession, the visual tempo intensifies the commotion of the onscreen action
of killing, the best example of which among the films examined is *Quantum of
Solace*. Furthermore, a diegetic opera performance makes the narrative parallels
between the onstage killing and the onscreen murder visually more immediate.
Another element that distinguishes the *Match Point* is that while in other films
the murder scene is the only place in the film to employ operatic music, in Allen's
film most of the other musical numbers on the soundtrack are also opera excerpts.
When opera is used only once throughout the film, its unique appearance attracts
stronger attention, and the resonance of death inherent in opera is exclusively
related to the act of killing in the film. In *Match Point*, then, how does opera still
highlight the death scene, in spite of its ubiquity throughout the film? How is the
Otello excerpt distinguished from other opera excerpts on the soundtrack? How
does it contribute to the sonic amplification of the onscreen action of killing,
despite its exclusion from the film's diegesis? These are the main issues to be
illuminated in this section.

The *Otello* excerpt first enters when Chris is leaving his office, heading toward
Nola's place to kill her. The Verdi excerpt begins with a short instrumental interlude
preceding the duet between Otello and Iago, "Desdemona rea!" ("Desdemona
false!") at the end of Act II, and ends with Iago's line "Non v'alzate ancor!"
("Do not rise yet!"). In this duet, Iago successfully makes Otello suspicious of
Desdemona's adultery with Cassio. On Allen's soundtrack, Verdi's music plays
continuously until the end of the murder scene, which lasts about ten minutes.
Below is the portion of the libretto excerpted in the film. As indicated with italics,
there is only one cut, near the end of the excerpt.

Otello: Desdemona rea!

Iago (aside):
  Con questi fili tramerò la prova
  Del peccato d'amor. Nella dimora
  Di Cassio ciò s'asconda.

Otello (to himself):
  Atroce idea!

Iago (observing Otello):
  Il mio velen lavora.

Otello: Rea contro me! Contro me!

Iago: Soffri e ruggi!

Otello: Atroce! Atroce!

Iago: Non pensateci più.

Otello: Tu? Indietro! Guffi!
  M'hai legato alla croce! Ahimè! …
  Più orrendo d'ogni orrenda ingiuria
  Dell' ingiura è il sospetto.
  Nell' ore arcane della suà lussuria
  (e a me furate!) m'agitava il petro
  forse un presagio? Ero baldo, giulivo …
  Nulla sapevo ancor; io non sentivo
  Sul suo corpo divin che m'innamora
  E sui labri mendaci
  Gli ardenti baci
  Di Cassio! Ed ora! … ed or …
  Ora e per sempre addio sante memorie,
  Addio, sublimi incanti del pensier!
  Addio schiere fulgenti, addio vittorie,
  Dardi volanti e volanti crosier!
  Addio, vessillo trionfale e pio,
  E diane squillanti in sul mattin!
  Clamori e canti di battaglia, addio!
  Della Gloria d'Otello è questo ilfin.

Iago: Pace, signor.

Otello: Sciagurato! Mi trova una prova secura
  Che Desdemona è impure …
  No sfuggir! Nulla ti giova!
  Vo una securra, una visibil prova!
  O sulla tua testa
  S'accenda e precipiti il fulmine
  Del mio spaventoso furor che si desta!

(He seizes Iago by the throat and throws him to the ground)

Iago: Divina grazia difendimi! Il cielo
  Vi protegga. Non son più vostro alfiere.

Otello: Desdemona false!

Iago (aside, hiding the handkerchief in his doublet):
  With these threads will I plot the proof
  Of the sin of love. Now this must be hidden
  In Cassio's dwelling!

Otello (to himself):
  Horrible thought!

Iago (observing Otello):
  My poison begins to work.

Otello: False towards me! Towards me!

Iago: Suffer and roar!

Otello: Horrible! Horrible!

Iago: Think no more of it.

Otello: You? Stand back! Begone!
  You have bound me to the cross. Alas! …
  More dreadful than the most dreadful
  Injury of injuries is suspicion.
  In the secret hours of her lust
  (stolen from me!) did a presentiment
  ever stir in my breast? I was bold,
  happy… As yet I knew nothing. I did
  not feel on the divine body I adored
  and on the lying lips
  the burning kisses
  of Cassio! And now! … And now!
  Now and forever farewell, holy memories,
  Farewell, sublime content of the mind!
  Farewell, brave troops, farewell, victories,
  Flying shafts and racing steeds!
  Farewell, triumphant sacred banner,
  And the reveille ringing in the morn!
  Sound and songs of battle, farewell!
  Otello's glory is gone.

Iago: Peace, my lord.

Otello: Villain! Find me sure proof
  That Desdemona is impure …
  Do not fly! 'Twill avail you nothing!
  I want sure and ocular proof!
  Or upon your head will fall
  The fiery thunderbolt
  Of my wakened and fearful fury

Iago: Divine grace defend me! Heaven
  Protect you. I am no more your ensign.

Voglio che il mondo testimony mi sia	I want the world to be my witness
Che l'onseta è periglio.	That honesty is not safe.

(He makes as if to go)

Otello: No … rimani. Forse onesto tu sei.	Otello: No … stay. Perhaps you are honest.
Iago: Meglio verebbe ch'io fossi un ciurmador.	Iago: 'Twere better were I a swindler.
Otello: Per l'universo!	Otello: The world be witness!
Credo leale Desdemona e credo	I believe Desdemona true and I believe
Che non lo sia; tu credo onesto e credo	She is not; I believe you honest and
Disleale … La prova io voglio!	I believe you disloyal … I want proof!
Voglio la certezza!	I want certainty!
Iago: Signor, frenate l'ansie.	Iago: My lord, curb your agitation
E qual certezza v'abbisogna?	And what certainty would you have?
Avvinti verderli forse?	To see them perhaps embracing?
Otello: Ah! Morte e damnizione!	Otello: Ah! Death and Damnation!
Iago: Ardua impresa sarebbe; e qual certezza	Iago: It would be a difficult task; and
Sognate voi se quell' immondo fatto	What certainty do you have if this
Sempre vi sfuggirà? … Ma pur se guida	monstrous deed forever eludes you? …
È la ragione al vero, una si forte	But if reason be guide to truth, I have
Congettura riserbo che per poco alla	A strong conjecture which soon
Certezza vi conduce, Udite.	Should bring you certainty. Listen.
Era la notre, Cassio dormia,	It was night, Cassio was sleeping,
Gli stavo accanto.	I lay beside him.
Con interrotte voci tradia	In halting accents he betrayed
L'intimo incanto.	His inmost rapture.
Le labbra lentre, lentre movea,	His lips moved slowly, slowly,
Nell' abbandono	In the abandon
Del sogno ardente; e allor dicea,	Of his burning dream; and then he said,
Con flebil suono:	In mournful tone:
"Desdemona soave!	"Sweet Desdemona!
Il nostro amor s'asconda.	We must hide our love.
Cauti vegliamo! L'estasi del ciel	Let us be wary! I am drowning in
Tutto m'innonda."	Heavenly ecstasy."
Seguia più vago l'incubo blando;	The nightmare grew ever more
Con molle angoscia	Passionate; with soft anguish
L'interna imago quasi baciando,	He seemed to kiss his fancy's image,
Ei disse poscia:	Then said:
"Il rio destino impreco	"I curse the fate
che al Moro ti donò"	that gave you to the Moor."
E allora il sogno in cieco	And then the dream subsided
Letargo si mutò.	Into blind oblivion.
Otello: Oh! Mostruosa colpa!	Otello: Oh, monstrous guilt!
Iago: Io ho narrai che un sogno.	Iago: I have but related a dream.
Otello: Un sogno che rivela un fatto.	Otello: A dream reveals a fact.

Iago: Un sogno che può dar forma di prova
  Ad altro indizio.
Otello: E qual?
Iago: Talor vedeste
  In mano di Desdemona un tessutro trapunto
  A fior e più sottil d'un velo?
Otello: E il fazzoletto ch'io le diedi,
  Pegno primo d'amor.
Iago: Quel fazzoletto ieri (certo ne son)
  Lo vidi in man di Cassio.
Otello: Ah! Mille vite gli donasse Iddio!
  Una è povera preda al furor mio!
  Jago, ho il cor di gelo.
  Lungi da me le pietose larve.
  Tutto il mio vano amor esalo al cielo,
  Guardami, ei sparve.
  Nelle sue spire d'angue l'idra m'avvince!
  Ah! Sangue! Sangue! Sangue!
  Si pel ciel marmorso giuro!
  Per le attorte folgori!
  Per la Morte e per l'oscuro mar sterminator!
  D'ira e d'impeto tremendo presto fia
  Che sfolgori
  Questa man ch'io levo e stando!
Iago: Non v'alzate ancor!
  Testimon è il Sol ch'io miro,
  Che m'irradia e inanima
  L'ampia terra e il vasto spiro
  Del Creato inter,
  Che ad Otello io sacro ardenti,
  Core, bracio ed anima
  S'anco ad opere cruenti
  S'armi il suo voler!

Iago: A dream that can give proof
  Of other evidence.
Otello: Of what?
Iago: Have you sometimes seen
  In Desdemona's hand a tissue embroidered
  With flowers and finer than gauze?
Otello: 'Tis the handkerchief I gave her,
  first pledge of love.
Iago: That handkerchief (I am sure)
  I saw yesterday in Cassio's hand.
Otello: Ha! God grant him a thousand lives!
  One is a poor prey to my fury.
  Iago, I have a heart of ice.
  Away from me piteous illusions!
  All my fond love thus do I blow to heaven,
  See, 'tis gone.
  The hydra entwines me in its snaky coils.
  Oh, blood! Blood! Blood!
  Yes, I swear by the marble heaven!
  By the forked lightning!
  By death and by the dark destroying sea!
  Let this hand which I raise and
  Stretch forth
  Soon blaze in wild transport of rage!
Iago: Do not rise yet!
  Witness is the sun that I behold,
  That shines on me and animates
  The broad earth and the vast soul
  Of all Creation,
  Witness that to Otello I solemnly
  Dedicate heart, hand and soul,
  If he will also arm his will
  For the bloody work!

As Chris knocks on the door of Mrs. Eastby's apartment, the cinematic sounds add a percussive effect to Verdi's turbulent music (Otello's "Nell' ore arcane della suà lussuria ... forse un presagio? Ero baldo, giulivo" ["In the secret hours of her lust ... I was bold"]). This added percussive sound heightens the agitating ambience of the film's impending murder. The volume of Verdi's music (Otello's lines, "Nulla sapevo ancor" ["Happy ... As yet I know nothing"]) grows softer during the dialogue between Chris and Mrs. Eastby, but resumes its original volume when their conversation ends at Otello's line, "Addio, vessillo trionfale e pio" ("Farewell, triumphant sacred banner"). The following lines—from Iago's "Pace, signor" ("Peace, my lord") to the fourth line of Otello's next entry, "Sciagurato! Mi trova una prova secura ... Vo' una secura, una visibil prova!" ("Villain! Find me sure proof ... I want sure and ocular proof!")—accompany Chris's loading the gun with bullets. Chris shoots Mrs. Eastby at Otello's next line, "O sulla tua testa" ("Or upon your head will fall"). In order to disguise his murder as a burglary, Chris scatters some books from the bookshelf on the floor during Iago's line "Meglio varebbe ch'io fossi un ciurmador" ("'Twere better were I a swindler") and takes the jewelry, including the ring, from Mrs. Eastby's corpse during Iago's "Signor, frenate ... Avvinti verderli forse?" ("My lord, curb your agitation ... To see them perhaps embracing?").

The next shot cuts to Nola, coming out of her work place and taking a cab. The images of Nola are cross-cut with those of Chris nervously waiting for her at Mrs. Eastby's apartment. During these cross-cuts, we hear Iago's lines from "Ardua impresa sarebbe" ("It would be a difficult task") to "Gli stavo accanto" ("I lay beside him"). At the next line of Iago's song, "Con interrote voci tradia" ("In halting accents he betrayed"), we see a medium shot of the theater with a neon-lit sign of *The Woman in White* on its façade. This shot cuts to Nola, getting out of the cab, which is accompanied by Iago's fabricated quotation of Cassio in his dream, "Desdemona soave! Il nostro amor s'asconda" ("Sweet Desdemona! We must hide our love"). At the next line, still quoting Cassio—"Cauti vegliamo! L'estasi del ciel" ("Let us be wary! I am drowning in heavenly ecstasy")—we see Mrs. Eastby's neighbor, Ian (Colin Salmon), coming down the stairs of the apartment building and knocking on her door to check if everything is all right, presumably having heard Chris's rifle. In the same way that Chris's knocking on Mrs. Eastby's door at the beginning of the murder sequence functioned, Ian's banging on her door serves as an added percussion instrument in the texture of Verdi's music, increasing the musical tension in the soaring crescendo of Iago's line, "Seguia piu vago ... quasi baciando" ("The nightmare grew ever more ... he seemed to kiss his fancy's image"). Giving up on hearing Mrs. Eastby's answer, Ian leaves as Iago sings, "Il rio destino impreco / che al Moro ti donò" ("I curse the fate that gave you to the Moor").

The next scene consists of several cross-cuts between Ian, who meets Nola in front of the apartment building, and Chris, coming out of Mrs. Eastby's apartment and waiting for Nola in front of the building's elevator. The music accompanying this scene starts at Iago's line, "E allora il sogno" ("And then the dream subsided"), but then cuts from "Un sogno che può dar forma di prova / ad altro indizio" ("A dream that can give proof of other evidence") to Otello's line, "Ah! Mille vite gli donasse Iddio!" ("Ha! God grant him a thousand lives"). At the next line, "Una è provera preda al furor mio!" ("One is a poor prey to my fury"), Nola comes out of the elevator. During the following line of Otello's song—"Jago, ho il cor di gelo. / Lungi da me le pretose larve" ("Iago, I have a heart of ice. / Away from me piteous illusions!"), Chris calls Nola's name and shoots her to death (Figure 3.2).

On his way out to the street, Chris bumps into a man, and the music that accompanies this scene is Otello's line, "l'idra m'avvince!" ("the hydra entwines

Figure 3.2   Chris points a shotgun at Nola in *Match Point*

me in its snaky coils"). At the following line, "Ah! Sangue! Sangue! Sangue!"
("Oh, blood! Blood! Blood!"), Chris's image cuts to Chloe, who is waiting for him
in front of the theater. She calls Chris and he answers the phone in the cab during
Otello's next two lines, "Si pel ciel marmoreo giuro! / Per le attorte folgori!"
("Yes, I swear by the marble heaven! By the forked lightning!"). Verdi's music
continues during the next shot of Chris in the cab and fades out at Iago's line, "Non
v'alzate ancor!" ("Do not rise yet!"), when Chris joins Chloe at the theater to see
The Woman in White.

The *Otello* excerpt suggests moderate parallels to the film. Like Desdemona,
Nola is killed by her beloved. Although Allen's heroine is not the same type of
woman as Verdi's heroine—Nola is a sensual femme fatale rather than a spiritual,
virtuous wife—Nola's death is a sacrifice to Chris's opportunistic greed and
selfishness as an ambitious social climber, just as Desdemona is sacrificed to
Otello's jealousy. The only musical cut should not fail to catch our attention.
Without that cut, the Verdi excerpt would have ended before reaching Otello's
furious cry, "Ah! Sangue! Sangue! Sangue!" ("Oh, blood! Blood! Blood!").
Considering the pertinence of this line for the act of murder, although no blood is
shown on screen, it is likely that the film director wanted to secure this line in the
murder scene. Although this operatic line is not synchronized with the murder, it
can still be regarded as a comment on the onscreen action. This delayed comment
has a function comparable to that of the *benshi*, a live narrator of Japanese silent
films who stood to the side of the movie screen and conveyed the story to the
audience, often with delayed storytelling, since his narration would occur after the
onscreen action.[10]

---

[10]   It is interesting that the camera does not show the murder victims after they
are shot; we only see Chris. Woody Allen's comedy *Crimes and Misdemeanors* (1989)
is often compared to *Match Point* because of the similarities between their themes: the
male protagonist's extramarital love affair and the murder of his lover. In *Crimes and*

Although all of the nondiegetic musical cues are opera excerpts in *Match Point*, the *Otello* excerpt blatantly stands out in several ways. First of all, it is the only recording *without* Caruso's voice (the duet is sung by Janez Lotric as Otello and Igor Morozov as Iago), and it is the only recording with the sound quality of modern recording technology, along with a full orchestral accompaniment. This stands in sharp contrast to the archaic, primitive sounds of Caruso's recording from the 1910s. More importantly, Verdi's excerpt is distinguished from other nondiegetic music in the film by its interaction with Chris. All of the Caruso recordings can be regarded as a sonic representation of Chris's mind. Some can even be considered to be actual music that Chris is hearing in his mind: in other words, metadiegetic music, according to Claudia Gorbman's definition, or psycho-diegetic music, to use Marcia Citron's preferred terminology.[11] This reading is diegetically suggested when Chris gives a CD of Caruso to Chloe to celebrate the first day of his job at her father's company. After describing it as "a rare recording," Chris adds, "His voice expresses everything that is tragic about life."[12] Although he does not mention the name of the singer, Caruso is strongly implied; at least, the film viewer would presume that it is Caruso, since up to this point in the film we have already heard several recordings of Caruso as nondiegetic music, always in association with Chris. The consistency of the sound quality of all of the Caruso recordings— primitive, archaic, and full of constant noise—makes stronger the interpretation that they are the music lingering in Chris's mind on different occasions.

As mentioned above, the film's first Caruso entry, "Una furtiva lagrima," is carried over from the opening credits to Chris's voiceover monologue about the match point in tennis as a metaphor for luck or misfortune, and it is the same recording that concludes the film and is carried into the closing credits. This ending creates a symmetrical weaving of the music into the diegesis of the film. In other words, "Una furtiva lagrima" serves to invite or suture the film audience to the fictional world of the film at its beginning, and at the end it moves the viewer away from the fiction. In this respect, the first and last Caruso excerpts do not function as metadiegetic music—that is, the music lingering in Chris's mind. In the most extended interpretation, they can partially be considered as such—only the portions that accompany Chris outside of the opening and closing credits.

Misdemeanors, the music that accompanies the murder scene is an excerpt from the first movement of Schubert's Quartet in G major, Op. 161 (D 887). In a previous scene, Schubert's association with death is foreshadowed in a conversation between the hero, Juda, and his lover Dolores: Juda says, "Schumann is flowery. Schubert is… reminds me of you. The sad one." The title of Jimmy McHugh's song, "Murder He Says," presented as a diegetic performance by Betty Hutton, alludes to the theme of murder but without a direct visual connection to the murder scene.

[11]   See n. 6 of this chapter.

[12]   When Tom's mother finds out about Nola's death in a newspaper, she flamboyantly shouts, "Oh, it's a tragedy," evoking Chris's description of Caruso's voice, as if Nola's death were destined by Caruso's voice.

All other Caruso excerpts can be regarded as psycho-diegetic music in relation to Chris, but each to a different degree. The strongest example is the second appearance of Donizetti's "Una furtiva lagrima" (no. 9 in Table 3.1). It enters the soundtrack when Chris sees a glimpse of Nola at the Tate Modern, but abruptly stops when he bumps into Chloe on his way to follow Nola. The excerpt returns as soon as Chris leaves Chloe and continues during his search for Nola. The music heard after the momentary silence continues immediately from where it was cut when it stopped, as indicated below:

[*Before Chris's Encounter with Chloe*]
    Un solo instante i palpiti
    Del suo bel cor sentir!
    ...
    per poco a'suoi sospir!

[*After Chris Leaves Chloe*]
    I palpiti, i palpiti sentir,
    ...
    Cielo! Si può morir! Di piu non chiedo, non chiedo.

The excerpt from Carlos Gomes's *Salvator Rosa* and that from Bizet's *Pearl Fishers* are also good examples of psycho-diegetic music, but to a lesser degree than the second entry of Donizetti's "Una furtiva lagrima" discussed in the previous paragraph. As examined earlier in this chapter, Gomes's excerpt functions as a leitmotif for Chris's affection for Chloe, while Bizet's excerpt, his lust for Nola. These two leitmotifs address a gender issue. Among the opera excerpts used on the soundtrack, *Salvator Rose* and *Pearl Fishers* are the only operas written by non-Italian composers. Given this, the two female protagonists are musically distinguished from Chris as exotic beings. However, the degree of musical exoticization is different. While Bizet's *Pearl Fishers*, and especially the excerpt used in Allen's film, "Mi par d'udir ancora," emphatically evokes otherness through the opera setting in Sri Lanka and such musical elements as harmony and instrumentation, Gomes's opera is fundamentally an Italian opera, despite the composer's Brazilian nationality. Gomes primarily worked in Italy and his operas are mostly written in the post-Rossinian style. Although in some of his operas, such as *Fosca* (1873), he incorporated Brazilian elements, musical and others, *Salvator Rosa* is solidly Italian in terms of opera's subject and musical style. It is even patriotically Italian, as the story dramatizes the Neapolitan resistance against the Spanish domination (and the excerpt used in *Match Point*, "Mia piccirella," is a Neapolitan song). The musical magnification of Nola's otherness through strong exoticism echoes the binary musical portrayal of women—as either a femme fatale or a virtuous wife—in the operatic tradition (Bizet's characterization of Carmen and Michaela is a standard example), and also conforms to film music conventions, especially those from what is known as the "classical period" of Hollywood, as Kathryn Kalinak has demonstrated.[13]

While all of the Caruso recordings can be regarded as Chris's psycho-diegetic music to varying degrees, the diegetic status of the *Otello* excerpt is ambiguous, not only because of the absence of Caruso's voice but also because of the way the operatic music interacts with the dialogue of the film. One should recall the second instance of "Una furtiva lagrima" in the Tate Modern sequence that stops when Chris is engaged with a conversation with Chloe, a strong indication of its psycho-diegetic status. Except for the opening and closing Donizetti excerpts ("Una furtiva...") and the second entry of the *Salvator Rosa* excerpt at the wedding scene, all other Caruso excerpts are used for silent images. As has been noted earlier in this book, this is a standard practice when using vocal music on a soundtrack, in order to avoid the interference of song lyrics with the film's dialogue. During the *Otello* excerpt, however, we hear the operatic singing voice and the cinematic speaking voice simultaneously. Considering the strong clash between the two voices, it is problematic to interpret Verdi's *Otello* either as typical musical underscoring or as Chris's psycho-diegetic music. Charalampos Goyios describes the murder scene as a "dramatic polyphony," by which he means "letting simultaneous dramatic strands, each with its own dramatic texture and rhythm, coexist on the screen, allowing for their points of convergence and spaces of divergence."[14] Certainly, the *Otello* excerpt impresses as an externally added "polyphonic" voice rather than one originating from the internal fictional world of the film. Here I find Jerrold Levinson's theory of the "narrative" versus "additive" functions of nondiegetic music to be insightful in illuminating the effect of Verdi's music in the murder sequence.[15]

Levinson's distinction between the two functions of nondiegetic music is based on whether the music is "an element in the narrative process" (a narrative function) or "an element standing outside both the story and its narration" (an additive function).[16] Drawing on Seymour Chatman's study of filmic narration in *Coming to Terms: The Rhetoric of Narrative in Fiction and Film* (Ithaca: Cornell University Press, 1991), Levinson assigns narrative music to the voice of the cinematic narrator, and additive music to that of the implied filmmaker: "implied" because he or she should be distinguished from the actual film director. Here "voice" does not mean a physical sound, but voice as the agent or creator of the music, whether narrative or additive. The cinematic narrator, who is not automatically the same as the voice-over narrator, resides on the same fictional

---

[13] Kathryn Kalinak, "The Fallen Woman and the Virtuous Wife: Musical Stereotypes in *The Informer, Gone with the Wind*, and *Laura*," *Film Reader* 5 (1982): 76–82.

[14] Charalampos Goyios, "Living Life as an Opera Lover: On the Uses of Opera as Musical Accompaniment in Woody Allen's *Match Point*," *Senses of Cinema* 40 (2006). http://sensesofcinema.com/2006/feature-articles/match-point (accessed March 11, 2013).

[15] Levinson, "Film Music and Narrative Agency," pp. 248–82.

[16] Ibid., p. 251.

plane of the film as a presenter of the story who is a component of the fiction, whereas the implied filmmaker is the inventor of the fiction and the discourse. For the implied filmmaker, the film's story is acknowledged as fictional, as it is for the film viewer. In contrast, a cinematic narrator is "a fictional or fictionalized being" created by the implied filmmaker.[17]

Narrative nondiegetic music serves to advance the storytelling of the filmic fiction rather than simply producing a general mood in viewers. Levinson discusses the "Shark" theme in Steven Spielberg's original *Jaws* (1975) as one of the most obvious narrative uses of soundtrack music, for it sometimes serves as "the only reliable signifier" of the shark.[18] The restaurant sequence in Alfred Hitchcock's *Vertigo* (1958) is another example of the narrative use of nondiegetic music, but not as a signifier of a tangible object in the film but as an indicator of something subtle, unspoken, and unseen: the music indicates "the overwhelming psychic effect" that Madeleine (Kim Novak) has on Scottie (James Stewart). Levinson notes that it is the cinematic narrator who endows the music with the function of *fictionally* informing the film viewers of the inner lives of the characters.[19]

According to Levinson's theory, nondiegetic music has an "additive" function when it contributes more to the aesthetic construction of *the film* than to its storytelling: for instance, when music helps define the formal structure of the film by being placed at symmetrical locations of the film, such as at the beginning and the ending, or when the visuals are edited so that their rhythm or phrasing corresponds to the musical rhythm or phrasing, as in the mickey-mousing.[20] This type of music cannot be created by someone who is within the fiction of the film; instead, it is attributable to "an intelligence standing outside" the fictional plane of the film—in other words, an implied filmmaker. One of Levinson's examples of additive music is the way Monteverdi's *Magnificat* is used nondiegetically in Robert Bresson's *Mouchette* (1967). Monteverdi's music is heard at the opening of the film, during which the titles are projected, and at the end when the heroine Mouchette (Nadine Nortier) commits suicide. For Levinson, the Magnificat functions to frame the fictional narrative from without, "like a pair of musical bookends," as opposed to shaping it from within.[21] In addition to its structural function, the Monteverdi excerpt, especially through its verbal content, acts as a commentary on the action of the film, something like the film director's requiem for the heroine. But Bresson's

---

[17]   Ibid., pp. 253–4.

[18]   Ibid., p. 261.

[19]   Ibid., pp. 266–7.

[20]   Claudia Gorbman describes the latter case as "manipulating the characters' actions so that they submit to musical division of time rather than dramatic or realistic time." She mentions Fellini's *Nights of Cabiria* (1957) as an example. See Gorbman, *Unheard Melodies*, p. 24.

[21]   Levinson, "Film Music as Narrative Agency," p. 272. In *Match Point*, the role of the first and the last entries of Donizetti's "Una furtiva lagrima" is strongly similar to that of the Monteverdi excerpt in Bresson's film.

commentary, according to Levinson, is not "an attitude literally directed on the suicide of the heroine," as in the case of narrative nondiegetic music attributable to a cinematic narrator, for whom the event of the suicide is real; instead, it is "an attitude bound up with the film's *representation* of that event, or directed toward events of the sort represented by the film" (my italics).[22]

Let us now apply Levinson's distinction between the narrative and additive functions of nondiegetic music to the *Otello* excerpt in *Match Point*. According to Levinson, pre-existing music is less likely to be purely narrative in function, because it has its own strong identity independent of the fictional world of the film, "deriving from the original context of composition or performance or distribution."[23] Anahid Kassabian, too, distinguishes the function of the "compiled score"—that is, a film score that includes pre-existing music—from that of the "composed score," which consists of music composed specifically for a particular film. Exploring the functions of film music in terms of the process of identification, she uses the term "assimilating identifications" to refer to the kind of identification that a composed score encourages and "affiliating identifications" in association with a compiled score.

> Composed scores, most often associated with classical Hollywood scoring traditions, condition what I call *assimilating identifications*. Such paths are structured to draw perceivers into socially and historically unfamiliar positions, as do larger scale processes of assimilation ... More often, compiled scores offer what I call *affiliating identifications*, and they operate quite differently from composed scores. These ties depend on histories forged outside the film scene, and they allow for a fair bit of mobility within it. If offers of assimilating identifications try to narrow the psychic field, then offers of affiliating identifications open it wide. This difference is, to my mind, at the heart of filmgoers' relationships to contemporary film music.[24]

But the Caruso excerpts in *Match Point* function differently from what is normally expected from the compiled score, or "the appropriated score," to use Levinson's term.[25] Caruso's music is not purely extradiegetic but is integrated into the fictional world of the film when Chris gives a Caruso CD to Chloe; moreover, Chris's description of Caruso's voice as the expression of "everything that is tragic about life" renders Caruso's diegetic—invisible but audible—presence stronger. As a sonic delineation of the non-verbalized domain of Chris's life, the function of Caruso excerpts is closer to narrative than additive, providing additional information about the film fiction beyond the film script. The *Otello* excerpt,

---

[22]   Ibid., pp. 276–7.

[23]   Ibid., p. 249.

[24]   Anahid Kassabian, *Hearing Film: Tracking Identifications in Contemporary Hollywood Film Music* (New York: Routledge, 2001), pp. 2–3.

[25]   Levinson, "Film Music and Narrative Agency," p. 249.

however, does not have the kind of diegetic anchoring that the Caruso excerpts do. Because of its uniqueness as the only recording without Caruso's voice and the only recording with the modern orchestral accompaniment, the *Otello* excerpt stands out so distinctively when it enters the soundtrack that it asserts its status as an outsider to the film's fiction. In other words, it has an additive function as an externally interpolated contrapuntal voice to the fictional world of the film; or to cite Charalampos Goyios's expression again, one that contributes to a "dramatic polyphony."[26] The fact that this musical cue does not have Caruso's voice, which often functions as Chris's unspoken voice, further supports my argument that this music does not represent Chris's psycho-diegetic world: in other words, this music resides outside the fictional world of the film.

Although there are some broad narrative parallels between the source opera and Allen's film, such as the murder of the heroine, this narrative or thematic parallelism should not be confused with the narrative function of nondiegetic music, as theorized by Levinson. This is because the function of the music is determined by the way it interacts with the film's fictional world. Like Monteverdi's *Magnificat* in Bresson's *Mouchette*, the *Otello* excerpt in *Match Point* can be considered to generate a commentary, but it does so in "a mode of distanced and reflective juxtaposition" to the film's event,[27] which is more attributable to the implied filmmaker who stands outside the film's fictional world than to the film's internal storyteller. The fact that the *Otello* excerpt is the only duet among the opera excerpts in *Match Point* can be symbolically interpreted as a metaphor for the two polyphonic voices—one from the filmic fiction (the literal voices of the cinematic characters, such as Chris and Mrs. Eastby) and one from the filmmaking (the intangible voice of an implied filmmaker, vocalized by Verdi's opera).[28] The status of the *Otello* excerpt as additive music is more convincing, considering its formal function of connecting the cross-cuts among multiple locations during the murder sequence: Nola's apartment building, where the double murders are executed; Nola's workplace and the street where she is waiting for a cab; and the theater of *The Woman in White*, where Chloe is waiting for Chris. As Levinson indicates, this type of formal function of providing continuity and achieving unity makes most sense as a construction of the implied filmmaker rather than the cinematic narrator.[29] This is because such formal and aesthetic properties as continuity and unity in the film do not contribute to the advance of the *storytelling* of the filmic fiction but belong to the domain of *filmmaking*.

---

[26]   Goyios, "Living Life as an Opera Lover"; and Levinson, "Film Music and Narrative Agency," p. 273.

[27]   Levinson, "Film Music and Narrative Agency," p. 272.

[28]   The *William Tell* excerpt and the *Woman in White* excerpt are also duets, but the portion of each excerpt used in Allen's soundtrack is only one character's voice—William Tell's and Walter's, respectively.

[29]   Levinson, "Film Music and Narrative Agency," p. 277.

Match Point and *La Cérémonie*: Covert Echoes

In the final section of this chapter, I will discuss some intriguing parallels between the murder scene in Allen's *Match Point* and that in Claude Chabrol's *La Cérémonie* as an extension of Marcia Citron's discussion of the Orphic interplay between sight and sound and the cultural implications of the opera versus a boom box (a CD player in case of *The Match Point*) and a television. I do not interpret the echoing of *La Cérémonie* in *Match Point* as an intentional allusion to the earlier film on the part of the filmmaker(s) of the later film. Instead, I focus on the possible meanings that can be drawn from the semiotic accumulation resulting from the reappearance of certain signifiers, such as a boom box or a television, in the later film.

In both *Match Point* and *La Cérémonie*, opera functions as a social signifier for high cultural status: both the Hewett family and the Lelièvres are portrayed as opera connoisseurs, or perhaps as consumers of opera. For Chris in *Match Point*, opera is a means to associate with upper-class people and advance socially; and it does work for him, since it is at a performance of *La traviata* at Covent Garden that Chris meets Chloe.[30] In *Match Point* there is a further hierarchy between live opera and recorded opera heard from a mechanically reproducing apparatus: the Hewett family always goes to live opera at Covent Garden, while Chris's primary experience of opera had been through CDs until his opera outing to Covent Garden with the Hewett family. In Chabrol's film, television, which like a CD player is an apparatus intended for mass cultural entertainment, is associated with both classes of characters—high and low—while a "portable" boom box, "in contrast to the stationary (immobile) television," suggests a crossing of class borders, according to Marcia Citron.[31] In *Match Point*, neither television nor CD player takes any recognizable role as a cultural indicator, but their covert presence, briefly mentioned or implied in the film script without showing their images, evokes these two machines prominently inscribed in Chabrol's film as socio-cultural signifiers

---

[30] As mentioned in the film's synopsis above, it is not only opera but also literature that serves as a means for social climbing for Chris. At the beginning of the film, Chris is shown reading Dostoyevsky's *Crime and Punishment*, but he soon abandons the novel and moves to *The Cambridge Companion to Dostoyevsky*. Like opera, Dostoyevsky connects Christ to the high-cultural Hewitt family: after Chris's first visit to the Hewitt's residence, Chloe comments on him, "He is not trivial. We had a nice conversation about Dostoyevsky yesterday." This is the moment when the father of the Hewett family is persuaded enough to admit Chris as a family friend in spite of his lower social class. In contrast, Nola, who is presumably from a social and cultural background similar Chris's, does not have Chris's pretentious, calculative, and opportunistic interest in high culture, and one can arguably claim that her lack of such an interest contributed to her failure to become a member of the Hewett family, and perhaps even to her death—her cultural demise.

[31] Citron, *When Opera Meets Film*, pp. 140 and 161.

along with opera. This process, which I call "semiotic accumulation," creates more hermeneutic room for inferring cultural meanings.

Although no CD player is shown in *Match Point*, its invisible presence permeates the entire film through Caruso's disembodied voice. This is because when Chris gives a CD of Caruso to Chloe, a CD player is the implied machinery that plays the recording. They almost listen to the CD immediately, but instead decide to join Tom and Nola for their movie outing. Since the Caruso excerpts serve as psycho-diegetic music representing the unspoken domain of Chris's life, as analyzed above, their presumable sound source, a CD player, looms in the film whenever Caruso's voice is heard. Later in the film, a CD player is mentioned by the minor character Ian, who knocks on Mrs. Eastby's door after she was murdered and on his way out bumps into Nola in front of the apartment building.

> Ian: Did you ever get the portable CD player we talked about?
> Nola: Yes, thanks for your help.

Ian mentions a CD player once more, to Inspector Dowd during the murder investigation:

> Ian: I bumped into her. We talked and we chatted. I recommended a piece of music equipment... She'd bought it. Yeah, and...
> Inspector: Music equipment? What was that?
> Ian: Nothing, it was a portable CD player, which reads MP3s, CD rewrites ...

Ian's mentioning of a portable CD player is out of context, but it associates Nola with this machinery and in so doing, connects her to Chris's (original) cultural apparatus. When Nola was engaged to Tom, both she and Chris would attend live opera performances with their prospective in-laws. Nola ceases to attend live theater after her breakup with Tom, but Chris continues to go. In fact, we learn that he goes to live performances even when not accompanied by the Hewett family, when Chloe asks him one day how he has enjoyed a ballet. Given this association of live performances and the Hewett family, an unseen CD player functions as a signifier of a lower social class and cultural tastes. In this context, it should not be overlooked that Chris joins Chloe at a live theater to see *The Woman in White* immediately after the double murder, during which a CD player is mentioned in association with Nola—another foregrounding of the cultural dichotomy and hierarchy between the live and the reproduced.

Television, too, serves as an indicator of social status, although in a much weaker way than a CD player does. There is only one mention of television throughout the entire film and, like Ian's reference to the CD player, it's out of context: when Chris visits Mrs. Eastby to kill her, he fabricates a story so that he can enter her apartment, saying that the television reception is not good at Nola's apartment and he wants to check it at Mrs. Eastby's place to find out whether it's a problem with the reception in the apartment building or something else.

So the apparatus of television is associated with Nola and Mrs. Eastby, who are presumably from the same (under-cultured) social class because they live in the same apartment building. It should be recalled that the same two machines, a television set and a boom box, are prominently foregrounded in the murder scene in Chabrol's *La Cérémonie*. Once more, I am not arguing that Woody Allen or anybody else involved in the filmmaking of *Match Point* is intentionally making a reference to Chabrol's film. However, by echoing the murder scene and the cultural implications of the television and boom box in Chabrol's film, these two machines in *Match Point* are endowed with a stronger symbolic meaning through semiotic accumulation.

Match Point also stages the cultural tension and the hierarchical relationship between opera and cinema through the characters associated with them: Nola is a struggling *movie* actress, while the Hewett family's primary venue for cultural activities is live *opera*. Considering Nola's American nationality in contrast to the British Hewett family, cinema in *Match Point* can be regarded as an emblem of American-ness, particularly of Hollywood and the prominence of popular culture, while opera represents British/European-ness as the origin of high art. Chris's nationality, Irish, can be regarded as in between because of the relative cultural otherness of Ireland in Europe—compared to, say, England, France, Italy, or Germany.

Chris's love for Caruso can also be contextualized within this cultural spectrum. Caruso was an Italian opera singer, and on the soundtrack of *Match Point* he sings Italian operas (even the excerpt from Bizet's *Pearl Fishers* is an Italian rendition); in other words, he represents the mainstream of operatic high culture. However, Caruso's active engagement with popular culture as "the world's first blockbuster recording artist"[32] makes Chris's love for him more appropriate for his social class. This association is more convincing considering Caruso's strong commitment in cinema. In 1911, he appeared in Thomas Edison's experimental "opera short" as Edgardo in Donizetti's *Lucia di Lammermoor*, and in two commercial silent films directed by Edward José, *My Cousin* (1918) and *The Splendid Romance* (1919), both of which were produced by Paramount.

The final point I consider in this section is the social implications of the murder weapons in *La Cérémonie* and *Match Point*. In both films, they are the property of the upper-class families with which the murderers are conducted, rather than their own possessions. Given this, the rifles in *La Cérémonie* could be interpreted as instruments of self-destruction, since the Lelièvre family is killed by its own possessions. In *Match Point*, however, the rifle belonging to the cultured and privileged Hewett family kills the lower-class Nola, and the film ends as a victory for the murderer. A social implication drawn from the role of the murder instrument could be that *Match Point* represents the triumph of the bourgeoisie, while in *La Cérémonie* it represents the opposite, the punishment of the bourgeois as symbolized by the demise of the Lelièvre family. But both films show the

---

[32]   Goyios, "Living Life as an Opera Lover."

reversal of the "Orphic strife,"[33] in that voice is endowed with not a redeeming power but a destructive power, the power not to overcome but incur death, like that of Orpheus's gaze in the myth. One could argue that in *Match Point* it is Caruso's voice that brings Nola's death, described as "a tragedy" by Chloe's mother, since Caruso's voice expresses "everything that is *tragic* about life," as Chris describes. In *La Cérémonie*, it is the triumph of the aural—with Sophie, a visual dyslexic, as the embodiment of the aural—that brings the death of the Lelièvre family.

---

[33]   Michal Grover-Friedlander, *Vocal Apparitions: The Attraction of Cinema to Opera* (Princeton, NJ: Princeton University Press, 2005), p. 56.

Chapter 4
Is Cinema's Anxiety Opera's Envy?[1]

Mercanteggini: But you must finish the performance!
Galas: I can't! I wish to God I could. But I can't. The voice ... the voice is slipping.
Mercanteggini: Slipping?
Galas: Yes, slipping! Slipping! The voice will not obey.
Mercanteggini (Growing more and more alarmed): How can that be?
Galas: I told you, sometimes the voice obeys and sometimes it will not. Tonight it will not!
Mercanteggini: You're speaking of your voice as though it had a will of its own.
Galas (With horror): It has! It does! Tonight it will not obey.
Mercanteggini: You've got to get hold of yourself. It's your voice. You must command it.
Galas (In a hoarse whisper): It's no use.

So begins Act I, scene 5 of Charles Ludlam's 1983 play about Maria Callas entitled *Galas: A Modern Tragedy*.[2] The above quote is a dramatization of the (in)famous "Rome walkout," Callas's cancellation after the first act of her 1958 performance in the Rome Opera production of *Norma*.[3] The endowment of the voice with its own will in this scene points to the central issue explored in this chapter: the uncanny autonomization of the voice in opera and film. Focusing on a recent trend in operatic theater that explores what has been called cinema's "castration anxiety" over the separation of the voice from the body, I examine how the mediatized unity of voice and body of the cinematic apparatus has affected the

---

[1] This chapter was evolved from the conference paper I presented at the annual conference of the International Federation of Theater Research (FIRT) held in St. Petersburg in May 2004.

[2] Charles Ludlam, *Galas: A Modern Tragedy*, in *The Mystery of Irma Vep and Other Plays* (New York: Theatre Communications Group, 2001), pp. 88–9.

[3] Callas was cast for the title role of *Norma*, which was the opening piece of the 1958 season for the Rome Opera House. The day before opening night, Callas was not feeling well and suggested to opera management that there should be a standby. But she was told, "No one can double Callas." After the first act on the opening night, Callas did not feel well enough to continue singing and so cancelled the performance, whose audience included the president of Italy, Giovanni Gronchi. Callas was accused of walking out on the president of Italy in a fit of temperament, and the press coverage aggravated the situation. Callas brought a lawsuit against the Rome Opera House and won, although it took thirteen years to settle the case.

embodied-ness of the operatic voice in live performance. In psychoanalytically oriented film theory, cinema's castration anxiety is interpreted as the origin of its envy of a live medium, such as opera, in which the voice is naturally embodied.[4] Thus, the separation of voice and body in recent operatic theater can be read as a reverse envy on the part of opera. I trace this "envy" of cinema's anxiety to cinema's privileging of the voice and sound in spite of the seeming dominance of the visual in this medium, as Slavoj Žižek argues.[5] I support my argument by demonstrating a parallel between what Žižek calls an "uncanny autonomization of the voice" in sound film[6] and "the uncanny aspects" of operatic performance: namely, the notion of the performer as a lifeless musical instrument, an automaton animated by the force of music, as Carolyn Abbate argues in her book *In Search of Opera*.[7]

Drawing on film theories developed by Kaja Silverman, Slavoj Žižek, and other scholars writing from a psychoanalytic perspective, and contextualizing these theories with Abbate's discourse on opera performance, I intend to show how they provide a methodological perspective from which the re-negotiated relationship between voice and body in the live theater of opera can be analyzed. In doing so, I hope to demonstrate how these theories expand and enrich the hermeneutic scope for examining the opera–cinema encounter. I cannot emphasize enough that what I argue in this chapter—that the separation of voice and body in opera reflects cinema's privileging of voice over body, sound over image—is only one of the possible interpretations that may not have much, if anything, to do with intentionality, be it the composer's, the stage director's, or the film director's. The voice–body split in operatic theater can be found at the level of production: in other words, a split that was not intended by the composer but added by stage directors (Julie Taymor's Saito Kinen Festival production of Stravinsky's *Oedipus rex* in 1992 is an example, in which Oedipus is portrayed by a dancer-mime and a masked singer [Figure 4.1]). In this chapter, I focus on works in which such a split is employed at the compositional level. Four operas will be analyzed in detail: two works from Alexander Goehr's *Triptych* (1968–71)—*Naboth's Vineyard* (1968) and *Sonata about Jerusalem* (1971); Harrison Birtwistle's *The Mask of Orpheus* (1986); and Philip Glass's *La Belle et la bête* (1994). My usage of the terms "opera"

---

[4]   See for instance Kaja Silverman, *The Acoustic Mirror: The Female Voice in Psychoanalysis and Cinema* (Bloomington: Indiana University Press, 1988).

[5]   Slavoj Žižek, "'I Hear You with My Eyes'; or The Invisible Master," in *Gaze and Voice as Love Objects*, ed. Renata Salecl and Slavoj Žižek (Durham, NC: Duke University Press, 1996), pp. 90–127.

[6]   Ibid., p. 92.

[7]   Carolyn Abbate, *In Search of Opera* (Princeton, NJ: Princeton University Press, 2001), pp. 5–7.

Figure 4.1   Oedipus, represented by the singer (Philip Langridge) with an extended mask above his head and by the dancer-mime (Min Tanaka), in the scene immediately before Oedipus pierces his eyes; from the Saito Kinen Festival production of Stravinsky's *Oedipus Rex* (1992)

and "operatic" throughout the chapter encompasses both conventional opera and "music theater," as defined by W. Anthony Sheppard,[8] unless specified otherwise.

The "Castration Anxiety" of the Cinematic Apparatus

Sam Abel contends that, in live theater, performing bodies are the primary condition for emotional and psychological communication between performers and the audience, whose bodies occupy the same space at the same time of performance.[9] In cinema, direct communication between performers and the audience through their bodies disappears. Film theorist Christian Metz defines this difference between live theater and cinema in terms of *absence*:

> During the screening of the film, the audience is present and aware of the actor, but the actor is absent and unaware of the audience; and during the shooting, when the actor was present, it was the audience which was absent … The exchange of seeing and being-seen will be fractured at its center.[10]

---

[8]   W. Anthony Sheppard, Part 1.1: "Defining Music Theater," in *Revealing Masks: Exotic Influences and Ritualized Performance in Modernist Music Theater* (Berkeley: University of California Press, 2001), pp. 3–9.

[9]   Sam Abel, *Opera in the Flesh: Sexuality in Operatic Performance* (Boulder, CO: Westview Press, 1996), pp. 164–5.

[10]   Christian Metz, quoted in Jeremy Tambling, "Towards a Psychopathology of Opera," *Cambridge Opera Journal* 9, no. 3 (1997): 266.

Metz notes that, in theater, reality is "physically present in the same space as the spectator," while cinema presents reality as "primordial *elsewhere*" (my italics).[11] In live theater real actors depict fictional characters, but film is the representation of a representation in that the screen image constitutes another level of representation—the two-dimensional representation of *the real actors* who represent *fictional characters*. Other film scholars, such as André Bazin and Jean-Louis Comolli, also argue that because of the absence of the real object in cinema, the cinematic apparatus is characterized by a "fundamental" *lack*. Metz uses the term castration to describe cinema's "structuring" lack, the ontological condition of the cinematic text that exists in "perfect isolation" from the viewer. In Freudian theory, the concept of castration is explained in terms of a baby's separation from its mother's body—the loss of the object and the entry into language:[12]

> It has been urged that every time his mother's breast is withdrawn from a baby he is bound to feel it as a castration (that is to say, as the loss of what he regards as an important part of his own body); that further, he cannot fail to be similarly affected by the regular loss of his faeces; and finally that the act of birth itself (consisting as it does in the separation of the child from his mother, with whom he has hitherto been united) is the prototype of all castration.[13]

The Freudian concept of castration can be applied to another dimension of absence in cinematic apparatus—namely, the lack of natural unity between voice and body. Unlike in live theater, where the voice is embodied, in cinema, voice and body—sound and image—are separated in the process of recording, and they are preserved on and reproduced from physically separate tracks (image tracks and soundtracks). Instead of the biological unity between voice and body characteristic of live theater, a technologically mediated unity between the two is the "primordial" condition of the cinematic apparatus. For Michel Chion, lip-synching—"assiduous but never perfect"—represents the ontological condition of the cinematic medium—that is, "the impossible unity" of voice and body.[14] In an attempt to disavow its anxiety about its irretrievable loss of the natural unity between voice and body, mainstream cinema, especially Hollywood classical cinema, has tried to synchronize the soundtrack (voice) and the image track (body)

---

[11]   Ibid.

[12]   See Silverman, "Lost Objects and Mistaken Subjects," in *The Acoustic Mirror*, pp. 1–41. Silverman explains that "to admit that the loss of the object is also a castration would be to acknowledge that the male subject is already structured by absence prior to the moment at which he registers woman's anatomical difference—to concede that he, like the female subject, has already been deprived of being, and already been marked by the language and desires of the Other" (p. 15).

[13]   Freud quoted in ibid., p. 15.

[14]   Michel Chion, *La Voix au cinéma* (Paris: Cahiers du Cinéma, 1982), p. 125; translation mine.

as tightly as possible. This synchronization is where cinema's simulation of live theater, its envy of opera, can be located.

As a reaction to mainstream tradition, some film directors, mostly those working outside Hollywood, have shown different approaches in dealing with voice and body. Marguerite Duras (1914–96)—an alternative French film director and writer whose representative works include *India Song* (1975), based on her play—is distinguished by the radical dissociation between sound and image and the destruction of the "reality effect" of synchronization. For instance, in the script of *La Femme du Gange* (1974), Duras literally announces the split between the soundtrack and the image track as constituting two separate films, "the film of the voice" and "the film of the image."[15] In general, Duras uses voice-off (i.e., offscreen voices) in very unusual ways, creating a strong sense of separation between voice and body. In the opening scene of *Nathalie Granger* (1972), for example, Isabelle (Lucia Bosé) and her husband are having a meal with their two children and the parents' voices are heard as voice-off during the entire sequence. After their children leave the dining table, the parents' conversation continues as voice-off while the camera shows the empty chairs on which the children had been sitting. A piano lesson sequence later in the film is fascinating for the way it expresses the separation between sound and image. It begins with Nathalie practicing a simple tune, the sound of which is heard synchronized with her fingers. Later, the camera pans to the desk nearby, which is covered with music scores, including one of Bach (Figure 4.2). The camera pans back to the piano keyboard and shows in close-up Nathalie's hands and those of her piano teacher, guiding the student's hand position. Nathalie is now playing different music from that heard in the opening scene. What is striking in this scene is the superimposition of the music from the opening scene over the piece she is currently playing; in other words, two

Figure 4.2   Music scores on the table near the piano, in the piano-lesson sequence in *Nathalie Granger*

---

[15]   Renate Günther, *Marguerite Duras* (Manchester and New York: Manchester University Press, 2002), p. 25.

Figure 4.3   Nathalie's hands and her piano teacher's, in the piano-lesson
              sequence in *Nathalie Granger*

different tunes are heard simultaneously, and the current tune is gradually eclipsed
by the previous one, resulting in a complete dissonance between sight and sound,
between what is seen and what is heard (Figure 4.3).

Hans-Jürgen Syberberg is another director who has explored non-synchronous
sounds, as against the general practice in mainstream (especially Hollywood)
cinema of using embodied voices. In his cinematic production of *Parsifal* (1982),
Syberberg intentionally employs inaccurate (that is, asynchronous) lip-synching
in order to demystify the seeming unity between voice and body in the cinematic
medium—a kind of Brechtian aesthetic strategy.[16] Chion describes the great
disparity between Amfortas's voice (sung by Wolfgang Schöne) and his body
(performed by the conductor of the recording, Armin Jordan) as follows:

> Here Syberberg focuses his camera, as nobody has ever done or ever would
> again, on the bewildering face of Armin Jordan, who is miming the voice of
> Wolfgang Schöne for the character of Amfortas, and one sees the black abyss of
> the mouth, the monstrosity of the lips in action, the strange beast of the tongue
> coming forward from the bottom of the throat, all of which attempt to seize the
> voice—and one is completely moved.[17]

Duras's and Syberberg's films, however, represent an exception and reaction to the
dominant politics of body and voice in mainstream cinema.[18]

---

[16]   For a detailed discussion of the Brechtian elements of Syberberg's *Parsifal*, see
my article "Hans-Jürgen Syberberg's *Parsifal*: The Staging of Dissonance in the Fusion of
Opera and Film," *Music Research Forum* 13 (1998): 1–21.

[17]   Chion, *La Voix au cinéma*, p. 126; translation mine.

[18]   Syberberg's antagonism towards mainstream cinema, especially Hollywood, can
be traced to his association with the New German Cinema, the members of which include
Rainer Werner Fassbinder, Werner Herzog, Alexander Kluge, and Wim Wenders. Emerging

As psychoanalytically oriented film scholars have argued, the common aesthetic strategy of mainstream cinema to tightly synchronize the voice with the body functions as a "fetish" against the cinematic apparatus's castration anxiety. Freud describes a fetish as something that a man who is incapable of accepting the woman's lack of a penis substitutes for the missing part—another part of the female anatomy or something attached to it, such as a shoe or a garment—in order to allay the fear of his own castration. In short, Freud ties fetishism to female lack—as the "male defense against the female condition of castration"—and the male defense against possibility of his own insufficiency.[19] This Freudian concept of female lack resembles Friedrich Nietzsche's vision of women as "a being without visible essence, an unseeable core, concealed by a sheen of adornment (cosmetics, ribbons, false hair, jewelry, and more intangible ornaments such as physical beauty)."[20] Feminist film scholars such as Kaja Silverman, Laura Mulvey, and Amy Lawrence argue that the embodied female voice functions as a fetish for cinema, a way to help conceal its primordial lack of natural unity between voice and body. Psychoanalytically oriented feminist film theories have been criticized by such scholars as David Bordwell, Noël Carroll, and Britta Sjogren, in part because such theories do not consider the audience and spectatorship (Bordwell and Carroll) and because of their ontological approaches to the cinematic apparatus (Sjorgren). However, those theories are still relevant to my argument in this chapter, since I focus on the "apparatus" of cinema precisely viewed from its ontological—that is, technological—condition.[21]

---

in the early 1960s, the New German Cinema directors established their identity less by their cohesive filmic style or aesthetics than by their ideological reactions against the "prostitution" of cinema to commercial expedience (Syberberg even called Hollywood a "great whore of showbusiness"). The "Oberhausen Manifesto," promulgated at the eighth Oberhausen Film Festival in February 1962, epitomizes their ideology: "This new cinema needs new freedoms. Freedom from the customary conventions of the trade. Freedom from the influence of commercial partners. Freedom from the tutelage of vested interests. We have a concrete notion of the production of the new German cinema at the intellectual, formal, and economic levels. We are collectively prepared to take economic risks. The old cinema is dead. We believe in the new one." See Joe, "Hans-Jürgen Syberberg's *Parsifal*," pp. 5–6.

[19]   See Silverman, *The Acoustic Mirror*, pp. 13–18.

[20]   Quoted in Carolyn Abbate, "Opera; or, the Envoicing of Women," in *Musicology and Difference: Gender and Sexuality in Music Scholarship*, ed. Ruth A. Solie (Berkeley: University of California Press, 1993), p. 226.

[21]   See David Bordwell and Noël Carroll, eds, *Post-Theory: Reconstructing Film Studies* (Madison: University of Wisconsin Press, 1996; and Britta Sjogren, *Into the Vortex: Female Voice and Paradox in Film* (Urbana and Chicago: University of Illinois Press, 2006). In her book, Sjogren offers alternative interpretations of select films from the classical Hollywood cinema by showing how female subjectivity and discourse are articulated through aural means, especially the female voice-off. See Chapter 5 for my further engagement with Sjogren's study.

Separation of Voice and Body in Opera

Considering the theory that a tightly synchronized sound and image, voice and body, characterizes dominant cinema and represents its aspiration to simulate the condition of live theater, the separation of voice and body in operatic theater is an intriguing phenomenon. Conventional opera is not devoid of disembodied voices—for instance, voices from the dead, such as Titurel in Wagner's *Parsifal*, and Antonia's mother in Jacques Offenbach's *Tales of Hoffmann*. More recently, Michael Daugherty used an offstage voice in an intriguing way in his opera *Jackie O* (1995), the libretto of which was written by Wayne Koestenbaum.[22] Near the end of the opera, Jackie is endowed with the power to communicate with her dead husband, who is not seen on stage but only heard as an offstage voice. She calls JFK and forgives him for his past infidelity in their duet, "Jack's Song," a mixture of the embodied and disembodied voices, which concludes with an allusion to Mozart's *Marriage of Figaro*, "Contessa perdona."[23] Although, for Abbate, disembodied singing is an "operatic cliché," I would argue that it is only recently that the separation of voice and body has noticeably increased in operatic theater.[24] The first and last works of Alexander Goehr's *Triptych*—*Naboth's Vineyard* (1968) and *Sonata about Jerusalem* (1971)—are other examples of works characterized by an innovative use of the voice–body split.[25] *Naboth's Vineyard*, dedicated to Olivier Messiaen on the occasion of his sixtieth birthday, is described as a "dramatic madrigal," and *Sonata about Jerusalem* as "a cantata—music theater III." In these works, the characters' physical presence is represented by mimes, while their voices are projected by onstage singers, creating "stylized forms of separation

---

[22]   When the Houston Grand Opera commissioned Daugherty, they did not specify a topic for the opera. It was Kostenbaum who suggested Jacqueline Kennedy Onassis as the heroine and topic of the opera, inspired by the book he was writing at that time, *Jackie under My Skin: Interpreting an Icon* (New York: Farrar, Straus, and Giroux, 1995).

[23]   The libretto of the entire duet is as follows. JACKIE: I don't know what I feel. It's impossible to probe my own shadows. Is it time to make my long-awaited, long-deferred call to the other side? *(She picks up the phone.) The dial tone. (With effort she dials.)*; JFK: Jackie!; JACKIE: Jack? Jack? Is that your voice?; JFK: Jackie! Forgive me; JACKIE: Is that your voice? I listen to your speeches, again and again; JFK: Jackie!; JACKIE: He's calling to me. I shed my bitterness. If only I could start all over again!; JFK: Together, in state, lonely cold: I have been waiting for this moment to arrive. Let's synchronize our breathing; JACKIE: In; JFK: Out; JACKIE: Out; JFK: We are back together, quiet, in the shattered limousine. That's all we have until eternity—the memory of being, once, years ago present together, in a bloody car. Do you believe in my voice?: JACKIE: I believe in oracles. I believe in silhouettes; JFK: Jackie! Forgive me; JACKIE: *Son qui.* I am here and I forgive you. I pardon you. *Contessa perdona*; JFK: Jackie!; JACKIE: *Contessa perdona.*

[24]   Abbate, *In Search of Opera*, p. xv. It seems to me that Abbate's claim is an exaggerated statement to support her argument for the ontological autonomy of voice in opera performance.

[25]   The second work in Goehr's *Triptych* is *Shadowplay* (1970).

between the silent performer physically representing a given character and the sung text associated with that character," to use Anthony Sheppard's description.[26]

The plot of *Sonata about Jerusalem* is based on a twelfth-century chronicle about how the Jews of Baghdad came to believe in the Messiah and returned to Jerusalem. In Goehr's work, the Jewish women are split into three dimensions of representation: the female chorus constitutes the aural dimension—that is, the voice; the narrator provides a verbal description of the visual element; and the mimes enact the bodily dimension of the women. *Naboth's Vineyard* is a dramatization of the biblical story included in chapter 21 of the first book of Kings from the Old Testament. King Achab wishes to acquire Naboth's vineyard and suggests a trade, but Naboth declines Achab's offer. Queen Jezebel (Achab's wife) falsely charges Naboth with blasphemy and Achab becomes the owner of Naboth's vineyard. God sends Elijah to reproach Achab; Achab repents and God decides not to punish him. In his operatic setting, Goehr uses two mimes, who represent various characters by wearing multiple masks, while the voices of those characters are provided by the singers. John Cox, the producer of the premiere of this piece, describes his staging as follows, which is included in the score:

> In the original production of *Naboth's Vineyard* the action was presented by two mimes wearing identical costumes. They put on or carried masks to represent the characters in the drama, exchanging them as the exigencies of the action required. Every attempt was made to keep the mimes indistinguishable from one another, so that the masks were the only "characters."[27]

The indistinguishableness among the characters, except for their masks, creates the "lifeless-ness" of the bodies, and, in so doing, intensifies the separation of the voice from the body—or the disembodied-ness of the voice—rendering the voice as if it were from "elsewhere."[28] Goehr's intention for the original staging, as described by Cox as follows, further supports my argument, as it minimizes the performer's bodily action.

> The composer insisted at the outset that the mime should not be choreographed, or even musical in feeling ... Nor is continuous mime required. Certain sections of the work are purely musical and need no action; at other points stillness is the most effective action ...
>
> In the ideal performance, instrumentalists, singers and mimes should all be visible and equal in visual importance, there being constant and close dramatic

---

26   Sheppard, *Revealing Masks*, p. 160.

27   John Cox, in Alexander Goehr, *Naboth's Vineyard* (London: Schott and Co., 1973), no page number given. It appears between the title page and the instrumentation.

28   For "elsewhere," see Abbate, *In Search of Opera*, pp. 5–7; and Metz, quoted in Jeremy Tambling, "Towards a Psychopathology of Opera," p. 266.

rapport amongst all the component parts of the work. An orchestra pit and all the
other conventions of "opera" must be avoided at all costs.[29]

Goehr's *Naboth's Vineyard*, then, is quite Brechtian in the sense that the highly
illusionistic theater of the Wagnerian *Gesamtkunstwerk* is avoided, most of all by
using a visible orchestra on stage rather than the sunken orchestra under the stage.
Bertolt Brecht has described his epic theater, intended as an aesthetic antidote to
Wagnerian theater:

> When the epic theatre's methods begin to penetrate the opera the first result is a
> radical *separation of the elements* ... So long as the expression "Gesamtkunstwerk"
> (or "integrated work of art") means that the integration is a muddle, so long as the
> arts are supposed to be "fused" together, the various elements will all be equally
> degraded, and each will act as a mere "feed" to the rest.[30]

For Brecht, a dangerous effect of the Wagnerian theater of illusion is an "emotional
infection," the direct transfer of onstage emotions to the audience. In order to
prevent the spectator from developing an emotional empathy with the characters,
Brecht demands a radical separation between each component of the drama in
order to achieve an effect of alienation (*Verfremdungseffekt*). "The alienation
effect intervenes," explains Brecht, "not in the form of the absence of emotion,
but in the form of emotions which need not correspond to those of the characters
portrayed."[31] For Brecht, the emotional manipulation of the audience through
the Wagnerian *Gesamtkunstwerk* is a kind of aesthetic totalitarianism that is
ideologically dangerous as well—a "phantasmagoria," to use Theodor Adorno's
description of Wagnerian theater.[32]

Although not as aggressive as Brecht's or Adorno's anti-Wagnerian aesthetics,
Goehr's operatic practice shares the essence of Brechtian epic theater, and his
voice–body split creates an alienation effect. In my interview with Goehr on
July 4, 2007, he acknowledged a Brechtian element in his *Naboth's Vineyard*. He
noted that for him the subject of the work itself is "Brechtian," and that Kurt
Weill, Brecht's main collaborator in his operatic work, once considered setting the
story of Naboth as an opera. During the interview, Goehr also revealed Charlie
Chaplin as another influential source for his operatic oeuvre in general and pointed
to the aesthetic connection between Brecht and Chaplin: the latter's silent films,

---

[29]   Cox, in Goehr, *Naboth's Vineyard*, no page number given.

[30]   Bertolt Brecht, *Brecht on Theatre: The Development of an Aesthetic*, ed. and trans.
John Willett (New York: Hill and Wang, 1964), p. 37.

[31]   Ibid., p. 94.

[32]   Theodor Adorno, *In Search of Wagner*, trans. Rodney Livingstone (London: NLB,
1981).

especially *The Gold Rush* (1925), significantly influenced the former.[33] In silent film in general, there is no such thing as an embodied representation of the voice simply because the voice is absent. Another motivation for the separation of voice and body in his *Triptych*, Goehr mentioned, was that he wanted to let the singers "act through their voice," which is for him the fundamental condition of opera, and not through physical gesture.[34] It is perhaps in this respect that Goehr's *Triptych* is considered to have a strong kinship with the Japanese Noh theater in which singers represent only the vocal dimension of characters, while their bodily representation is enacted by dancers.[35]

Philip Glass's *La Belle et la bête* (1994) is another example of the split representation of a character's body and voice. Since the 1990s, Glass has shown a strong interest in the operatic exploration of cinema. His three works *Orfée* (1993), *La Belle et la bête* (1994), and *Les Enfants terribles* (1996) form the "Cocteau Trilogy," each adapting Cocteau's corresponding work in different ways. *Orfée* is a straightforward operatic setting of Cocteau's film, using a condensed version of the film's screenplay as the libretto. The last work, *Les Enfants terribles*, is a dance opera in which dance is an equal partner with music in the expression

---

[33] Another affinity between Brecht and Chaplin can be found in their strong interest in the Chinese Peking Opera actor Mei Lanfang (1894–1961). For Brecht, Peking Opera was a model for his epic theater: "Traditional Chinese acting also knows the alienation effect, and applies it most subtly … Above all, the Chinese artist never acts as if there were a fourth wall besides the three surrounding him. He expresses his awareness of being watched. This immediately removes one of the European stage's characteristic illusions." See Brecht, *Brecht on Theatre*, pp. 91–2.

[34] Interview with Alexander Goehr on July 4, 2007, at a coffee shop near the train station in Cambridge, England. He also mentioned to me that he was invited to score a film that was to be directed by Michael Powell and featuring Bing Crosby, but it did not materialize.

[35] Melanie Daiken, "Notes on Goehr's *Triptych*," in *The Music of Alexander Goehr*, ed. Bayan Northcott (London: Schott, 1980), p. 40. In Noh, a character is vocally represented by the chanting chorus, which sometimes collectively functions as a narrator or a commentator who describes events from the perspective of another character in a similar way to how a chorus functions as a commentator in ancient Greek drama. Given these multiple functions of the singers, the separation between voice and body is more complex in Noh. Anthony Sheppard notes that, in a telephone conversation, Goehr informed him that his early interest in the films and theories of Eisenstein had aroused his interest in Japanese theater. (Eisenstein had repeatedly acknowledged the influence of Japanese theater on his work.) Following the composition of *Naboth's Vineyard*, Goehr planned to set two of Yukio Mishima's modernized Noh plays and traveled to Japan to meet with the writer and to study Noh, but Mishima committed ritual suicide before the meeting could occur. However, Goehr has recently composed music for these plays. See Sheppard, *Revealing Masks*, pp. 297–8.

of the drama.[36] Most of the characters are portrayed by one singer and one or more dancers. Lise, the heroine, for instance, is represented by a singer and three dancers. By doubling or tripling characters, Glass and choreographer Susan Marshall intended to amplify the characters' emotions or express their conflicting and divided emotions.

La Belle et la bête demonstrates the most noteworthy fusion of opera and cinema, especially in terms of a renewed relationship between voice and body. An adaptation of Jean Cocteau's 1946 film, the opera uses Cocteau's cinematic images for its visual content while Glass's operatic music replaces the original soundtrack.[37] During the performance of Glass's *Belle*, there is no acting. Singers perform while standing on stage below a gigantic film screen on which Cocteau's images are mutely projected (because Cocteau's *Belle* is a sound film, Glass had to silence its original soundtrack, composed by Georges Auric, in order to replace it with his live music). Using Cocteau's original scenario as the libretto, which he wanted to keep intact, Glass designed his music so as to ensure a reasonable synchronization between the singing and the projected images. The technical problem, then, was how to synchronize the singing with the onscreen characters' lip movements. Glass originally planned to time the dialogue with a stopwatch and compose music to match it. But this method was too crude, and he finally ended up using a digital time code—a black bar showing elapsed minutes, seconds, and fractions of seconds—added to a print of the film.

Unlike traditional operatic theater, in which live bodies are an essential part of the operatic spectacle, Glass's opera makes the singers' live bodies superfluous from a visual and representational point of view, because acting and the visual content of the opera are provided by Cocteau's film. While in traditional operatic performance the singer's body becomes a physical manifestation of the voice, in Glass's *Belle*, the singers' voices are re-embodied as cinematic images, destroying the traditional unity between voice and body in live theater. Once the film starts to run, the singers do not act but simply sing (and according to Goehr, this is an ideal condition for opera, for singers should "act through their voices," as quoted above). When Cocteau's cinematic images replace the opera's visuality, the singers' bodies lose their signifying function. By simply standing on stage, fixed and immobile, powerless to act, Glass's singers—or more precisely, their

---

[36]   Cocteau wrote the screenplay of *Les Enfants terribles*, based on his novel of the same title. The film was directed by Jean-Pierre Melville.

[37]   I examine this opera in detail in "The Cinematic Body in the Operatic Theater: Philip Glass's *La Belle et la Bête*," in *Between Opera and Cinema*, ed. Jeongwon Joe and Rose M. Theresa (New York: Routledge, 2002), pp. 59–73. Another substantial study of Glass's opera is Aaron Ziegle's "Reshaped and Redefined: Watching Cocteau's *La Belle et la Béte* with Auric and Glass," *Music Research Forum* 26 (2011): 45–74. Ziegle's article focuses on the comparison of Auric's original score for the film and Glass's new operatic music.

bodies—no longer function as a tool to represent the emotions and psychology of the opera's characters.[38]

Harrison Birtwistle's *The Mask of Orpheus* (1986) offers a further example of the voice–body split. It consists of multiple narratives of the Orpheus myth told from different characters' perspectives, reflecting the various versions of the original myth itself. The stage is divided into different areas to distinguish the different narratives. Each of the major characters—Orpheus, Euridice, and Aristaeus—is represented in three forms: as a singer, a mime, and a puppet. All of the singers are to wear masks, following the tradition of Greek tragedy. As in Goehr's *Naboth's Vineyard*, the masks engender an alienation effect by further distancing the singers' voices from their bodies and, in so doing, disrupting the hearing and viewing senses.[39] This alienation effect, re-formulated in the aesthetics of neoclassicism, was exactly what Stravinsky intended to produce when he instructed his singers to wear masks in his *Oedipus Rex*. Masks, as Robert Wilson notes, create "a distance between the sound and image," voice and body, and, in so doing, contribute to the disruption of hearing and viewing senses.[40] The use of puppets in *The Mask of Orpheus* creates an additional degree of distancing between voice and body. Unlike in his earlier opera *Punch and Judy* (1967), which features singers pretending to be puppets, Birtwistle uses actual puppets in *The Mask of Orpheus*, and their voices are provided by offstage singers. The separation of voice and body, then, is more radical than it is in Glass's opera: in *La Belle et la bête*, the surrogated body is still a human body, even though it is two-dimensional cinematic image; in Birtwistle's work, the human body is replaced by an inanimate puppet, which enhances the disembodied-ness of the singing voice.

---

[38]   There are a couple of points during the opera when the singers imitate the position of Cocteau's cinematic images: for instance, in the dinner sequence, in which the Beast is standing behind Belle. But the operatic singers are mostly immobile on stage throughout the opera.

[39]   Robert Wilson used microphones to create an effect similar to that of masks in Greek theater. He notes, "It's like the Greek theatre in that when the Greek actor was on stage he wore a mask, which presented an image that was different from what he was saying. It's in this way that what I'm trying to do is similar to Greek theatre—the entire stage is a mask. That's one reason I use microphones—to create a distance between the sound and the image." Quoted in Johannes Birringer, *Theatre, Theory, Postmodernism* (Bloomington: Indiana University Press, 1991), p. 224.

[40]   For more detailed information about Stravinsky's neoclassical aesthetics, see Chapter 6.

The Power of the Bodiless Voice—the Voice from Elsewhere—in Film and Opera

How can we explain the recent fascination in opera with the separation of voice and body? Given the "castration anxiety" of the cinematic apparatus, why would opera embrace something that has been an "anxiety" for cinema? Why would opera relinquish the very quality that cinema aspires to simulate, the embodied voice? I propose that one possible reason is cinema's ironic privileging of the voice in spite of the seeming dominance of the visual in film.

When the voice is isolated from the body that produces it, the voice acquires a more autonomous power. In fact, this phenomenon of the autonomous voice is inherent, although hidden from and elusive to our perception, in the cinematic apparatus. Slavoj Žižek's argument is illuminating on this matter. He contends that, contrary to people's expectations, the effect of adding a soundtrack to silent film is the exact opposite of a realistic imitation of life:

> What took place from the very beginning of the sound film was an uncanny autonomization of the voice, baptized "acousmatisation" by Chion: the emergence of a voice that is neither attached to an object (a person) within diegetic reality nor simply the voice of an external commentator, but a spectral voice, which floats freely in a mysterious intermediate domain ... The voice acquires a spectral autonomy, it never quite belongs to the body we see, so that even when we see a living person talking, there is always some degree of ventriloquism at work: it is as if the speaker's own voice hollows him out and in a sense speaks "by itself," through him.[41]

The autonomous and uncanny power of voice in the cinematic media (i.e., film, video, and television) is readily experienced when the synchronization of image and sound tracks falters. Even a split-second discrepancy in synchronization yields a fatal destruction of what Roland Barthes calls the "reality effect," as images, whose illusion is created by synchronized sound, are transformed into a shadow play of flat pictures, losing their flesh. This is the moment that unveils the intrinsic authorial power of the soundtrack, the power of the voice, in the cinematic media. Michal Grover-Friedlander's discussion of Franco Zeffirelli's film *Callas Forever* (2002) insightfully addresses the primacy of sound over image.[42] The film is a fictionalization of Callas's last few years in Paris and it focuses on a cinematic production of *Carmen*, using a recording of Callas as the sound text, to which Zeffirelli's Callas is simply lip-synching. As Grover-Friedlander indicates, we assume that a voice searches for the right body to be anchored in, that it would

---

[41]   Slavoj Žižek, "'I Hear You with My Eyes,'" p. 92.

[42]   Michal Grover-Friedlander, "The Afterlife of Maria Callas's Voice," in *Operatic Afterlives* (New York: Zone Books, 2011), pp. 45–75. An earlier version of this chapter was published in *Musical Quarterly* 88, no. 1 (Spring 2005): 35–62.

remain incomplete if detached from a body or were off screen or disembodied. But she argues for the primacy of sound over image by demonstrating how Zeffirelli's film suggests that it is the image that struggles to satisfy the demands of the voice, and that its phenomenal (in the Kantian sense) power is diminished if not annulled by the voice. *Callas Forever*, she contends, "unleashes a 'Voice-Callas' that overpowers its vessel and resists any anchoring in a body."

> Dubbing, playback, and post-synchronization have little to do with voice–body accommodation, when it comes to Callas's voice, because reattaching a body to the voice of Callas does not put that voice to rest. Here is a voice absolutely and unconditionally marked, a voice already uncomfortably hosted in its originating body (as the weight loss and the Hepburn fixation make manifest). *Callas Forever* tells the more haunting tale: pairs of *voices* ominously searching for, reliving, recalling, and remapping themselves one onto another.[43]

Grover-Friedlander concludes that the multiplicity of voices born of the representation of Callas's voice demonstrates a rejection of the anchoring body. Various theories postulate that such a rejection results from a notion that the voice itself has a body,[44] just as the voice of Charles Ludlam's Callas has its own will, as I discussed at the beginning of this chapter.

Glass's *La Belle et la bête* also unveils the intrinsic autonomy of the voice by accentuating the two-dimensionality of Cocteau's screen images. In standard film, a significant function of sound is to flesh out the play of flat images on the screen. Various visual techniques are employed to create a sense of spatial depth: for instance, a camera continuously moves toward or away from objects in order to articulate the space in between.[45] But, as Rudolph Arnheim stresses, sound can create a much stronger sense of spatiality than image does.[46] Béla Balázs contends that "[w]e accept seen space as *real*, only when it contains sounds as well, for these give it the dimension of depth."[47] As indicated earlier, Glass silenced Cocteau's original soundtrack in order to re-embody the singers' voices in the cinematic bodies. When cinematic images lose their sounds, they lose their flesh as well. Of course, Cocteau's cinematic bodies are re-envoiced with the operatic music in Glass's *Belle*, and music in cinema does function to

---

[43]   Grover-Friedlander, "The Afterlife of Maria Callas's Voice," in *Operatic Afterlives*, p. 58.

[44]   Ibid., p. 62.

[45]   Lucy Fischer, "*Applause*: The Visual and Acoustic Landscape," in *Sound and the Cinema: The Coming of Sound to American Film*, ed. Evan William Cameron (Pleasantville, NY: Redgrave Publishing, 1980), p. 185.

[46]   Quoted in ibid., p. 182.

[47]   Béla Balázs, *Theory of the Film: Character and Growth of a New Art* (New York: Dover Publications, 1970), p. 207.

compensate for the lack of spatial depth in photographic images.[48] Hanns Eisler and Theodor Adorno argue that music serves, more than the speaking voice, "to breathe into the pictures some of the life that photography has taken away from them." In their view, the talkie without music is not very different from a silent movie.[49] However, as I argue elsewhere,[50] the spatial function of music is only metaphorical: *music* creates a *general* sense of space through its three-dimensionality, but does not correspond to the particular images shown on the screen. In contrast, diegetic (or ambient) *sounds* articulate the very space that the shown image represents, and thus these sounds more realistically, rather than metaphorically, corporealize the images. According to Marcia Citron, an effect of diegetic sounds is "the imposition of a frame of reality—as if the sounds are marking off events in real time and space."[51] Considering these dynamics between image and sound, we can see how Glass's *Belle* deactivates the "reality effect" (à la Barthes, or "the imposition of reality" à la Citron) through reinforcing the two-dimensionality of the screen images and, in so doing, accentuates the autonomy of the voice.

A more exaggerated and radical example is the "Teatro Silencio" scene in David Lynch's *Mulholland Drive* (2001). In this scene, a female singer (Rebekah Del Rio) is lip-synching to her recording of Roy Orbison's song "Crying" in a Spanish rendition ("Llorando"), and her recorded singing voice continues after she collapses on stage in the middle of the song. This is the moment Žižek describes as the autonomization of the voice as "a pure spectral apparition of a bodiless 'undead' voice."[52] I argue that the "uncanny autonomization of the voice" in film can be regarded as one reason for opera's unconscious attraction to cinema. This is because in opera performance, too, the voice acquires an autonomous power, separated from the singer's body, in spite of the embodied performance.

---

[48]   This is why music accompanied silent cinema in addition to its function of masking noises from the projector. See Claudia Gorbman, "Narrative Film Music," *Yale French Studies*, no. 60 (1980): 186. The entire issue of this journal is devoted to the subject of cinema and sound.

[49]   Hanns Eisler, *Composing for the Films*, reprint ed. (New York: Books for Libraries Press, 1971), pp. 59 and 77.

[50]   See Joe, "The Cinematic Body in the Operatic Theater: Philip Glass's *La Belle et la Bête*."

[51]   Marcia Citron, "A Night at the Cinema: Zeffirelli's *Otello* and the Genre of Film-Opera," *Musical Quarterly* 78, no. 4 (Winter 1994): 719.

[52]   Slavoj Žižek, *Organs without Bodies: Deleuze and Consequences* (New York: Routledge, 2004), p. 169. Žižek compares the undead voice in the "Teatro Silencio" scene in *Mulholland* to the telephone ringing at the opening of Sergio Leone's *Once Upon a Time in America*: a phone is ringing loudly and the ringing continues after a hand picks up the receiver.

At the beginning of her book *In Search of Opera*, Carolyn Abbate discusses Orpheus's last song emanating from his decapitated and floating head as a "master symbol" for central issues her book addresses: "the complications of the performance network."[53] Orpheus's postmortem singing, she argues, is also a literal embodiment of the music that comes not from the human body but from *elsewhere*, just as cinema's reality resides in a "primordial elsewhere," according to Christian Metz as quoted above. Abbate regards Orpheus's postmortem singing as representing the uncanny aspect of musical performance in general and operatic performance in particular. For Abbate, "a powerful metaphysics of absence"—of elsewhere—in spite of the visible presence of the singing body characterizes the state of voice in opera performance. In her theory, dead (musical) instrument and live performer are considered the same because both are inanimate objects given life by music. To illustrate the lifelessness of the performer whose master is the music, whether vocal or instrumental, Abbate quotes Ange Goudar's 1777 review of Italian keyboard players:

> When I saw the celebrated virtuoso Anf[.] for the first time in Venice, I believed myself to be witnessing an automaton, a machine mounted on brass wires. One has to imagine a man from another world who ignores everything that happens in this one, who says nothing, does nothing, knows nothing, with whom one can have no conversation, who has no expression except that drawn from quarter notes, eighth notes, and sixteenth notes. Since he had left his soul on the lid of his clavichord, I begged him to retrieve it, that is, to play an arietta of his own composition, that I might know that he existed; but he didn't want to exist: so on that day, I had a conversation with his cadaver.[54]

In light of Abbate's theories, the voice–body split in the four examples I have examined in this chapter can be considered to be the visualization of the intrinsic condition of operatic voice and performers. The mimes in Goehr's *Triptych*, the fleshless onscreen cinematic images in Glass's *La Belle et la bête*, the puppets in Birtwistle's *The Mask of Orpheus*, and the collapsed singer in Lynch's *Mulholland Drive*—these all represent the lifelessness of the performers, whose voices are emanated from "elsewhere." This is the voice having "a will of its own," just as Ludlam's Callas does—the voice whose autonomization, whose power, comes from its bodiless-ness. This power is not a phantom of scholarly metaphysics but a physical entity that touches a diva's consciousness when she hears another diva's voice on stage. In her autobiography, Mary Garden, a Scottish diva dubbed as "the Sarah Bernhardt of opera," notes:

> You know, the last note of the first act of *La Bohème* is the last note that comes out of Mimi's throat. It is a high C, and Mimi sings it when she walks out of

---

53   Abbate, *In Search of Opera*, p. 5.
54   Ibid., pp. 196–7.

the door with Rodolfo. She closes the door, and then she takes the note. The way Melba sang that high C was the strangest and weirdest thing I have ever experienced in my life. The note came floating out of the auditorium at Covent Garden: it left Melba's throat, it left Melba's body, it left everything, and came like a star and passed us in our box and went out into the infinite … My God, how beautiful it was![55]

---

[55]   Quoted in Richard Somerset-Ward, *Angels and Monsters: Male and Female Sopranos in the Story of Opera* (New Haven, CT: Yale University Press, 2004), p. 291.

Chapter 5
Film Divas: The Problem and the Power of the Singing Women[1]

In her essay "Music in *The Piano*," Claudia Gorbman argues that depictions of musicians in film, especially in melodramas from Hollywood's classical era, are fairly consistent in their gendered representation of the protagonists' profession: male characters are portrayed as serious, committed, and accomplished musicians, while female musicians are rarely presented with the same degree of commitment to their profession. As an example, Gorbman discusses Irving Rapper's *Deception* (1946), based on Louis Verneuil's play *Monsieur Lamberthier* (1927). The film's heroine, Christine Radcliffe (Bette Davis), is a pianist and music teacher, but her career does not get much attention in the film: in Gorbman's words, "the fabric of film is curiously uninterested in what she does musically."[2] Instead, Christine's musical qualifications only function as an instrument for her to be associated with "real" musicians—her ex-lover and genius composer, Alexander Hollenius (Claude Rains), and her cellist husband, Karel Novak (Paul Henreid). Christine is a professional musician just like the male characters she is associated with, but there is not a single shot of *her* performing. Instead, Christine is only shown as an audience member, marveling at their virtuosity as composer (for Alexander) and performer (for Karel). Gorbman notes, "Women characters frequently serve as the audience's stand-in, the audience within the story, anchoring our reception of diegetic music or art in a context of values. Women's production must ordinarily be confined to the internal or at least domestic sphere, tamed, transformed into an attribute of femininity." Based on her analysis of *Deception* and several other films about musicians, such as John Brahm's *Hangover Square* (1945) and Jean Negulesco's *Humoresque* (1946), Gorbman concludes that "Hollywood film codes serious art as a masculine enterprise."[3] Since artistic areas in general have been regarded as a "dangerously feminine sphere" in Western culture—in the United

---

[1]   The second part of the subtitle of this chapter is a reference to the subtitle of the first chapter ("The Pleasures of Echo: The 'Problem' of the Speaking Woman") of Amy Lawrence's book, *Echo and Narcissus: Women's Voices in Classical Hollywood Cinema* (Berkeley: University of California Press, 1991). This chapter was developed from my presentation at the workshop "Intersections of Opera and Film," held at Rice University in March 2006, organized by Marcia J. Citron.

[2]   Claudia Gorbman, "Music in *The Piano*," in *Jane Campion's "The Piano,"* ed. Harriet Margolis (Cambridge: Cambridge University Press, 2000), p. 44.

[3]   Ibid., pp. 44–5.

States, classical music in particular[4]—Western cinema has imbued male artist protagonists with a strong masculinity to compensate for the anxiety about art's feminine association.

> The serious musician is a man who expresses the depth of his soul through consummate knowledge, skill, and passion … Music is a business, a career, but also a higher calling, showing the male artist to have something godlike about him … The classical cinema rarely presents a woman musician similarly accomplished or committed.[5]

Gorbman finds that, in spite of the accelerated women's movement of the early 1970s, Hollywood films have not changed much in the gendered representation of musician characters since its classical era. In more recent films, however, musician heroines shown to have successful careers are not entirely absent. Gorbman observes that such heroines "tend to be" singers, as in Sidney J. Furie's *Lady Sings the Blues* (1972) and Mark Rydell's *The Rose* (1979), biopics of Diana Ross and Bette Midler, respectively. I find this cinematic tendency to be very prominent and to encompass operatic divas as well as pop singers.

Biopics of historical divas started at an early stage of sound film, including two Jenny Lind films by MGM, starring Grace Moore, Sidney Franklin's *A Lady's Morals* (1930) and Arthur Robinson's *Jenny Lind* (1932); Lewis Milestone's *Melba* (1953), about the Australian diva Nellie Melba; and Curtis Bernhardt's *Interrupted Melody* (1955), based on the autobiography of another Australian diva, Marjorie Lawrence, who struggled with polio. Werner Schroeter's *The Death of Maria Malibran* (1972) is another diva film, about the legendary nineteenth-century Spanish mezzo-soprano Maria Malibran. Schroeter's film is not a standard biopic but rather a non-narrative and extremely abstract representation of its main character: as in many of Schroeter's films, a traditional narrative plot is replaced with a poetic representation through pure (that is, non-narrative) images, sounds, and gestures, similar to Robert Wilson's "theater of images," an example of which is his collaboration with Philip Glass, *Einstein on the Beach* (1976).[6]

---

[4]   Robynn Stilwell's article about John McTiernan's original *Die Hard* (1998) demonstrates how classical music is feminized and stigmatized as un-American in contrast to popular music, and how this dichotomy was promoted during the Reagan era. See Stilwell, "'I just put a drone under him …': Collage and Subversion in the Score of *Die Hard*," *Music and Letters* 78, no. 4 (November 1997): 551–80.

[5]   Gorbman, "Music in *The Piano*," p. 44. Gorbman argues that the heroine in Jane Campion's *The Piano* (1993), Ada McGrath (Holly Hunter) represents a departure from the gender ideology of movie musicians, as she is located in between "the heritage of the serious public-sphere male artist and the casual private-sphere female artist" (p. 45). Moreover, Ada not only plays music but also composes it (p. 46).

[6]   One of the few substantial studies of Schroeter's *Malibran* in English is James Clark Farmer's dissertation, "Opera and the New German Cinema: Between Distance and

A more recent example of diva biopics is Franco Zeffirelli's *Callas Forever* (2002), a fictional dramatization of Maria Callas's final years in Paris. Among the films that feature completely fictional diva heroines are Bernardo Bertolucci's *La Luna* (1979); Jean-Jacques Beineix's *Diva* (1981); István Szabó's *Meeting Venus* (1991); Claude Miller's *The Accompanist* (1992); and Don Boyd's *Lucia* (1998), a film about producing Donizetti's opera *Lucia di Lammermoor*, featuring the director's daughter Amanda Boyd in the title role.

This chapter addresses the issue of cinema's representation of diva heroines in comparison to that of instrumentalist heroines, paying particular attention to the gendered identity of vocal and instrumental music.[7] Based on the films I examine as case studies, I will show that the dichotomy between "the serious public-sphere male artist" and "the casual private-sphere female artist" that Gorbman observes among movie musicians also appears *within* the realm of female musician heroines: namely, what determines the public or private persona among female musicians is whether the heroine's profession is vocal or instrumental music. I discuss this dichotomy in the context of the sexual identities associated with vocal music and instrumental music in Western culture, as theorized by such scholars as Daniel Chua. In so doing, I will show how cinema, as represented by the films I analyze in this chapter, conforms to the Western tradition of gendering vocal music as a feminine prerogative and instrumental music as a male domain. I focus on the films that deal with fictional divas rather than biopics, because I have found the former group to be a more intriguing representation of the gendered difference from instrumental heroines in terms of their music-making. Films about fictional musicians have more flexibility in handling scenes of their musical performances than do biopics, in which the inclusion of the scenes of public performance are to a certain degree unavoidable, because they were historical events. As I have noted several times throughout this book, what I argue is not meant to be a general and absolute theory that covers the entire cinematic tradition. There is nothing further from my intention than creating a "master theory" of the cinematic convention. Rather, I examine how a gendered representation of instrumentalist versus diva heroines in certain films corresponds to a gendered dichotomy between vocal and instrumental music. My occasional use of the term "cinema" in this chapter, and in some other contexts throughout this book, is not intended to refer to the entire genre but only as represented by the specific films I analyze as case studies.[8]

Fascination (Alexander Kluge, Werner Schroeter, Hans-Jürgen Syberberg)" (PhD diss., University of Iowa, 2003). Caryl Flinn's book *The New German Cinema: Music History, and the Matter of Style* (Berkeley: University of California, 2004) does not focus on *The Death of Maria Malibran* but it is a good source for situating Schroeter's operatic film in the context of the New German Cinema.

[7]   In this book, the term "diva" refers to female singers.

[8]   In his review of Michal Grover-Friedlander, *Vocal Apparitions: The Attraction of Cinema to Opera* (Princeton, NJ: Princeton University Press, 2005), Matthew W. Smith notes that Grover-Friedlander's argument is not "true of opera and film taken as a whole,"

Instrumental Heroines

Just as female musicians are shown more often in private spheres than public ones as compared to their male counterparts, the music-making of instrumentalist heroines tends to be confined to domestic and private arenas, while diva heroines are mostly immune from such domestic restrictions. Claude Sautet's 1992 film *A Heart in Winter* (*Un cœur en hiver*) serves as an example. The plot of the film centers on a romantic triangle between a beautiful violin virtuoso, Camille Kassler (Emmanuelle Béart), who is obsessed with the composer Maurice Ravel; Maxime (André Dussollier), a violinist and violin shop owner; and Stéphane (Daniel Auteuil), a violin craftsman who works for Maxime. Maxime leaves his wife for Camille, but Camille becomes attracted to Stéphane, a detached, aloof, indifferent, and extremely introverted character. Stéphane, too, is interested in Camille, but the film ends with his cruel rejection of Camille, severely breaking her heart and wounding her ego as a virtuoso artist and an attractive woman. The reason for Stéphane's rejection of Camille's affections remains enigmatic. There are numerous performance scenes throughout the film, but Camille is never shown in a public concert; instead, her performance scenes are limited to recording studios or private venues (Figures 5.1 and 5.2). In the entire film, there is only one scene of a public concert, and in that scene the performer is not Camille but Maxime, whose career as a violinist is not even comparable to that of Camille.

Ingmar Bergman's *Autumn Sonata* (1978) serves as another example that demonstrates the domestic confinement of instrumentalist heroines' music-making. Bergman's film is a story about the formidable emotional tension between Charlotte Andergast (Ingrid Bergman) and her daughter Eva (Liv Ullmann). Charlotte is a celebrated concert pianist whose success was achieved at the expense of her motherly duties. The film begins with Charlotte's visit to Eva's house after having abandoned Eva and her other daughter, Helena (Lena Nyman), for a long time. Helena is mentally impaired and was placed in a mental institution many years ago. Until her visit to her first daughter, Eva, Charlotte does not know that Eva has removed Helena from the institution in order to take care of her at home. The tension between Charlotte and Eva slowly builds, climaxing in an intense conversation one night as Eva pours out her long-accumulated anger at her mother.

Compared to Sautet's *A Heart in Winter*, there are fewer performance scenes in *Autumn Sonata*, as Bergman's film is highly focused on the psychological states of the protagonists. But in the few performance scenes, Bergman's pianist heroine, like Sautet's violinist, is exclusively shown in domestic settings such as her childhood practice room, shown as a soundless flashback (Figure 5.3), or at

---

but "is true, in surprising ways, of" the particular films she analyzes in her book. I think that Grover-Friedlander is not claiming the validity of her argument for the entire genre of film and cinema. It seems to me that, as I clarified above, she too uses the terms "opera" and "cinema" as represented by the works she analyzes. For Smith's review, see *The Opera Quarterly* 22, no. 1 (2007): 170–200.

Figure 5.1   Camille in a recording studio, in *A Heart in Winter*

Figure 5.2   Camille performing in a string quartet at a private concert, in *A Heart in Winter*

her daughter's house, where she plays Chopin's Prelude no. 2 in A minor to show her interpretation of the piece to her daughter Eva, the only audience member in the room (Figure 5.4).[9] Charlotte's public concerts are mentioned only verbally in a telephone conversation with her manager, Paul, when she is arranging a concert in London. This conversation reveals her status as a celebrated performer, which is

---

[9]   For a discussion of the two different interpretations of this Chopin piece as provided by Charlotte and Eva, see Lawrence Kramer, "Music, Metaphor, and Metaphysics," *Musical Times* 145 (Autumn 2004): 5–18. According to Kramer, this scene reverses conventional wisdom about musical performance by suggesting that "the standard performance is not the realization of the formal pattern indicated by the score" but "an understanding of what the piece means, what it 'tells of'" (pp. 5–6). Kramer contextualizes Bergman's scene in the recent musicological discourse surrounding performance, stimulated by Carolyn Abbate's article, "Music—Drastic or Gnostic?" *Critical Inquiry* 30, no. 3 (Spring 2004): 505–36.

Figure 5.3   Charlotte in her practice room as a child, in *Autumn Sonata*

Figure 5.4   Charlotte playing Chopin's A minor Prelude for Eva, in *Autumn Sonata*

especially implied by the amount (although unspecified) that the concert sponsor is willing to pay her: "What, another concert? ... Oh no, that's impossible. That's my time off and you know that very well ... How much do they pay did you say? Good Lord. All right. If they can make that concert on Wednesday, the 17th, it will be all right."

Frank Borzage's film *I've Always Loved You* (1946) is about a pianist heroine, Myra Hassman (Catherine McLeod),[10] who is torn between a professional and

---

[10]   Perhaps Borzage's film was a tribute to British concert pianist Myra Hess. I thank Scott D. Pauline for bringing Borzage's film to my attention.

romantic attraction to the despotic and arrogant conductor Leopold Goronoff (Philip Dorn) and a warm—gentle but not passionate—love for her long-time friend George Sampter (Bill Carter). Myra decides to marry George out of her despair—a kind of escapism—after a humiliating concert debut at Carnegie Hall, where she played Rachmaninoff's Second Piano Concerto. Leopold conducted the concert but out of jealousy for her talent, combined with his sexism, he intentionally derails her performance by accelerating the tempo to the point that she cannot follow the orchestra. After that traumatic concert, Myra withdraws from the stage and concert life and does not play the piano at all, although her husband, George, always encourages her to go back to concert performance. In the meantime their daughter, Georgette, "Porgy" (Gloria Donovan plays Porgy at five, and Vanessa Brown plays the adult Porgy), is taking piano lessons. When Porgy wins a piano competition and is chosen to be a soloist at Carnegie Hall, to be conducted by Leopold, George suggests that Myra should go to New York with Porgy and meet Leopold. Myra reluctantly follows his suggestion. The final scene is the concert at Carnegie Hall, but there is an announcement that the soloist will not be Porgy but her mother Myra. The change has been arranged by Leopold to compensate for the damage he inflicted at her concert debut a long time ago. Myra plays the same piece, Rachmaninoff's Second Piano Concerto.

In contrast to the heroine of Bergman's *Autumn Sonata*, Borzage's pianist heroine is shown performing in a public concert twice, the second of which is a performance sequence for a substantial amount of time, a little over nine minutes, into which all of the three movements of Rachmaninoff's Second Piano Concerto are condensed. In several places in the film, Leopold is shown in a very relaxed posture, while Myra is portrayed with a much more serious attitude about her profession (Figure 5.5). Furthermore, near the end of her second performance at Carnegie Hall, the once-sexist maestro, Leopold, even acknowledges Myra's

Figure 5.5   Myra and Leopold in the maestro's living room, in *I've Always Loved You*

greatness as a musician through his voiceover ("I was wrong, Myra. There is a woman in music."). However, the film ends, severely undermining Myra's professionalism. Immediately following Leopold's aforementioned voiceover, Myra leaves the stage of Carnegie Hall without completing her performance and goes to her husband George, who is standing behind the curtain at the side of the stage. Myra tells George with tearful eyes, "I've always loved you!" and they kiss, which is followed by the film's closing credits. This scene is a clear culmination of what Claudia Gorbman regards as the perpetuation of Hollywood's sexist encoding of serious art as a male territory.

Joel Oliansky's *The Competition* (1980) is particularly intriguing for examining a gendered representation of film instrumentalists, because its protagonists are two pianists, one female and one male. The story features an international piano competition held in San Francisco, whose six finalists include the protagonists Paul Dietrich (Richard Dreyfuss) and Heidi Joan Schoonover (Amy Irving). For the preparation for, and the rehearsal of, the final competition concerts, all the finalists are summoned to San Francisco, where Paul and Heidi first meet each other and fall in love. But because they have to compete with each other, they both agonize about the conflict between career and love. Unlike the instrumentalist heroines in Bergman's film and Sautet's, Heidi is shown performing in public, just like Paul, which might have been unavoidable given the storyline of the film. Unlike the musician heroines of the films Gorbman examines and those of many other films, Heidi is portrayed as a "serious" musician, and her professional ambition and achievement are represented as important as, if not more important than, her personal and domestic concerns. The choice of the piano concerto she selects for the final competition, Prokofiev's Third Piano Concerto, too, is a metaphor for her almost "aggressive" ambition, as it is replete with brilliant virtuosity (Figure 5.6). In terms of the technical virtuosity, then, Prokofiev's concerto can even be considered more "masculine" than Paul's choice for the final competition, Beethoven's "Emperor" (Figure 5.7)[11] Furthermore, Heidi is portrayed as a more accomplished pianist than Paul, for she is selected as the winner of the competition, while Paul wins the second-place prize.

Throughout the film, however, one can find interesting differences between the representation of Heidi's performance and that of Paul's. First of all, private spheres are still more associated with Heidi than with Paul: for a significant amount of the film, she is shown in a private practice room, offered to her by a former pianist who lives in the competition city of San Francisco. Moreover, the sequence of her (public) rehearsal with the orchestra is not only significantly shorter (about four minutes) than that of Paul's (about nine minutes),[12] but hers is

---

[11]   It is interesting that Heidi's first choice is Mozart's G major Concerto, but she immediately changes her mind.

[12]   Although orchestral rehearsals are not public concerts, they are relatively more public than playing in a private practice room because multiple people (the conductor and orchestral members) are involved and thus are a kind of social, as well as artistic, activity.

Figure 5.6   Heidi playing Prokofiev's Third Piano Concerto at the final concert, in *The Competition*

Figure 5.7   Paul playing Beethoven's "Emperor" Concerto at the final concert, in *The Competition*

also interrupted by news about the illness of Tatjana Baronova (Vicki Kriegler), a Russian prodigy who is another finalist.[13] In contrast, the artistic intensity of

---

[13]   The film addresses some interesting issues related to race and ethnicity. For instance, when Ty Henderson (Michael Humphries), the only African American among the six finalists, is shown practicing in a private room, he is naked, which I interpret as the exoticization of his race. Tatjana, too, is exoticized, as she is treated as a political "other"— at least, the film does not fail to acknowledge her political otherness in that the plot includes her teacher's pursuit of political asylum in the United States.

Paul's orchestral rehearsal scene is exceptionally strong. Paul is portrayed with charismatic power as he challenges the despotic conductor, Andrew Erskine (Sam Wanamaker), about his interpretation of the "Emperor" Concerto in the middle of his rehearsal.[14] Erskine asks Paul to conduct the passage in question. He first hesitates, telling the maestro that he is a pianist, not a conductor, and that he has never conducted before. However, Paul ends up charismatically leading the orchestra and convincing the maestro of his point of view (Figure 5.8).

Figure 5.8   At the maestro's request, Paul conducts the orchestra; conductor Andrew Erskine (Sam Wanamaker) is shown behind Paul

The scene of Heidi's performance for the final competition also shows a thought-provoking contrast to that of Paul's. Both performances are public concerts and each has a similar length, about seven minutes. Whereas Paul's scene is strongly focused on his performance, with extremely dexterous cut-and-paste edits of Beethoven's "Emperor" Concerto, Heidi's final performance scene, like her orchestral rehearsal scene, is interrupted by the cross-cut between Heidi's performance on stage and the backstage, where Heidi's teacher, Greta Vandemann (Lee Remick), and Paul are anxiously listening to Heidi's performance. There are also the cross-cuts between Heidi's performance and shots of Paul restlessly walking up and down outside the concert hall; his

---

14   The real maestro of the entire soundtrack is Lalo Schifrin, with the Los Angeles Philharmonic Orchestra playing the orchestral part of the soundtrack. Schifrin is also a prolific film composer: most recently, he scored Brett Ratner's martial arts/action-comedy series *Rush Hour* (1998, 2001, and 2007), starring Jackie Chan. Schifrin is a four-time Grammy award winner and has received six Oscar nominations, including Best Original Song for *The Competition* at the 1980 Academy Awards (the song title is "People Alone," with lyrics by Wilbur Jennings and sung by Randy Crawford).

facial expressions and bodily gestures are indicative of psychological struggle, his admiration for Heidi's masterful final performance bifurcated with his jealousy of it. Although Heidi and Paul are portrayed equally in terms of the balance between career and love at the plot level, the film's visual text still shows a relative anxiety and uneasiness about female performers' presence in the public sphere. The gendered dichotomy between "the serious public-sphere male artist" and "the casual private-sphere female artist"—a dichotomy that, according to Gorbman's study, was "surprisingly consistent" in classical Hollywood melodramas about musicians[15]—is only *partially* improved in Oliansky's film. Here, the female performer is portrayed as being as serious as the male performer, but a public (male territory) versus private (female territory) dichotomy still remains and the seriousness of Heidi's performance is compromised by the distracted and interrupted representation of it, intercut with other shots. This dichotomized representation of musical performance is analogous to Heather Laing's distinction between "conventional" and "personal" depictions of diegetic performance: while conventional performance refers to a more objective depiction of performance that focuses on the performer's technical musical prowess, personal performance highlights the performer's subjective, internalized, and privatized domain, removed from the public domain of conventional performance.[16]

The domesticity of instrumentalist heroines shown in *Autumn Sonata* and *A Heart in Winter* (and in *Deception*, Gorbman's example) demonstrates a fascinating twentieth-century resurrection of the sexual politics of music performance characteristic of Renaissance England. As Linda Austern explores in her essay "Sing Againe Syren: The Female Musician and Sexual Enchantment in Elizabethan Life and Literature," female musicians in England during this period were discouraged from performing in public because of the danger of their sensual beauty. The music performed by women was sometimes associated with such positive attributes as heavenly rapture and redemption, and even Stephen Gosson, a notorious anti-feminist and anti-musician English writer (1554–1624), allowed music in women's lives. But the beauty and spirituality of female music performance was always perceived as being intertwined with destructive carnal lust, motivating and justifying Gosson's claim that women should only perform in private spheres.[17] Since most Elizabethan women of the gentry indeed practiced their musical arts exclusively in domestic settings, Austern contends that Gosson had codified patriarchal prescriptions and expectations for the female music performance during his era: "When women sing or play for themselves alone, the

---

[15] Gorbman, "The Music in *The Piano*," p. 45.

[16] Heather Laing, "Wandering Minds and Anchored Bodies: Music, Gender and Emotion in Melodrama and the Woman's Film" (PhD diss., University of Warwick, 2000); quoted in Stilwell, "Hysterical Beethoven," *Beethoven Forum*, 10, no. 2 (2003), pp. 173–4.

[17] Linda Austern, "Sing Againe Syren: The Female Musician and Sexual Enchantment in Elizabethan Life and Literature," *Renaissance Quarterly* 42, no. 3 (Autumn 1989): 420-48.

pure spiritual essence of their music remains untouched by feminine beauty or the passion of love, and reaches their immortal souls simply and directly."[18] Although Linda Austern's study focuses on the Elizabethan England, the discouragement, if not prohibition, of female musicians' public performance was not limited to England but prevalent in Western Europe and continued in the eighteen and nineteenth centuries except for the domain of opera.

Film Divas

The films I examine in this chapter demonstrates the continuation of the gendered politics of female musical performance in Western Europe during the Elizabethan period throughout the nineteenth century, but the twentieth-century cinematic tendency, as represented by the films examined earlier in this chapter, distinguishes instrumental music from vocal music: to slightly modify Gosson's statement quoted above, "When women ... *play*" (that is, instrumentalist heroines), their performance venues are limited to private (such as a personal practice room) or semi-private (such as a recording studio) settings; "When women *sing*" (that is, diva heroines), they are immune from confinement to domestic performance. Film divas are usually shown in splendid public concerts, flamboyantly displaying their enchanting voice and virtuosity and often showered with thunderous applause. Claude Miller's *The Accompanist* is one such example. Set in Nazi-occupied Paris, the film's plot centers around the affair of a celebrated singer, Irène Brice (Elena Safonova), with a young man, Jacques Fabert (Samuel Labarthe), as seen through the eyes of Irène's accompanist, Sophie Vasseur (Romane Bohringer), whose admiration for Irène is almost an obsession. The film ends with the suicide of Irene's husband, Charles (Richard Bohringer), prompted by his wife's affair mixed with his guilty feelings about helping the Nazis for the sake of his business. Unlike Sautet's violinist heroine Camille and Bergman's pianist heroine Charlotte, Irene is shown in a public concert setting several times throughout the film, and each of her performances is greeted with huge applause.

Jean-Jacques Beineix's *Diva* is another example that shows a film diva's unrestricted public display of her virtuosic performance. It is a thriller based on Daniel Odier's crime novel of the same title, which was published in 1979 under Odier's pseudonym, Delacorta. The plot surrounds the diva Cynthia Hawkins (Wilhelmenia Fernandez), who adamantly refuses to have her singing recorded. Jules (Frédéric Andréi), a motorcycle-riding postman, is an opera fan and at one concert, he makes an illicit recording of Hawkins's singing of the aria "Ebben? Ne andrò lontana" from Alfredo Catalani's opera *La Wally*; he also steals her gown. The tape is confused with crime-related goods and the police pursue it. The film begins with the diva's concert performance, which is a central scene of the film (Figure 5.9). Beineix's diva is shown not only in public concerts but also in

---

[18]   Gosson quoted in ibid., p. 436.

Figure 5.9   Cynthia Hawkins's concert, at the beginning of *Diva*

other types of public and social contexts, such as a press interview, which further magnifies her public presence through media publicity.

Bernardo Bertolucci's *La Luna* also features a diva heroine, a recently widowed American singer, Caterina Silveri (Jill Clayburgh). Although the film's plot does not center on the musical aspect of the heroine's life but instead focuses on her incestuous relationship with her fifteen-year-old son, Caterina is shown in a number of public performances. István Szabó's *Meeting Venus* also contains numerous scenes of public performance by its diva heroine, Karin Anderson (Glenn Close). Szabó's film is a love story about the Hungarian conductor Zoltan Szanto (Niels Arestrup) and Karin, a celebrated Swedish prima donna who is chosen for the much-anticipated new production of Wagner's *Tannhäuser*, to be conducted by Szanto.

Even the alien diva in such sci-fi films as Luc Besson's *The Fifth Element* shares the glorious display of film divas' public performance. Plavalaguna, the alien diva, sings the "Mad Scene" from Donizetti's *Lucia di Lammermoor*, and this opera scene is one of the most prominent scenes in the film from both visual and narrative points of view: it is the moment when the "fifth element" is found inside the diva's body (Figure 5.10).[19] Plavalaguna's audience, like that of human film divas, is shown mesmerized by the enchanting beauty of her voice, and at the end of the performance she is showered with clamorous applause (Figure 5.11).

---

[19]   For plot details of *The Fifth Element*, see Chapter 1.

(a)

(b)

Figure 5.10 (a)–(b)   Alien diva Plavalaguna's performance of Donizetti's *Lucia*, in *The Fifth Element*

Gendered Dichotomy between Vocal and Instrumental Music

> Silence gives grace to a woman—though that is not the case likewise with a man.
>
> (Aristotle, *Politics*)

> As in all the congregations of the saints, women should remain silent in the churches. They are not allowed to speak, but must be in submission, as the Law says. If they want to inquire about something, they should ask their own husbands at home; for it is disgraceful for a woman to speak in the church.
>
> (1 Corinthians 14:34–35)

> In the beginning was the Word, and the Word was with God, and the Word was God. He was with God in the beginning.
>
> (John 1:1–2)

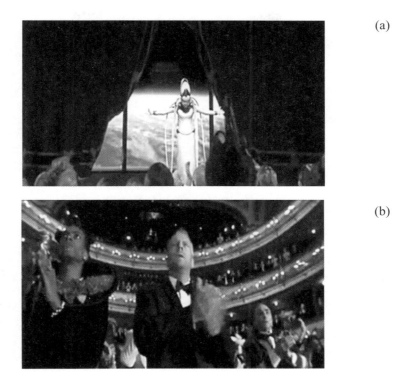

Figure 5.11 (a)–(b)   The mesmerized audience, including the protagonist Korben Dallas (Bruce Willis), applauding after Plavalaguna's performance, in *The Fifth Element*

The liberation of diva heroines from the confinement to the private sphere experienced by instrumentalist heroines demonstrates cinema's tendency that inscribes vocal music as a feminine domain. Cinema's tendency to gender vocal music as feminine, as shown in the films discussed above, can be contextualized in the sexual biology of instrumental and vocal music that have operated within Western culture. In his book *Absolute Music and the Construction of Meaning*, Daniel Chua has shown that the gender identity of instrumental music has suffered a Tiresias-like fate, oscillating between male and female identity. To be more specific, instrumental music has undergone "sex changes" with a very "messy operation" performed during the Enlightenment. The musical discourse at the beginning of the eighteenth century coded instrumental music as feminine, as "voluptuously soulless music," but it was eventually reborn with a phallus after several operations and has remained "male" since then.[20]

In contrast, the gendering of vocal music as feminine has been fairly stable. One reason for this stability is "sirenology"—the study of siren figures of the Greek mythology and beyond that period in various cultures. Instrumentalist sirens are not entirely absent, but in most episodes in Western mythology, literature, and folklore that feature siren characters, vocal music has been territorialized, if not stigmatized, as sirens' queendom and, by extension, a feminine prerogative. The genre of opera has further reinforced the sexual identity of vocal music as feminine, for the opera stage was one of the first public spheres where female performers' public presence was not only allowed but also celebrated. The epigraphs quoted from First Corinthians and from Aristotle's *Politics* might have provided a rationale for the emergence of castrati, but the operatic stage, unaffected by Aristotle's or St Paul's guidance, made a significant contribution to the coding of vocal music as feminine. My point is that the relative stability of the feminine gendering of vocal music is supported by the prominence given to public performance by film divas, as compared to that by instrumentalist heroines, suggesting that cinema has also encoded vocal music as a feminine domain.

Even the film musical, a genre that requires both female and male singers, tends to confirm the gendering of vocal music as primarily a woman's domain by preferring a more natural, less refined voice for male singers. As Edward Baron Turk argues in his study of the dualistic attitude toward male and female voices in the American film musical, this preference reveals the patriarchal culture's anxiety about singing as a threat to masculinity. According to Turk, post-Civil War American ideology reinforced the suspicion of singing by men, especially classical singing, as testified by Hollywood's preference for the more natural voices of Al Jolson (the songster in the very first sound film *The Jazz Singer* [1927]), Fred Astaire, and Bing Crosby over the more formally trained operatic voices of Dennis King, Lawrence Tibbett, and John McCormack.[21] This could be an excuse for the amateurish vocal quality of male singers in Robert Wise's *The Sound of Music* (1965): in this film, female singers overpower male singers, most notably in the pairing of Julie Andrews and Christopher Plummer. The unbalanced vocal virtuosity between female and male singers continues in more recent film musicals, such as Lars von Trier's *Dancer in the Dark* (2000), Baz Luhrmann's *Moulin Rouge!* (2001), and Rob Marshall's Academy Award–winning film *Chicago* (2002). In *Dancer in the Dark*, winner of the Palme d'Or

---

[20]   Daniel K.L. Chua, *Absolute Music and the Construction of Meaning* (Cambridge: Cambridge University Press, 1999); see especially "On Women" (pp. 126–35) and "On Masculinity" (pp. 136–44).

[21]   Edward Baron Turk, "Deriding the Voice of Jeanette MacDonald: Notes on Psychoanalysis and the American Film Musical," in *Embodied Voices: Representing Female Vocality in Western Culture*, ed. Leslie C. Dunn and Nancy A. Jones (Cambridge: Cambridge University Press, 1997), p. 106.

and Best Actress Award at the Cannes Film Festival in 2000, the heroine Björk's splendid vocal power cannot be compared to that of any male singer. Neither *Moulin Rouge!* nor *Chicago* features a diva as virtuosic as Björk, and both female and male singers are somewhat amateurish in these films, but male singers far exceed female singers as unrefined voices: one can think of the pair of Satine (Nicole Kidman) and Christian (Ewan McGregor) in *Moulin Rouge!* and that of Roxie (Renée Zellweger) and Billy (Richard Gere) as well as Billy and Velma (Catherine Zeta-Jones) in *Chicago*.

In her essay "Ophelia's Songs in *Hamlet*: Music, Madness, and the Feminine," Leslie C. Dunn notes that Ophelia is a woman "who becomes even more 'Woman' when she sings," as her sexual otherness, as well as her psychological otherness, is confirmed and reinforced by the discursive otherness of her singing. Dunn argues that the solidification of the association of vocal music with women has much to do with the bodily elements in singing.[22] In the singing voice, there is literally more body—"more breath, a more open mouth"—because of the intensified and exaggerated vocalization, especially in operatic singing. Singing is an inherently more embodied, more sensual experience than playing an instrument in that sound is produced within the performer's body, from her throat rather than outside the body, as with a piano or violin or other instrument. Considering the highly bodily aspect of singing and the patriarchal construction and representation of women first and foremost as a bodily entity, the gendering of vocal music as feminine is a logical consequence. From this, the privileged status of diva heroines among male-dominated movie musicians can be read as a reflection of this gendered categorization of vocal music.

Is the unrestricted display of film divas' virtuosity in the public sphere entirely positive—something to be celebrated as a liberation from the privatized and domestic confinement of instrumentalist heroines' performances? In previous studies, the issues surrounding the diva movie heroine have been discussed either at the plot level or in connection to cinema's ideological representation of opera through divas. As I discussed in the Prologue, cinema's employment of opera divas has a long history that begins with the silent film era. For Jeremy Tambling, this phenomenon is indicative of cinema's aspiration to the high-culture status of opera through the presence of opera divas onscreen.[23] Susan Leonardi and Rebecca Pope consider the phenomenon from a different angle. In their essay "Divas Do the Movies," they address a gender issue implied in the use of opera singers in silent films: "But singers in silent films? Voiceless or de-voiced divas?" They argue that "the spectacular silencing of the very women known to have voices, of women whose professional lives and authority were grounded in their voices" shares the masculinist cinematic convention of silencing women prevalent during

---

[22]   Leslie C. Dunn, "Ophelia's Songs in *Hamlet*: Music, Madness, and the Feminine," in Dunn and Jones, eds, *Embodied Voices*, pp. 50–64.

[23]   Jeremy Tambling, "Film Aspiring to the Condition of Opera," in *Opera, Ideology and Film* (Basingstoke: Palgrave Macmillan, 1987), pp. 41–67.

the classic Hollywood period.[24] Leonardi and Pope find another gender issue concerning movie divas at the plot level of the film.[25] As in Claudia Gorbman's study discussed at the beginning of this chapter, Leonardi and Pope problematize diva heroines' lack of subjectivity and seriousness about their profession. Their priority is not their artistic achievement or career development, but love or family concerns. Most of the opera-themed films of the 1930s are repetitions of what they call "a masculinist diva domesticated" narratives, an example of which they discuss is John Cromwell's *I Dream Too Much* (1935), a story about a reluctant opera singer Annette Monard (Lily Pons) and her husband Jonathan Street (Henry Fonda), a struggling opera composer. When Jonathan discourages her singing of popular songs, warning that such songs will ruin her voice, Annette answers: "We should forget about my voice … I don't want to be an opera singer, I just want to be your wife."[26] Unlike Gorbman, however, Leonardi and Pope do recognize positive aspects of film divas, as they see the coexistence of "the constructive closure of women's films—heroines choose lover over career and thereby suggest that a woman's real career is marriage and motherhood"—and the depiction of divahood's attractions—"wealth, glamour, independence, and power."[27] Whether it is film divas' domesticated narratives or their attractions, Leonardi and Pope's argument is based on the plot level, as is Gorbman's. In what follows, I discuss the problem of diva heroines from a different perspective. Like Leonardi and Pope, I consider gender issues but I approach those issues from the tension between the two art forms: opera as a live medium and cinema as a technologically mediated apparatus.

Diva's Embodied Voice on Stage and Screen

Carolyn Abbate contends that the embodied voice of female singers has an authorial power *on stage*. Challenging what Catherine Clément calls "the undoing of women" in opera[28]—that is, a feminist reading of operatic heroines' death, whether sacrificial as in the case of many Wagnerian heroines, a patriarchal punishment for excessive feminine sexual promiscuity as in the case of Carmen and Lulu, or for other reasons as in Tosca and Madame Butterfly—Abbate has explored

---

[24]   Susan J. Leonardi and Rebecca A. Pope, *The Diva's Mouth: Body, Voice, Prima Donna Politics* (New Brunswick, NJ: Rutgers University Press, 1996), p. 177. However, Leonardi and Pope indicate a positive aspect of "a silenced Carmen," as the silent presence of the divas in film stimulated the film audience's wish to hear their voices in another medium, opera. (pp. 177–8).

[25]   Ibid., pp. 175–96.

[26]   Ibid., pp. 180 and 184.

[27]   Ibid.

[28]   Catherine Clément, *Opera, or the Undoing of Women*, trans. Betsy Wing (Minneapolis: University of Minnesota Press, 1988).

"how traditional assumptions of the male composing voice may be challenged by perceptions of multiple voices," one of which is the female "singing" voice at the time of performance. Abbate locates the empowerment rather than undoing of women in opera; but this is opera as a performed, phenomenal event rather than the one existing as a score or libretto. Women in opera are empowered by the "phenomenology of performance": although female *characters* die in the plot of opera, they outlive their narrative and bodily deaths in performance through the singers' voices, which carry the physical force of music and compete with the composer's authorial voice. When discussing Wagner's *Ring* cycle as an example, Abbate differentiates the "voice-Brünnhilde" (a concept that is only indirectly related to Poizat's operatic voice-object) and "the plot-Brünnhilde" (the woman in the plot), and argues that the former transcends the death of the latter."[29] For Abbate, opera is "a genre that so displaces the authorial musical voice onto female characters and female singers that it largely reverses a conventional opposition of male (speaking) subject and female (observed) object.[30] Hence the title of Abbate's rebuttal article against Clément's position—"Opera; or the Envoicing of Women."[31]

Abbate interprets Patrick Conrad's film *Mascara* (1987) as allegorizing the transfer of the authorial voice from the male composer ("a male composing voice") to the female performers (their "singing voice").[32] Conrad's film is a murder mystery featuring a police inspector, Bert Sanders (Michael Sarrazin), who is a fervent opera fan and the owner of a nightclub called "Mister Butterfly." The transfer, or reversal, of the authorial voice is enacted when male transvestites at "Mister Butterfly" lip-synch recordings of arias sung by opera heroines, for their lip-synching unveils the fact that the authorial voice is the female voice.

> In lip-synching drag acts, the text being performed is not the operatic passage in question (an excerpt from *Orfeo*, authored by Gluck) … Rather, the text is the female singer's voice, Eurydice-sound, authored by, say, Benita Valente, and caught forever on tape. This taped voice is the permanent material basis for generating a performance (Pepper's lip-synching and miming), just as a score of *Orfeo*—paper and ink and binding—constitutes a permanent musical basis for any live performance of the opera. On the Mister Butterfly stage, female

---

[29]   Carolyn Abbate, *Unsung Voices: Opera and Musical Narrative in the Nineteenth Century* (Princeton, NJ: Princeton University Press, 1991), p. 242; Michel Poizat, *The Angel's Cry: Beyond the Pleasure Principle in Opera*, trans. Arthur Denner (Ithaca, NY: Cornell University Press, 1992), pp. 25–31.

[30]   Ibid., pp. 228–9.

[31]   Abbate, "Opera; or, the Envoicing of Women," in *Musicology and Difference: Gender and Sexuality in Music Scholarship*, ed. Ruth A. Solie (Berkeley: University of California Press, 1993), pp. 225–58.

[32]   It is also an interesting transfer of the intangible, abstract, and figurative voice (voice as subjectivity) to the literal, physical voice (voice as a sounding entity).

voices make the sound-text that sets biologically male puppets spinning in an interpretive dance. In this sound-text, the women's singing voices themselves have an explicitly *authorial* force, and these strange lip-synching scenes represent women as the *makers* of the musical sonority in opera.[33]

The opera scene in Stephan Elliott's *The Adventures of Priscilla, Queen of the Desert* (1994) can also be interpreted according to the same Abbatean operatic phenomenology that finds an authorial force in the female voice. *The Adventures of Priscilla* is a story about two drag queens, Tick/Mitzi (Hugo Weaving; Figure 5.12) and Adam/Felicia (Guy Pearce), and one transsexual, Bernadette (Terence Stamp), who together form an ensemble that impersonates ABBA, the Swedish pop vocal group founded in 1972, among other performers. As the ensemble drives a bus across the desert, Tick/Mitzi lip-synchs "Sempre libera," an aria sung by Violetta in Verdi's *La traviata*, from the top of the bus (Figure 5.13). As in *Mascara*, the sound-text of the diva's voice (Joan Carden) carries the authorial force in Elliott's film.

It is opera's "phenomenology"—opera as a live performance that unavoidably involves female *singers*, as opposed to *characters*[34]—that imbues women's embodied voices on stage with authorial power. The opera lip-synching scenes in both films—*Mascara* and *The Adventures of Priscilla, Queen of the Desert*—are illuminating as a metaphor for the phenomenal power of the female voice in opera that transcends the death of the heroines at the plot level. These scenes are also significant in that the female voice endowed with authorial power is a *disembodied* voice—that is, recorded female arias—and thus they address a fundamental issue concerning the ontological condition of the cinematic apparatus—that is, its castration anxiety—which has been criticized by many feminist film scholars.

As examined in detail in Chapter 4, sound and image—voice and body—are separated in the cinematic apparatus in the process of recording, and those separated tracks of image and sound are synchronized at the time of reproduction. Unlike

---

[33]   Abbate, "Opera; or, the Envoicing of Women," p. 228. The excerpt from Gluck's *Orfeo* is played when Bert asks Pepper (Eva Robin's), who is in love with Bert, to perform Eurydice's Act III recitative, in which Eurydice reflects on her feelings, observing the stricken Orfeo. Pepper's Eurydice performance is followed by an excerpt from Strauss's *Salome*—the heroine's final passage—and, backstage, Pepper takes off her Eurydice costume, exposing her secret—her male genitalia. Abbate describes this scene as the film's "primal scene (female object unveiled as male)" and argues that the "opera scenes" in *Mascara* (i.e., the male transvestites' lip-synching) enact a dangerous reversal of *Mascara*'s primal scene. What follows the "primal scene" is a parallelism between onstage (operatic) action and backstage (filmic) action—a double murder. While the final line of Strauss's opera—Herod's scream, "Let this woman be killed!" ("man töte dieses Weib!")—is heard as a taped voice, Bert strangles Pepper out of his horror at what he has *seen*. While Salome is being killed on stage, Pepper is murdered backstage; and Pepper's death, like Eurydice's, is caused by her lover's *gaze* upon her—in this case, her male genitalia (see pp. 226–8).

[34]   Abbate, "Opera; or, the Envoicing of Women," p. 228.

Figure 5.12   Hugo Weaving playing Tick/Mitzi, in *The Adventures of Priscilla, Queen of the Desert*

Figure 5.13   Hugo Weaving lip-synching "Sempre libera" from Verdi's *La traviata*, in *The Adventures of Priscilla, Queen of the Desert*

the embodied voice in live theater, an artificial unity (one that is technologically reconstructed) between voice and body is the ontological condition of cinematic apparatus. Psychoanalytically oriented scholars explain cinema's lack of the natural unity between voice and body in terms of the "castration anxiety" and theorize it as the origin of cinema's envy of a live medium such as opera. For Michel Chion, diegetic performance in film is a way of suturing the audience in the movie theater to the live audience within the film. Put another way, the movie theater and its audience are deluded and transported into the diegetic space and time of the film—that is, the onscreen live theater. By simulating the condition of live theater, diegetic performance in cinema serves to approximate the phenomenal power of live performance.[35]

Another way of simulating live theater, especially its natural unity between voice and body, is through the embodied presentation of the voice. Cinema's castration anxiety and its use of female voice as a fetish, which I examined in the previous chapter, should be recalled here. As explored by many feminist film scholars specializing in film sound,[36] cinema, especially classical Hollywood cinema, has shown a strong tendency that while the female voice is presented in an "emphatically embodied form," the male voice is usually not confined to such embodied-ness.[37] In other words, the female voice serves as a "fetish" that enables cinema to disavow its castration anxiety. Given this cinematic dichotomy, the unrestricted display of film divas' public performance—that is, their embodied singing—is problematic, for it can be read as a continuation of cinema's use of the female voice to cover up its castration anxiety by anchoring the divas' voices to their bodies. The containment of a film diva's voice in her body, then, is analogous to the confinement of the instrumental heroines' performance to domestic and privatized arenas. The "power" of the embodied voice in opera—i.e., in live theater—transforms into a "problem" in cinema, an apparatus that depends on the technology of reproduction.

Cinema's embodied presentation of the female voice points to another gender issue, as it places female characters in the inferior position in the diegetic hierarchy. Amy Lawrence notes that classical Hollywood cinema has shown a strategy of trying to confine the female voice to a "recessed area of the diegesis"—"recessed" because diegetic interiority implies discursive inferiority. Lawrence argues that the diegetic interiority positions female characters as a "sign rather than as signifying subject," depriving them of their subjectivity.[38] The disembodied voice, or the *acoustmêtre* to use Michel Chion's term, is omnipresent and omniscient, if not omnipotent, because it has the power to reside outside and beyond the film's diegesis. Chion traces the origin of the word "acousmatic" back to the time of ancient Greece. At that time, the word referred to a Pythagorean sect whose members had a tradition that, when the Master spoke, he stood behind a curtain so that the body of the speaker would not distract them from what he says.[39] In this respect, the power of the invisible voice is evocative of the *divine* power—the

---

[35]   Michel Chion, *Audio-Vision: Sound on Screen*, trans. Claudia Gorbman (New York: Columbia University Press, 1994), p. 151.

[36]   For instance, Silverman, *Acoustic Mirror*; Lawrence, *Echo and Narcissus*; Mary Ann Doane, *The Desire to Desire: The Woman's Film of the 1940s* (Bloomington: Indiana University Press, 1987); and some articles in Dunn and Jones, eds, *Embodied Voices*.

[37]   Nancy Jones, "Music and the Maternal Voice in *Purgatorio* XIX," in Dunn and Jones, eds, *Embodied Voices*, p. 36.

[38]   Lawrence, *Echo and Narcissus*, p. 149.

[39]   Michel Chion, *The Voice in Cinema*, ed. and trans. Claudia Gorbman (New York: Columbia University Press, 1999), p. 19.

power of the *invisible voice*—because "God's authority," Carolyn Abbate contends, "is predicated on the presence of his voice in the absence of his body."[40] Abbate's claim is based on the fact that in the Bible, God and his power are represented as a vocal entity, while the description of his body is rare. One can recall Psalm 29, the entire chapter of which is the glorification of God's voice and its power:

> Give unto the Lord, O ye mighty, give unto the Lord glory and strength.
> Give unto the Lord the glory due unto his name; worship the Lord in the beauty of holiness.
> The voice of the Lord is upon waters the God of glory thundereth: the Lord is upon many waters.
> The voice of the Lord is powerful; the voice of the Lord is full of majesty.
> The voice of the Lord breaketh the cedars yea, the Lord breaketh the cedars of Lebanon.
> He maketh them also to skip like a calf; Lebanon and Sirion like a young unicorn.
> The voice of the Lord divideth the flames of fire.
> The voice of the lord shaketh the wilderness; the Lord shaketh the wilderness of Kadish.
> The voice of the Lord maketh the hinds to calve, and discovereth the forests; and in his temple doth every one speak of his glory.
> The Lord sitteth upon the flood; yea, the Lord sitteth King for ever.
> The Lord will give strength unto his people; the Lord will bless his people with peace.
>
> (King James version)

It has become a classical theory in cinema studies that the diegetic interiority of the female voice is indicative of Hollywood's gendered politics of the voice, and this explains why voiceover narration, in both documentaries and narrative films, is predominantly, although not exclusively, conveyed by the male voice in classical Hollywood cinema.[41] For Nancy Jones, the gendered politics of the voice has a long history, dating back to Dante's time. In her study of the Siren episode in Dante's *Purgatorio*, she argues that the siren song is characterized first and foremost by its embodied-ness. It is also at the level of narratology that Jones finds the inferior quality of the siren song:

---

[40] Carolyn Abbate, "Debussy's Phantom Sounds," in *In Search of Opera* (Princeton, NJ: Princeton University Press, 2001), p. 148.

[41] From the perspective of the gendered politics of the voiceover, Barbet Schroeder's film *Reversal of Fortune* (1990) is thought-provoking. There are two main voiceovers—one by the male protagonist Claus von Bülow (Jeremy Irons) and the other by Claus's wife Sunny (Glenn Close)—and the male and female voices show an intriguing reversal of the standard diegetic hierarchy (interiority and exteriority): Irons's flashback voiceover resides within the diegesis, addressing his onscreen audience, while Close's voice speaks directly to the film viewers, transcending the film's diegesis.

the episode of the Siren, presented as a quasi-hallucinatory experience, represents a false dream narrative embedded within a true dream narrative. In narratological terms, the episode is relegated to a secondary level of the poem's diegesis.[42]

Jones conceives the diegetic status of Dante's Siren as a poetic counterpart of the typical discursive strategy of classical Hollywood cinema that imprisons the female voice in the diegetic interiority—a "recessed area of the diegesis," to quote Amy Lawrence again.[43]

From Ontology to Vortexicality

The disembodied female voice, whether singing or speaking, is not entirely absent in cinema, and in some films it does articulate female subjectivity and facilitate feminine discourse. It is in this respect that Britta Sjogren, a film scholar and director, challenges the film theories that entirely preclude the possibility of feminine subjectivity and discourse in cinema. In her book, *Into the Vertex: Female Voice and Paradox in Film*, she argues for the possibility of the feminine discourse in film through the female voice-off. Rejecting the traditional definition of voiceover versus voice-off, Sjogren uses the term "voice-off" to refer to all asynchronous voice in order to explore the way the voice "slips free of the image, glides in and out of its attachments to its apparent body, moving from (in Doane and Silverman's terms) voice-over to voice-off to embodied voice-over to badly synched sound and back again."[44] For Sjogren, the main problem in the work by such feminist film theorists as Silverman and Doane—although "brilliantly written and groundbreaking in one way or another"[45]—is that they propose a "globalizing theory"[46] at the expense of the particularities of individual films. As Silverman has elucidated, it is the ontological condition of the cinematic apparatus that the unity between the voice and the body is not natural but technologically manufactured. But when she argues that the use of the embodied *female* voice serves as a fetish to conceal cinema's castration anxiety, she identifies the cinematic apparatus as a male entity—to be more precise, a male body from which his voice is castrated to be preserved on the soundtrack. The irony of this feminist agenda is that it pronounces a male-centered position. Since the cinematic apparatus itself is male and thus can only projects male desire, there is no room for female subjectivity to step in, and the embodied voice that functions as a fetish to conceal castration anxiety *has to be* a female voice.

---

[42]   Jones, "Music and the Maternal Voice in *Purgatorio* XIX," pp. 47–8.

[43]   Lawrence, *Echo and Narcissus*, p. 149.

[44]   Britta Sjogren, *Into the Vortex: Female Voice and Paradox in Film* (Urbana and Chicago: University of Illinois Press, 2006), p. 9.

[45]   Ibid., p. 10.

[46]   Ibid., p. 145.

Doane, Lawrence, Silverman, and other film scholars who share the same feminist agenda do acknowledge the existence of the female voice-off, but according to their analyses of the films, which are mostly from Hollywood's classical era, the female voice-off is not endowed with the discursive power that characterizes the male voice-off—the power that transcends the film's diegesis. Renovating the male-centered position of those scholars, Sjogren's book provides alternative analyses of the four films from the same time period, one of which is Max Ophüls's *Letter from an Unknown Woman* (1948). Set in Vienna in the early 1900s, the story of Ophüls's film centers on Lisa Berndle's fatal infatuation with the renowned pianist Stefan Brand. Lisa (Joan Fontaine) firsts meets Stefan (Louis Jourdan) as her neighbor when she is a teenage girl. She leaves Vienna because of her mother's marriage with a man in Linz. Several years after her move to Linz, Lisa meets Stefan again in Vienna as a young lady. He does not recognize Lisa but is drawn to her. At the end of their long romantic date one day, they make love and she gets pregnant. Without knowing her pregnancy, he leaves Vienna for a concert in Milan. Stefan promises to come back but he doesn't, and while waiting Lisa gives birth to their child. After some years, Lisa marries an old wealthy man in Vienna. When they go to an opera in Vienna, Lisa, now transformed into an elegant, aristocratic-looking woman draped in a fur coat, bumps into Stefan at the opera house.[47] Stefan still does not recognize Lisa but is again strangely drawn to her. Utterly distressed when realizing that Stefan has never loved her, Lisa leaves Stefan for good and, a few years later, she dies of typhus.

Ophüls's film begins with Stefan's reading of a letter from an unknown woman. It's the letter Lisa wrote when she was hospitalized because of typhus. The rest of the film visualizes the story in the letter in flashback, occasionally cross-cut with shots of Stefan's present time. While reading the letter, Stefan's memories of Lisa comes back to his mind: Lisa as a teenage neighbor, as a young woman with whom he made love, and as a mature woman whom he met at the opera house. As noticed by many film scholars, *Letter from an Unknown Woman* is distinguished by the extensive female voice-off, as the letter is narrated by Lisa's (Joan Fontaine's) voice throughout the film. In spite of this, many film scholars have criticized the absence of female subjectivity in *Letter* based on the plot and the visual text of the film: Lisa is a forgotten and abandoned woman who eventually dies. They also address the problem that Lisa's voice-off is still contained in the diegetic interiority, unlike the male disembodied voice that resides outside of the diegesis, in the sense that her letter/voice-off is addressed to Stefan—a narration within a narration like Dante's Siren song as discussed above—and that her voice is not entirely liberated

---

47 The opera performed is Mozart's *Magic Flute*. The opera-house sequence starts during the intermission before Act II, as the recommencement is announced by the ushers. But the music that is heard from the unseen stage—unseen because the camera only shows the audience seats—begins with the first three chords of the opera's overture, after which the music is cut to Papageno's entrance aria. The length of the opera-house sequence is about six minutes.

from her body, because her voice-off is sometimes heard over her image. Among the scholars in this camp that Sjogren cites in her book is Edward Branigan, who argues that Lisa's subjectivity is solely compromised by a "hidden and powerful masculine discourse" to the extent that Lisa is nowhere in the film.[48]

In light of Sjogren's interpretation of Ophüls's *Letter*, however, Lisa is *everywhere* in the film through "the mobility of the voice-off, its 'hovering' spatiality, its strange verticality across the narrative's trajectory through represented time." Lisa's voice-off traverses time, mobilizing multiple temporalities across the film through flashbacks and thus evoking a "consciousness of her 'place.'"[49] The narrative structure articulated by Lisa's voice-off is not linear but "vortexical" (the term referenced in her book title refers to vertical, spiral, or spinning). In this context, Sjogren claims, "That Stefan's memory itself exists *grace à* the spiral reverie brought on by the instigation movement of Lisa's voice-off is something Branigan never addresses adequately in his essay."[50] In other words, Lisa's voice-off has a discursive power in the sense that it activates Stefan's memory and its visualization, and in this respect it is the soundtrack that begets the visual text of the film. Sjogren also indicates that Lisa's letter as narrated by Joan Fontaine's *voice* is not exactly the same as the *words* written in the letter, since there's another dimension in the voice—the voice as pure sounds that directs our attention to its texture, its "grain" (à la Barthes), or "geno-song," as I discussed in detail in the first chapter. Sjogren notes, "The quality of her voice here is at least as remarkable as the words." Fontaine's "celebrated voice with its hushed mellifluousness," she continues, captivates Stefan and the spectator of the film, and in so doing, it adds an additional power—an aural and quasi-musical power—to Lisa's capacity to project her subjectivity and desire through her voice-off. According to Sjogren's study, many female voice-offs are "expressly musical," evoking pre-Symbolic maternal voice that a fetus experiences in the mother's womb, while the male voice-off tends to be "matte" and "dry," more aligned with a pheno-song, the linguistic dimension of the voice.[51] For some scholars, Christianity promotes the alignment of the male voice with words and the consequent privileging of the logocentrism of the voice, considering, for instance, the biblical passage quoted in the third epigraph of this section: "In the beginning was the Word, and the Word was with God, and the Word was God. He was with God in the beginning" (John 1:1–2).

Sjogren's book is illuminating in challenging the ontological and essentialist assumption that cinema can only allow for male subjectivity—the ontology

---

[48]   Edward Branigan, *Narrative Comprehension and Film* (New York: Routledge, 1992), pp. 177–9; quoted in Sjogren, *Into the Vortex*, pp. 58–9.

[49]   Sjogren, *Into the Vortex*, p. 59.

[50]   Ibid., p. 58.

[51]   Ibid., 65. Sjogren uses "speech" rather than "pheno-song," but my replacement of the word does not affect her argument and it provides a better context for this book, especially the first chapter.

inferred in the studies by such scholars as Kaja Silverman, Mary Ann Doane, and Amy Lawrence, among others. Their works are indispensible in the theory of film sound, especially the voice, which challenges the primacy of the visible in film studies. By incorporating a feminist perspective, they certainly extended those seminal studies of film sound by Rick Altman and James Lastra, rectifying what Altman called "historical fallacy" about sound—the fallacy that sound is only secondary because its primary function is to add realism.[52] Several times in the book, Sjogren herself acknowledges that her own study is considerably indebted to those pioneering feminist studies of film sound. But through her alternative interpretations of select films, such as *Letter from an Unknown Woman*, she has shown that feminine subjectivity can be expressed within the classical Hollywood cinema especially through the female voice-off. The separation of the voice and the body is an ontological condition of the cinematic apparatus in that it is a technologically unavoidable condition. Given this, using the term "separation anxiety" will be pertinent to illuminate cinema's technological necessity to *reconstruct* the unity between the voice and the body, between the sound and the image, and the term "separation anxiety," it seems to me, is more appropriate than the "castration anxiety," to avoid a heavily gendered overtone. Embodied voice, whether female or male, then, is a convenient means to solve the separation anxiety of the cinematic apparatus. However, it is undeniable that disembodied voice, or voice-off, is considerably more common for male characters than female characters, and if one considers the embodied voice to be cinema's "fetish" in the Freudian sense, cinematic tradition has clearly shown a gendered management of the voice.

Sjogren proposes her book as an inquiry into "the possibility of any voice— embodied or not—to speak of the feminine,"[53] and she has brilliantly illuminated the power of the voice as a venue of enunciating female subjectivity and countering apparently patriarchal discourse of the film at its visual and narrative levels.[54] The cinematic heroine liberated from "her scripted fate"[55] through her voice in

---

[52] Rick Altman, "Four and a Half Film Fallacies," in Altman, ed., *Sound Theory Sound Practice* (New York Routledge, 1992), p. 35.

[53] Sjogren, *Into the Vortex*, p. 9.

[54] Sjogren's analysis of the final scene of Jean Negulesco's *Humoresque* (1946) is enlightening. She interprets the music that the male protagonist Paul Boray (John Garfield) is performing on stage, which the heroine Helen Wright (Joan Crawford) is hearing from the radio broadcast, as the "voice" between Helen and Paul in that scene. But Paul's music in general is his "voice" created by Helen, Paul's patroness. So she has the authorial power of Paul's voice (his music). Although Sjogren's extension of the concept of "voice" into non-vocal sonic elements, such as music, is illuminating, her interpretation of Helen's suicide as an expression of her subjective power, not a mortal end but an ecstatic culmination of her desire—her "apotheosis" (!)—is for me a little far-fetched. See Sjogren, *Into the Vortex*, p. 131.

[55] Ibid., p. 195.

Sjogren's study is analogous to the death-ridden operatic heroines empowered by their voices on stage—the voice-Brünnhilde redeemed from the plot-Brünnhilde, for instance—in Abbate's study examined above. In film, however, I argue that the voice has more potential to exert the redeeming and enunciating power when it is disembodied, because, as the voice-off, it has the capacity, at least *more* capacity, of intervening and subverting the visual and linear discourse of the film by providing what Sjogren calls a "vortexical" force. And that explains, it seems to me, why her study focuses on the female voice-off despite her acknowledgement of the possibility of "any voice—embodied or not—" as a premise. Indeed, she herself notes in the Epilogue that she locates "the female voice-off as a particularly powerful formal feature that provokes an awareness of heterogeneous consciousness, plural point of view and discursive paradox…"[56]

The ontological pessimism that cinema only allows male subjectivity, which is dominant in previous studies of the cinematic voice, is redeemed by Sjogren's brilliant alternative perspectives. However, film divas' embodied singing can still be a "problem" because of the lack of the vortexical force in the embodied voice compared to the voice-off. In the Epilogue of her book, Sjogren discusses Lars von Trier's film musical *Dancer in the Dark* as an example in which the heroine's (embodied) singing voice transcends and overcomes her "scripted fate" to be executed by functioning as a means to express her subjective perception and inner world otherwise unknown to the film audience. In *Dancer*, the musical scenes represent what the blind heroine Selma, played by a celebrated pop diva Björk, fantasizes—in other words, Selma's internal vision—and it is true that her singing in these scenes functions as "windows into the invisible world of Selma's consciousness."[57] However, film musical is a special genre in which embodied singing is required and *a priori* privileged, and the status of embodied voice is different from that in narrative film. Perhaps, it was an acknowledgement of that special status when Sjogren described Selma/Björk's voice in the musical scenes as "almost a voice-off."[58]

Voice-Off Divas

Not almost but truly voice-off singing does appear in narrative films (what I mean by voice-off singing in this section is recorded songs).[59] Among the most powerful

---

56   Ibid., p. 197.

57   Ibid., p. 191.

58   Ibid., p. 194.

59   In her essay on Michael Powell and Emeric Pressburger's cinematic production of Jacques Offenbach's opera, *The Tales of Hoffmann* (1951), Marcia Citron compares Olympia's quasi-disembodied voice—a "free-floating voice," in Citron's words—when she sings the "Doll Song" to Dapertutto's completely disembodied singing in the "Diamond Aria," and she notes that, in film, completely disembodied singing is more common for

examples are Maria Callas's "La mamma morta" from Umberto Giordano's opera *Andrea Chénier* used in Jonathan Demme's *Philadelphia* (1993) and the "Letter Duet" from Mozart's *Marriage of Figaro* in Frank Darabont's *The Shawshank Redemption* (1994).[60] In both films, the disembodied operatic voice is heard in the key moment of the film. In *The Shawshank Redemption*, Mozart's duet heard as a disembodied song is the voice that makes every prisoner at Shawshank feel free, as Morgan Freeman's voiceover narrates.[61] In *Philadelphia*, the much acclaimed opera scene is the turning point when the attorney Joe Miller (Denzel Washington) becomes truly sympathetic to the agony of his client Andrew Beckett (Tom Hanks), who was fired by his law firm because he is an AIDS patient. In the opera scene, Callas's disembodied (i.e., recorded) song serves as the voice through which the hero, like Selma in *Dancer* and Lisa in *Letter*, expresses his existential inner realm, and during his monologue over Callas's voice he even identifies himself with the operatic heroine, Maddalena, who sings the aria.

In light of Wayne Koestenbaum's perspectives, Callas's voice in *Philadelphia* is a special property for the gay protagonist Andrew Beckett because of the prominence of the diva worship, especially Callas, in the gay community.[62] The death scene of this film is also accompanied by Callas's voice-off singing, although almost inaudibly because of the soft volume. Perhaps it is because of the covert presence of her voice that this scene has slipped away from most scholars' attention. The function of the voice-off opera in this scene is more complex and subtle in articulating the protagonist's inner world and unspoken desire, as it requires the mediation of Koestenbaum's book to have access to the inner state of the film's protagonist Andrew Beckett; or perhaps, one even needs to identify Beckett with Koestenbaum. Indeed, Tom Hanks's appearance in the film surprisingly evokes Koestenbaum (Figure 5.14).[63]

While Demme's protagonist is lying on his soon-to-be deathbed surrounded by many visitors, Callas's voice sneaks in the soundtrack almost inaudibly: the aria she sings is "Ebben? Ne andrò lontana" from Alfredo Catalani's opera *La Wally*. This mise-en-scène is an exact visualization of Koestenbaum's wish for his

male than female singers. See Citron, *Opera on Screen* (New Haven, CT: Yale University Press, 2000), pp. 121–3.

[60]   For an extensive discussion of the scene in *Philadelphia*, see Marc Weiner, "Why Does Hollywood Like Opera?" in *Between Opera and Cinema*, ed. Jeongwon Joe and Rose M. Theresa (New York: Routledge, 2002), pp. 75–92; for *The Shawshank Redemption*, see Mary Hunter, "Opera *In* Film: Sentiment and Wit, Feeling and Knowing: *The Shawshank Redemption* and *Prizzi's Honor*," in Joe and Theresa, eds, *Between Opera and Cinema*, pp. 93–120.

[61]   For Freeman's full voiceover narration, see my first chapter "Opera as Geno-Song."

[62]   Wayne Koestenbaum, *Queen's Throat: Opera, Homosexuality, and the Mystery of Desire* (New York: Poseidon Press, 1993).

[63]   I thank Matteo Magarotto, who indicated this resemblance to me while he was taking my graduate seminar, "Opera and Gender" in the spring of 2010.

(a)

(b)

Figure 5.14   (a) Tom Hanks as Andrew Beckett in *Philadelphia*; (b) Wayne
Koestenbaum

deathbed as written in his book, although with a different opera aria and different singers on the soundtrack:

> If I die a peaceful death, I want to have an opera record playing in the room ... The end of opera is now: my moment of attentive, melancholy listening. My ear is the melody's mausoleum: when I listen to a phrase of a dated but priceless opera (a moment from Maddalena and Andrea's first-act love duet in Giordano's *Andrea Chénier*, sung by Beniamino Gigli and Maria Caniglia) ...[64]

Catalani's voice-off aria in the film, then, can be read as a surrogated voice of the film's protagonist as Koestenbaum's body double.[65]

David Cronenberg's *M. Butterfly* (1993) offers another intriguing use of female voice-off singing in articulating the subjectivity of the male protagonist, but in this case the hero is not homosexual but heterosexual who suffers from the unveiling of the disguised sexual identity of his lover. Like Puccini's opera *Madama Butterfly*, which permeates Cronenberg's soundtrack, *M. Butterfly* also addresses ethnic and cultural as well as gender issues. In a way, the film serves as a critique of the blatant Orientalism explicit in the opera by reversing the gender roles and cultural dynamics. Cronenberg's film is a cinematic adaptation of David Henry Hwang's 1988 play, a liberal dramatization of the romantic relationship between the two historical figures during the Cultural Revolution, French diplomat in China Bernard Bousicot and Shi Pei Pu, a female impersonator in Peking opera (as René Gallimard and Song Liling in the play, respectively). Gallimard (Jeremy Irons) falls in love with Song (John Lone) without knowing that his beloved is a man. The conversation between Gallimard and Song after her performance of Puccini's *Madama Butterfly* demonstrates the film's cynicism about the Orientalism in the opera:

> *Gallimard*: I've never seen a performance as convincing as yours.
>
> *Song*: Convincing? Me, as a Japanese Woman? Did you know that the Japanese used thousands of our people for medical experiments during the war? But I guess such an irony is lost on you.
>
> *Gallimard*: No, No. What I meant was you made me see the beauty of the story. Of her death. It's, it's pure sacrifice. I mean he's not worthy of it but what can she do? She loves him so much. It's very beautiful.

---

[64] Koestenbaum, *The Queen's Throat*, p. 192.

[65] Opera in film can signify not only male gayness but also lesbian sexuality and desire. Tony Scott's postmodern vampire film *The Hunger* (1983) is an example and it predates Koestenbaum's book by ten years. In Scott's film, "The Flower Duet" from Léo Delibes's opera *Lakmé* accompanies the film's signature scene, depicting lesbian sex between the vampire heroine Miriam (Catherine Deneuve) and Sarah (Susan Sarandon), a doctor who is investigating the premature aging of Miriam's vampire husband John (David Bowie).

Song: Well, yes, to a Westerner.

Gallimard: I beg your pardon?
Song: It's one of your favorite fantasies, isn't it? The submissive Oriental woman and the cruel Western man.

Irons: Oh, I don't think so.

Song: A blond cheerleader falling in love with a short Japanese man; if she commits suicide, you would think that she is stupid, not beautiful…

Irons: I got your point…

Gallimard and Song develop a romantic relationship and they leave China for Paris, where she spies on him for the government of her country. Gallimard ends up betraying his country and is charged for treason. During the investigation, Song's sexual identity is revealed to Gallimard. Horrified by the unbelievable and unbearable truth, Gallimard suffers a mental breakdown and is put in an asylum. The film concludes with Gallimard's suicide at the end of his performance of *Madama Butterfly* presented in the form of a mono-psychodrama, in which he takes the role of the opera's heroine Cio-Cio-San in her costume and geisha-looking makeup. The psychodrama scene is accompanied by Cio-Cio-San's signature aria, "Un bel dì," issued from a cassette tape recorder that Gallimard brought for his performance.

What renders the role of the *Butterfly* excerpts distinctive is its double function. First the operatic music serves as a sonic and racial index for Song when s/he performs the opera's heroine—a cliché for Puccini's opera. During the course of the film, however, the stereotypical role of this opera undergoes a transformation process by becoming a leitmotif for Galliard, more specifically his fantasy about and longing for Song: in other words, it represents both Song and Galliard. At the final sequence of the film, Puccini's *Butterfly* is solely identified with Galliard, a Western man, whose cultural and gender roles are reversed with those of Puccini's Oriental heroine. The sequence begins with a close-up of Galliard's trembling hand with his fingers manicured in red, slowly approaching to the cassette tape player. When he presses down the play button, we hear Mirella Freni's voice as Madam Butterfly. The opera excerpt begins with a spot in the libretto, "O Butterfly, piccina mogliettina" (O Butterfly, My tiny little child-wife) which appears several lines before "Un bel dì." This portion of Butterfly's song is unique in that it is what Pinkerton told her before he left Japan, as narrated by Cio-Cio-San, when she is passionately trying to convince her maid Suzuki (and herself) about his return:

(cerca imitate Pinkerton)	(imitating Pinkerton)
O Butterfly,	O Butterfly,
Piccina mogliettina,	My tiny little child-wife,
Tornerò colle rose	I'll return with the roses,

Alla stagion serena   The warm and sunny season

Quando fa la nidiata il pettirosso   When the red-breasted robins

                                            are busy nesting.

Considering that the above lines are Pinkerton's words enunciated by Butterfly's voice—in other words, the co-existence and multiplicity of the two voices, one male and one female, and one silent and one vocalized—this portion of Puccini's opera is an exquisite choice for representing Galliard's multiple and confused identity in terms of gender and culture—a metaphoric mutation of his identity from a Western man to a dragged Madam Butterfly. And it is through Mirella Freni's voice-off singing that Galliard voices his longing for his lover, his confused gender and cultural identity, and his wounded subjectivity. This operatic disembodied singing voice amplifies his own (male) spoken and embodied voice, whose monologue for the psychodrama begins with "There is a vision of the Orient. Slender women in Chong-sams and Kimonos, who die for the love of unworthy foreign devils" and culminates in "My name is René Gallimard, also known as Madam Butterfly" (Figure 5.15)—his final words before the ritualistic suicide by cutting his throat.[66]

Figure 5.15   Jeremy Irons as René Gallimard in the final scene of *M. Butterfly*

Opera in Duncan Tucker's *Transamerica* (2005) is associated with the transgender status of the protagonist Bree Osbourne, who is undergoing a male-to-female sex change procedure. When she is playing a vinyl record of Dido's lament, "When I am laid in Earth," from Henry Purcell's *Dido and Aeneas*, she momentarily slows down the speed of the turntable by holding the record with her finger, resulting in the lowering of the frequency of the playback sound—a literal "transgendering" of Dido's voice into a man's voice. Unlike the opera sequence in

---

[66]   In Hwang's play, Gallimard commits *harakiri*.

Philadelphia and *M. Butterfly*, the operatic moment in *Transamerica* is extremely brief and devoid of any visual extravaganza, such as the ritualistic suicide in *M. Butterfly*. Yet this short disembodied operatic voice succinctly and powerfully expresses the intensity of the protagonist's transgender aspiration.

Franco Zeffirelli's *Callas Forever*, too, can be contextualized in the issue of the disembodied voice of a diva. As discussed in the previous chapter, Zeffirelli's fictionalized biopic centers around the making of opera films with Callas's old recordings—the ones made before the decline of her voice as an opera singer—synchronized with her present body. The first attempt, Bizet's *Carmen*, was a huge success. Larry Kelly (Jeremy Irons), Maria's longtime friend and manager, proposes another opera film in which she would lip-synch her old recording, just like she did for *Carmen*. Callas (Fanny Ardant) refuses and instead she proposes to use her present "real" voice in the next work. Now it's her sponsor that refuses the proposal. At the end of the film, Callas demands that Larry should destroy her *Carmen* film, which is a "fake" for her: "It's not honest," she says. The reconstructed unity between voice and body, in other words, the faked unity, is a technological condition of and necessity for the cinematic medium. In light of the psychoanalytically oriented feminist interpretation of cinema's castration anxiety (or separation anxiety, my preferred term, as I explained above), Callas's denial of the *re*-embodiment of her old voice can be read as an allegory for her refusal to be used as a fetish. Michal Grover-Friedlander's reading of the film examined in the previous chapter is illuminating in the context of film diva's embodied voice. It should be recalled here that, for Grover-Friedlander, the two failures—the cinematic re-embodiment of Callas's old voice refused by the diva herself as a fake and that of her present voice rejected by her sponsor—allegorizes the elusiveness of Callas's voice that "overpowers its vessel and resists any anchoring in a body."[67] This elusiveness or stubbornness of the diva's voice, I argue, suggests the vortexical power of the female voice-off explored by Britta Sjogren in that this stubborn voice resists to be *contained* in the body and in so doing, challenges the hegemonic power of the visual in film and film studies. The failure of the re-embodiment of Callas's voice in Zeffirelli's film, then, signifies the paradox that the diva's voice, and by extension the cinematic voice, is empowered by remaining bodiless.[68]

---

[67]   Michal Grover-Friedlander, "The Afterlife of Maria Callas's Voice," in *Operatic Afterlives* (New York: Zone Books, 2011), p. 58. An earlier version of this chapter was published in *Musical Quarterly* 88 (Spring 2005): 35–62.

[68]   At the 2012 conference of Music and the Moving Image held at New York University, Alexis Luko presented a brilliant paper on the comparison of disembodied phantoms—Chion's *acousmêtre*—and its counterpart "voiceless being" in Ingmar Bergman's films.

Chapter 6

Behind the Discourse on the Opera–Cinema Encounter: Film Music Criticism and the "Great Divide" between Modernism and Postmodernism

Their [filmmakers'] primitive and childish concept of music is not my concept. They have the mistaken notion that music, in "helping" and "explaining" the cinematic shadow-play, could be regarded under artistic considerations. It cannot be … And there is only one real function of film music—namely, to feed the composer!

(Igor Stravinsky)

"Music," says Mr. Stravinsky, "probably attended the creation of the universe." Certainly. It was background music.

(David Raksin)

Cinema music is the cinema. That's part of making the picture, not something that's put in later.

(Bernard Herrmann)[1]

Tracing the Great Divide between Classical and Film Music

Andreas Huyssen's book *After the Great Divide: Modernism, Mass Culture, Postmodernism* is a groundbreaking work in the discussion of the cultural conflict

---

[1] Igor Stravinsky, "Igor Stravinsky on Film Music," *The Musical Digest* (September 1946); reprinted online by The Film Music Society, at www.filmmusicsociety.org/news_events/features/2003/101003.html (accessed November 3, 2007); David Raksin, "Hollywood Strikes Back: Film Composer Attacks Stravinsky's 'Cult of Inexpressiveness,'" *The Musical Digest* (January 1948); reprinted online by The Film Music Society, at www. filmmusicsociety.org/news_events/features/2003/101003.html (accessed November 3, 2007); Bernard Herrmann, quoted in Royal S. Brown, *Overtones and Undertones: Reading Film Music* (Berkeley and Los Angeles: University of California Press, 1994), p. 291.

between high and low in the context of modernism versus postmodernism.[2] In his second chapter, "Adorno in Reverse: From Hollywood to Richard Wagner," Huyssen focuses on Theodor Adorno's critique of Wagner's contribution to the culture industry in general and film industry in particular, in the context of modernist elitism and postmodern friendship with popular culture. As Huyssen discusses in his chapter on Wagner and Hollywood, Adorno's ideologically biased diagnosis of Wagner's music drama as a prototype of film[3] has already expressed a fundamental and ongoing contempt for film music addressed in the opening quotations from the famous debate between Stravinsky and David Raksin in *The Musical Digest*.[4] Stravinsky's skepticism about the function of film music partially derived from his larger aesthetic belief that "music is essentially powerless to express anything at all, whether a feeling, an attitude of mind, a psychological mood ..."[5]—to which Raksin sarcastically responded, "Mr. Stravinsky's music may indeed be more expressive than he himself suspects. For even when he sets out to say nothing he succeeds in saying much about himself." But Stravinsky's comments on film music not only show his fundamental anti-romantic position; they are a clear projection of an elitist and prejudiced attitude toward film music, as he equates the function of film music to that of wallpaper:

> The film could not get along without it, just as I myself could not get along without having the empty spaces of my living-room walls covered with wall paper. But you would not ask me, would you, to regard my wall paper as I would regard painting, or apply aesthetic standards to it?[6]

---

[2]   Andreas Huyssen, *After the Great Divide: Modernism, Mass Culture, Postmodernism* (Bloomington, IN: Indiana University Press, 1986).

[3]   Adorno wrote, "Nietzsche in his youthful enthusiasm, failed to recognize the artwork of the future in which we witness the birth of film out of the spirit of music. Theodor Adorno, *In Search of Wagner*, trans. Rodney Livingstone (London: NLB, 1981), p. 107.

[4]   Stravinsky, "Igor Stravinsky on Film Music," and Raksin, "Hollywood Strikes Back."

[5]   "Expression has never been inherent property of music. This is by no means the purpose of its existence. If music appears to express something, this is only an illusion and not a reality. It is simply an additional attribute." See Igor Stravinsky, *An Autobiography* (New York: W.W. Norton, 1998), p. 42. Stravinsky added, "Most people like music because it gives them certain emotions, such as joy, grief, sadness, an image of nature, a subject for daydreams, or—still better—oblivion from 'everyday life.' They want a drug—'dope' ... Music would not be worth much if it were reduced to such an end. When people have learned to love music for itself, when they listen with other ears, their enjoyment will be of a far higher and more potent order, and they will be able to judge it on a higher plane and realize its intrinsic value."

[6]   Raksin, "Hollywood Strikes Back," p. 7.

In a conversation with Walt Disney about the use of *The Rite of Spring* in the film *Fantasia*,[7] Stravinsky again confirmed his high-culture elitist stance against cinema:

> Disney: Think of the numbers of people who will now be able to hear your music.

> Stravinsky: Well, the numbers of people who consume music … are of no interest to me. The mass adds nothing to art.[8]

Schoenberg, too, expressed his strong disdain for cinema, particularly in the context of comparing it to opera, considering film to be the art for "the masses" and incapable of functioning as "pure art":

> I had dreamed of a dramatization of Strindberg's *To Damascus*, or the second part of Goethe's *Faust*, or even Wagner's *Parsifal*. All of these works … would have found the solution to realization in sound pictures. But the industry continued to satisfy only the needs and demands of the ordinary people who filled their theatres … do not assume that the industry, which at present produces moving pictures, could, or cares to start such a turn towards pure art … the opera of the future cannot be art for *the masses*. [italics added][9]

---

[7]   Bruno Bozzetto's animated film, *Allegro Non Troppo* (1976), is a strong parody of Disney's original *Fantasia*. It consists of six episodes, the last of which is an excerpt from Stravinsky's *The Firebird*—"The Princesses' Round Dance" and "The Infernal Dance of King Kashchei." The visualization of this episode is loosely the biblical story of Adam and Eve. The other five episodes are drawn from Debussy's "Prelude to the Afternoon of a Faun," Dvořák's Slavonic Dance No. 7, Op. 46, Ravel's *Bolero*, Sibelius's "Valse triste," and Vivaldi's Concerto in C major for 2 oboes, 2 clarinets, strings, and continuo. Each episode is preceded by a comic scene with spoken dialog.

[8]   Quoted in Nicholas Cook, *Analysing Musical Multimedia* (Oxford: Oxford University Press, 1998), pp. 174–5.

[9]   Arnold Schoenberg, *Style and Idea*, ed. Leonard Stein and trans. Leo Black (Berkeley: University of California Press, 1975), pp. 154–6 and 337. It is interesting that both Schoenberg and Stravinsky, Adorno's prime paradigms for the two poles of cultural progression and regression, respectively, shared Adorno's modernist disdain for the culture industry in general and the film industry in particular. For Adorno's discussion of Schoenberg and Stravinsky, see his "Schoenberg and Progress" and "Stravinsky and Restoration," in *Philosophy of New Music* (Minneapolis: University of Minnesota Press, 2006). The following quotes show that Stravinsky and Schoenberg themselves stimulated Adorno's polarized view of them: Stravinsky said, "Schoenberg, in my judgment, is more of a chemist of music than an artistic creator … I admire Schoenberg and his followers but I recognize that the chromatic gamut on which they are based only exists scientifically"; Schoenberg's response was, "Maybe for Stravinsky, art falls not into this last category but among the fashionable materials and neckties. In that case, he is right in trying merely to

Since the beginning of the motion picture history, those composers who are mainly involved in film scoring have been qualified as "film music composers" and this qualification itself reveals an implication that those composers are treated differently from classical composers. It is in this context that Bernard Herrmann considered it to be absurd to be called a "film music" composer,[10] just as Stravinsky hated being specified as a "Russian" composer. This type of nomenclature reveals that "film music" or "Russian" composers are a "marked" category, deviations from the mainstream.

The tension between classical and popular music was not only an issue for scholarly or artistic debates, but it was also dramatized in some early cartoons. Tex Avery's *Merrie Melodies* animated short, "I Love to Singa," is an example. Derived from the 1936 Wagner Bros. feature-length film *The Singing Kid*, Avery's short presents the story of a young owl who wants to sing jazz, against his parents' wish to make all of their children classical musicians. It mildly alludes to Alan Crosland's *The Jazz Singer*: Owl Jolson instead of Al Jolson (and Al Jolson, who played the title role in Crosland's film, was one of the three singers featured in the original feature-length film *The Singing Kid*). *Music Land* (1935), from Disney's *Silly Symphony* short series, is another example of dramatized tension between classical music and jazz.[11] Its story is the tension between The Land of Symphony and The Isle of Jazz, separated by The Sea of Discord (Figures 6.1 and 6.2).[12]

One day, the prince of the Isle of Jazz crosses the sea and meets the princess of the Land of Symphony. They play with each other merrily, but when the prince kisses the princess, she becomes infuriated and the prince is imprisoned. This begins a war between the two countries. The music that accompanies the Land of Symphony's bombing is "The Ride of the Valkyries" from *Die Walküre* in Wagner's *Ring* cycle (what else could it be?). During the war, the queen of the Land of Symphony accidentally falls into the sea but is rescued by the king of the Isle of Jazz. The short features a happy ending, concluding with a double wedding between the prince and the princess and the king and the queen, and its final frame

---

satisfy the customers." Quoted in Piero Weiss and Richard Taruskin, eds, *Music in the Western World: A History in Documents* (New York: Schirmer Books, 1984), pp. 466–7.

[10]   Brown, "Interviews: Bernard Herrmann," in *Overtones and Undertones*, p. 291.

[11]   The cultural status of jazz is different from that of popular music such as rock and roll and country music, and it is a complicated issue as to whether jazz can be included in the category of the culturally "low." For some jazz musicians and scholars, jazz *is* America's classical music. In the above discussion, however, jazz is considered to be on the opposite pole of "high" in the cultural spectrum, since that is the case for "I Love to Singa" and *Silly Symphony: The Music Land*, in which jazz and (European) classical music are dichotomized. As Jennifer Fleeger indicated, jazz functioned to describe "a collection of popular tunes" for Hollywood around cinema's conversion period, 1926–32. See Fleeger, "Opera, Jazz, and Hollywood's Conversion to Sound" (PhD diss., University of Iowa, 2009), p. 20.

[12]   I thank Frederic Rzewski for informing me of Disney's *Music Land* when he visited the University of Cincinnati in March 2010.

Figure 6.1   The Land of Symphony, in Disney's *Silly Symphony: The Music Land*

Figure 6.2   The Isle of Jazz, in Disney's *Silly Symphony: The Music Land*

shows the newly constructed Bridge of Harmony between the land and the island, brightly lit with a rainbow (Figure 6.3)—a visual allusion to the end of Wagner's first *Ring* opera, *Das Rheingold*.

In spite of the reservations toward film and film scoring arising from the cultural status of cinema as a popular entertainment, a number of early twentieth-century classical music composers were captivated by the then-inchoate art form of film. Paul Hindemith scored the music for Arnold Fanck's 1921 silent *Im Kampf mit dem Berg*, a film about mountain climbing in the Alps. Both the original silent and a shorter version with a soundtrack, produced in 1940, were believed to be lost, but a print of the silent version was discovered in an archive in Moscow in the 1970s. Hindemith's original score, the total length of which is about

Figure 6.3   The Bridge of Harmony at the end of Disney's *Silly Symphony: The Music Land*

90 minutes, was separately found in a different archive and now is preserved at the Hindemith Archives in Frankfurt, Germany.[13] Hindemith composed another film score in 1927, a player-piano score for a cartoon, *Felix at the Circus*, but the score is known to be lost. The film's premiere at the Baden-Baden festival was a serious disappointment to the composer because the machine selected to synchronize his pianola roll with the film projector malfunctioned.[14] Dmitri Shostakovich composed about a dozen film scores, including animated films such as *The Tale of the Priest and His Servant Balda* (Op. 36, 1934), his fourth film score and his very first for an animated film, and *The Silly Little Mouse* (Op. 45, 1939).[15]

Alban Berg, too, was tremendously interested in film and film scoring, as expressed in his letters to Schoenberg in 1930 and 1933 that are quoted in the Prologue.[16] Perhaps his use of a silent film in *Lulu* (1935), one of the earliest uses of a film screen in the operatic theater, was a substitute for his wish for film

---

[13]   A portion of this film with Hindemith's music is available as a YouTube clip, at www.youtube.com/watch?v=uz3rmWyfPIw (accessed March 4, 2011).

[14]   Neil Strauss, "Tunes for Toons: A Cartoon Music Primer," in *The Cartoon Music Book*, ed. Daniel Goldmark and Yuval Taylor (Chicago: A Cappella Books, 2002), p. 6.

[15]   The image track of *The Tale of the Priest and His Servant Balda* was never finished, and Shostakovich converted his score into an opera. Alfred Schnittke is another Russian composer who composed a substantial number of cartoon scores, including "Glass Harmonica," "Butterfly," and "Armoire," all of which were done in collaboration with Andrei Khrjanovsky. Some of the Khrjanovsky–Schnittke films were shelved by Soviet censors until released as a volume in the series *Masters of Russian Animation*, distributed by Image Entertainment in 1997.

[16]   See Prologue, p. 11.

scoring.[17] Unlike his pupil Berg, Schoenberg did have a chance at scoring an actual film. In 1934, Irving Thalberg, the production head of Metro-Goldwyn-Mayer (MGM) studios, invited Schoenberg to compose a film score. Impressed by *Verklärte Nacht*, a prime representative of the so-called late romantic period of Schoenberg's earliest compositional style, Thalberg asked the composer to score for the film adaptation of Pearl S. Buck's *The Good Earth*. "My terms are very simple," replied Schoenberg. "Fifty thousand dollars and an absolute guarantee that not a single note of my score will be altered." Furthermore, he wanted to control the pitch levels of the actors' voices.[18] Of course, Schoenberg's requests were not accepted. The amount of honorarium he requested, which was exceptionally high for film scoring at that time, was not a problem, but his demand for absolute control over every musical element of the film—in other words, absolute musical autonomy—was, and still is, an unrealistic condition in mainstream filmmaking. Considering Schoenberg's contempt toward entertainment for "the masses," his "Accompaniment to a Cinematographic Scene," a 12-tone orchestral piece he composed for an "imaginary" film, reveals an ambivalence toward film. The comparison he drew between opera and cinema suggests that this ambivalence was at least partially derived from Schoenberg's envy of the large number of people cinema attracts:

> I know only a very small number of people who have seen a movie more than once. Producers of movies can obtain an attendance of 100 per cent of the movie-going population only in the case of a great success. Suppose the audience which can be acquired for serious plays and operas is only five per cent of the people … and in four generations every single person of these audiences would see a work only five times; five times four generations means twenty times for each work. Twenty times five per cent of the population amounts to the same 100 per cent of the population for which the movie industry aims so badly.[19]

MGM approached not only Schoenberg but also Stravinsky shortly after Stravinsky had emigrated to the United States in 1939 (both Schoenberg and Stravinsky lived

---

[17]   Other early operas that used film screens include Kurt Weill's *Royal Palace* (1926), Darius Milhaud's *Christophe Colomb* (1928), and George Antheil's *Transatlantic* (1930). In these operas, film images serve for the operatic narrative. Film images in *Lulu*, however, have another function as a visual illustration of the musical structure that accompanies the film: the palindrome. Considering this relationship between music and image, the film music scene in Berg's *Lulu* can be regarded as the ancestor of music video in the sense that music has the authorial power over the visual images—i.e., the music was created first and the visuals serve the music—rather than the other way around, which is the case for most standard narrative film.

[18]   Quoted in Otto Friedrich, *City of Nets: A Portrait of Hollywood in the 1940's* (New York: Harper and Row, 1986), p. 36.

[19]   Schoenberg, *Style and Idea*, p. 156.

in the Hollywood area). The following is a report of a conversation between Stravinsky and Louis B. Mayer, the then-head of MGM, as chronicled by Miklós Rózsa:

> *Mayer*: I hear you are the greatest composer in the world.
> *Stravinsky*: Well, this is the greatest movie studio in the world.
> *Mayer*: How much will you charge for a music score?
> *Stravinsky*: How long is it?
> *Mayer*: Say 45 minutes.
> *Stravinsky*: [after doing a calculation based on the amount of work he did for such works as *Petrushka* and *The Rite of Spring*] $25,000.
> *Mayer*: That's a lot of money, Mr. Stravinsky… much more than we normally pay. But since you're the greatest composer in the world you shall have it. Now, when can I have the score?
> *Stravinsky*: In about one year.
> *Mayer*: [after staring at Stravinsky in disbelief] Good day, Mr. Stravinsky.[20]

As noted at the beginning of this chapter, Stravinsky's disdain for cinema was stronger than that of Schoenberg, and his contempt extended to filmmakers: "In all frankness, I find it impossible to talk to film people about music because we have no common meeting ground … The current cinematic concept of music is foreign to me; I express myself in a different way. What common language can one have with the films?"[21] When Stravinsky praised Schoenberg's "Accompaniment to a Cinematographic Scene," his comments were full of bitter sarcasm concerning film: "by far the best piece of real film music ever written, an ironic triumph if there ever was one, for the film itself was *imaginary*" (italics added).[22] In spite of his disdain for film and its creators, Stravinsky highly admired Charlie Chaplin, considering him a friend, and even attempted collaborating on a film with Chaplin. For his film project with Stravinsky, Chaplin suggested a surreal film about the Crucifixion at a decadent nightclub, but the project was aborted because Stravinsky considered the theme Chaplin suggested to be too sacrilegious. When Stravinsky later approached Chaplin about another collaboration, the film director's response was cool.[23]

Although his first few opportunities for film composing ended unsuccessfully, Stravinsky did get involved in some film projects later on, and it is known that he

---

[20]   Quoted in William H. Rosar, "Stravinsky and MGM," in *Film Music 1*, ed. Clifford McCarty (New York: Garland, 1989), pp. 114–15.

[21]   Stravinsky, "Igor Stravinsky on Film Music."

[22]   Igor Stravinsky and Robert Craft, *Memories and Commentaries* (New York: Doubleday, 1960), p. 102.

[23]   Charles Joseph, "The Would-Be Hollywood Composer: Stravinsky, the Literati, and 'The Dream Factory,'" in *Stravinsky Inside Out* (New Haven, CT: Yale University Press, 2001), pp. 114–15.

composed the music without seeing a single scene of film.[24] None of Stravinsky's film projects materialized, and he turned some of those aborted projects into concert music. Among those works are *Four Norwegian Moods* (1942), which originated as a score for John Farrow's 1942 film *Commandos Strike at Dawn*—a story about a Norwegian widower involved in the underground resistance against the Nazis; *Ode* (1943), originally intended to be part of Robert Stevenson's film adaptation of *Jane Eyre* (1943), starring Orson Welles in the leading role of Edward Rochester; and the second movement of the *Symphony in Three Movements* (1943), which Stravinsky conceived for the "Apparition of the Virgin" scene for a film adaptation of Franz Werfel's novel *The Song of Bernadette* (1942). *Scherzo à la Russe* (1944) was originally intended for a war film set in a Ukrainian village threatened by Nazis, with a script written by Lillian Hellman. Stravinsky later arranged this music for the Paul Whiteman Band.[25]

Hollywood's attempt to employ prominent classical composers such as Stravinsky and Schoenberg can be considered in the larger context of cinema's aspiration to the high-cultural status of classical music, as argued by Jeremy Tambling.[26] In addition to the works Tambling discusses, *A Midsummer Night's Dream* (1935), directed by Max Reinhardt and William Dieterle, serves as another example. It opens with an "Overture," during which Mendelssohn's overture (Op. 21) is heard in its entirety before the film's opening credits start to roll. In so doing, the film simulates the operatic theater. In addition, the film's opening credits present the film as Shakespeare's piece, describing it as "Midsummer Night's Dream by Shakespeare" rather than specifying that the film was *based on* Shakespeare's work. Similarly, the musical credits read "Mendelssohn arranged by Erich Korngold," rather than presenting the composer of the original music first, as in many later films that use the arrangement of pre-existing classical pieces.

Cinema's association with classical music was not just a cultural calculation on the part of filmmakers but was sometimes a pressure exerted on its patrons— film viewers—or their business partners, such as a recording company. Archival materials I examined for Jean Negulesco's *Humoresque* (1946) provide evidence of this. According to a telegram from Columbia Recording Corp. to Warner Bros. dated October 22, 1946, Columbia demanded that the commercial advertisement for their recording feature Isaac Stern, the real violinist who played all of the violin pieces performed in the film by protagonist Paul Boray (John Garfield).

---

[24]   Leah Branstetter, "Neoclassical Stravinsky Meets Classical Hollywood," term paper for the musicology seminar on "Neoclassical Stravinsky" I taught at the University of Cincinnati's College-Conservatory of Music in the fall of 2008 (p. 8).

[25]   Branstetter, "Neoclassical Stravinsky," p. 8. She provides detailed information about each of Stravinsky's aborted film projects (see pp. 7–14).

[26]   Tambling, "Film Aspiring to the Condition of Opera," in *Opera, Ideology and Film* (Basingstoke: Palgrave Macmillan, 1987), pp. 41–67.

ESSENTIAL IN OUR HUMORESQUE ALBUM THAT WE ANOUNCE
VIOLIN SOLOS IN MOVIE HUMORESQUE ARE PLAYED BY ISAAC
STERN. OTHERWISE THERE WOULD BE NO REASON FOR THIS
PARTICULAR TIE UP. WARNER BROS HERE SEEMS TO OBJECT TO
OUR MENTIONING IT EVEN THOUGH OUR ALBUMS WILL FOLLOW
PICTURE RELEASE RATHER THAN PRECEDE IT. DO YOU SEE ANY
REASON FOR THIS OBJECTION AND CAN YOU CLEAR IT?"[27]

As Jeremy Tambling has noted, the film industry's strategic association with, and
evocation of, high-cultural classical music began to diminish in the 1960s, in part
because, by that time, film as an art form had stabilized and the film industry,
confident of its own aesthetics and values supported by its financial success,
no longer envied the high cultural glamour of opera.[28] Also, the emergence of
postmodernism around the beginning of the 1960s contributed to the mitigation
of the "great divide" between high and low, as testified by those musical pieces
which blatantly incorporate popular tunes, such as, to name a few among many,
Philip Glass's *Low Symphony* and *Heroes Symphony*, both of which are based on
David Bowie's rock music, and Michael Daugherty's *Dead Elvis* for solo bassoon
and chamber ensemble, in which several tunes by Elvis appear in variation (the
composer even intended the solo bassoonist to be an Elvis impersonator by wearing
his signature costume). For William Bolcom, the esteem for "serious music" is an
artistic racism:

> To answer your question about "serious music"; that is, I assure you, not my own
> original term; in fact I hate it, as it implies that everyone not in it is not serious
> … ; it's almost racist … Your other question: "shouldn't classical, serious
> composers learn from the opposition" is one my whole life has addressed.[29]

In spite of the postmodern mitigation of the tension between classical and
popular music, I find a continued dichotomy between high and low in film music
criticism, specifically in those studies that are obsessed with the musical integrity
of classical music when it is used as a soundtrack. In what follows I will discuss
two issues recurrent in film music criticism in the context of postmodernism
versus modernism. The first issue I consider is the controversy among film-music
composers and scholars concerning the original score versus the compilation
score, the latter of which includes pre-existing music such as opera excerpts. Here
I place the artistic and scholarly skepticism about the compilation score within

---

[27]   Telegram from Columbia Recording Corp. to Warner Bros., 1946, USC Warner
Bros. Archives, School of Cinema–Television, University of Southern California.

[28]   Tambling, *Opera, Ideology and Film*, p. 76.

[29]   William Bolcom, "From *Something About the Music*," *Contemporary Composers
on Contemporary Music*, ed. Elliott Schwartz and Barney Childes (Cambridge, MA: Da
Capo Press, 1998), p. 482.

the modernist–postmodernist debate about originality and musical autonomy. The second issue is the "problem" of historical inaccuracy in biopics about musicians, which is frequently addressed in musicological studies. Problematizing the polarity between hypercritical reactions to historical inaccuracy in film and the generous condoning of such inaccuracy in operas based on historical events or figures, I argue that these dualistic responses reveal the modernists' disdain for a popular medium and an associated distrust of its consumers and filmmakers.

Musical Integrity, Historical Accuracy, and Film Music Criticism[30]

In his essay on Milos Forman's *Amadeus* (1984), Joseph Horowitz furiously criticized the soundtrack primarily because of its "mutilation" of Mozart's music, and the subtitle of his review, "*Mass* Snob Appeal" (italics added), echoes the view of Stravinsky and Schoenberg noted earlier—film as an entertainment for the masses.[31] Robert Craft endorses Horowitz's assessment when he notes, "Music bleeds at every splice, welling up, fading out, left suspended in mid-phrase."[32] The problem of mutilation for Horowitz and Craft lies in the fact that what is mutilated is Mozart's music (that is, classical masterpieces), and this issue—even the metaphor of "bleeding"—recurs in criticisms of the use of classical music in film: Derek Elley's review of *Meeting Venus* reads, "[T]he pic's main fault is the paucity of underscoring beyond the bleeding chunks of *Tannhäuser*."[33] This metaphor of bleeding replicates those furious criticisms of Disney's original *Fantasia*, which treat the classical pieces used in the movie as "sacred" by accusing the film for its "musical blasphemy."[34]

Along with the issue of the musical fragmentation, a lack of historical accuracy has also been a criticism of Forman's *Amadeus* and other biopics about musicians. For Paul Henry Lang, the film did an "injustice" to Mozart as well as Salieri.

> *Amadeus*, whatever its virtues as entertainment, is offensive in its injustice to both Mozart and Salieri, and will unfortunately give many in its extensive audience an enduringly twisted view of these composers … In the end, *Amadeus*

---

[30]   This section of Chapter 6 is partially based on my article about Milos Forman's film *Amadeus*. See Jeongwon Joe, "Reconsidering *Amadeus*: Mozart as Film Music," in Phil Powrie and Robynn Stilwell, eds, *Changing Tunes: The Use of Pre-Existing Music in Film* (Aldershot: Ashgate, 2006), 57–73.

[31]   Joseph Horowitz, "Mozart as Midcult: Mass Snob Appeal," *Musical Quarterly* 76 (1992): 11.

[32]   Robert Craft, "B-flat Movie," *New York Review of Books* 32, no. 6 (1985): 11.

[33]   Derek Elley, "*Meeting Venus*: British Romantic Comedy," *Variety*, September 6, 1991, p. 16.

[34]   Cook, *Analysing Musical Multimedia*, p. 175.

is an amorphous muddle of ideas crippled by their contradiction of recorded facts, yet slick and overlaid with a varnish of cinematic éclat.[35]

Lang is just one of many scholars annoyed by the distortion (or liberal dramatization) of historical facts in *Amadeus*. Many critics and amateur Mozartians were similarly outraged. At the very outset of the *Amadeus* project, however, Forman and Peter Shaffer, author of the original play *Amadeus* and the screenplay of the movie, clearly professed their intention: "We were not making an objective 'Life of Wolfgang Amadeus Mozart.'"[36] Shaffer declared that the film is "not a screen biography but a fantasia on events in Mozart's life."[37]

> This cannot be stressed too strongly. Obviously, *Amadeus* on the stage was never intended to be a documentary biography of the composer and the film is even less of one … We are also blatantly claiming the grand license of the story teller to embellish his tale with fictional ornament.[38]

Virulent objection to the lack of historical inaccuracy in *Amadeus* is thought-provoking given the reticence over historical distortions in Rimsky-Korsakov's *Mozart and Salieri*, an operatic adaptation of Alexander Pushkin's dramatic poem, which is based on the rumor that Salieri poisoned Mozart. Aren't Pushkin's dramatic poem (1830) and Rimsky-Korsakov's opera (1897) also each a "fantasia on events in Mozart's life"? It seems that what is problematic for the detractors of the film *Amadeus* is not its distorted representation of history but, more fundamentally, the popular/mass cultural appropriation of the great composer and his music. This view is supported by the absence of criticism of Shaffer's *play* on the grounds of historical inaccuracy, as well as of Pushkin's poem and Rimsky-Korsakov's opera. This double standard, emerging from disdain for a popular medium and distrust for its creators and consumers, can be regarded as the attribute of modernism as opposed to postmodernism, the latter of which is characterized by the collapse of the "great divide" between high and low, to use Andreas Huyssen's expression once more.

Musical autonomy in film, forcefully advocated by Hanns Eisler and Theodor Adorno, can also be situated in the same line of the modernist elitism against popular art. When they deplore the subordination of music to image, Eisler and Adorno are arguing not only for musical autonomy but, more importantly, for the autonomy of high art against mass culture. Throughout their book *Composing for*

---

[35]   Paul Henry Lang, "Salvaging Salieri (and Mozart) after *Amadeus*," *Opus* 1, no. 6 (1985): 21.

[36]   Quoted in Peter Brown, "*Amadeus* and Mozart: Setting the Record Straight," *American Scholar* 6, no. 1 (1992): 50.

[37]   Quoted in Herbert Kupferberg, *Amadeus: A Mozart Mosaic* (New York: McGraw-Hill, 1986), p. 240.

[38]   Quoted in Brown, "*Amadeus* and Mozart," p. 50.

the Films, Eisler and Adorno regard cinema first and foremost as a commercial and consumerist art, a shameful product of the culture industry.[39] Although a glimpse of change in Adorno's attitude toward film is present in his late writings, he adamantly excluded film from the area of art on account of, first of all, the equation of technique and technology in film.

> The late emergence of film makes it difficult to distinguish between technique and technology as clearly as is possible in music. In music up to the electronic period, the intrinsic technique—the sound structure of the work—was distinct from its performance, the means of reproduction. Film suggests the equation of technique and technology since, as Benjamin observed, the cinema has no original which is then reproduced on a mass scale: the mass product is the thing itself.[40]

Adorno attributes the dominance of technology in film to the genre's inherently "representational" as opposed to "autonomous" nature, resulting from photographic reproduction. For Adorno and Eisler as well, the peculiar cultural status of film music lies in the existence of a high art—music—within the popular medium, film: hence their desperate advocacy for the autonomy of music, in order to protect high art. It is on this basis that Robynn Stilwell contends that modernist elitism is "emphatically articulated" by Eisler and Adorno when they insist on musical autonomy in a film.[41]

Insistence on historical authenticity can also be contextualized within the larger cultural debate between modernism and postmodernism over the notion of history. For many postmodernists in various fields, historical facts are not stable but elusive; history is not an absolute truth but a construct. In their collaborative book, *Telling the Truth about History*, Joyce Appleby, Lynn Hunt, and Margaret Jacob draw an analogy between historians and novelists:

---

[39] Theodor Adorno and Hanns Eisler, *Composing for the Films* (London: The Athlone Press, 1994). The 1947 original edition was published under Eisler's name only and Adorno's name was added in later editions. The most recent edition was published by Continuum International Publishing Group in 2005, with a new introduction by Graham McCann.

[40] Theodor Adorno, "Transparencies on Film," trans. Thomas Y. Levin, *New German Critique*, no. 24–5 (1981–82): 200. Adorno revised his harsh criticism of film and the culture industry in general in his later writings, including "Culture Industry Reconsidered," written in 1967 and published in *New German Critique*, no. 6 (1975): 12–19, trans. Anson G. Rabinbach. Miriam Hansen notes that one of the major motivations for Adorno's positive reassessment of film was his encounter with Alexander Kluge, especially his 1966 film, *Abschied von Gestern*. See Hansen, "Introduction to Adorno, 'Transparences on Film,'" *New German Critique*, nos. 24–5 (1981–82): 192.

[41] Robynn Stilwell, "'I Just Put a Drone Under Him…': Collage and Subversion in the Score of *Die Hard*," *Music and Letters* 78, no. 4 (November 1997): 569.

The implication is that the historian does not in fact capture the past in faithful fashion but rather, like the novelist, gives the appearance of doing so. Were this version of postmodernism applied to history, the search for truths about the past would be displaced by fictively producing convincing "truth-effects."[42]

Whereas novelists make aesthetic and literary choices for their works, they continue, historians' choices are "political, social, and epistemological."[43] The much-presumed "objectivity" of historical knowledge is called into question not only in history but also in artistic areas. An example is what Linda Hutcheon calls "historiographic metafiction," a postmodern literary genre in which historical figures are liberally fictionalized. In E.L. Doctorow's novel *Ragtime*, for instance, numerous late nineteenth- and early twentieth-century historical personages are freely treated in a fictional frame—Theodore Roosevelt, the architect Stanford White, the painter Winslow Homer, and the magician Harry Houdini.[44] Hutcheon argues that in the process of abducting historical figures into the fictional frame without any pretense of accuracy, historiographic metafiction obscures the traditional hard-and-fast borderline between *history* and *story*, between the real and the fictive, and in so doing destabilizes the absolutism of historical truth.

> Historiographic metafiction, like postmodernist architecture and painting, is overtly and resolutely historical—though, admittedly, in an ironic and problematic way that acknowledges that history is not the transparent record of any sure "truth."[45]

Perhaps it was not a mere coincidence that Milos Forman also directed a cinematic adaptation of Doctorow's *Ragtime*, as we can see that his *Amadeus* shares the spirit of historiographic metafiction that challenges deterministic historiography.

The trend in film music criticism that privileges "evidence" over everything else can be situated in the same line of modernist sanctification of historical facts. Paul A. Merkley's masterful, award-winning article, "'Stanley Hates This but I Like It!': North vs. Kubrick on the Music for *2001: A Space Odyssey*," can serve as an example. In his conclusion, Merkley strongly supports empirical methodology over hermeneutic or interpretative approaches to film music by asking the reader to accept his conclusion *on the basis of the evidence offered*.[46] In his review of

---

[42]   Joyce Appleby, Lynn Hunt, and Margaret Jacob, "Postmodernism and the Crisis of Modernity," in *Telling the Truth About History* (New York: W.W. Norton, 1994), p. 227.

[43]   Ibid., p. 229.

[44]   Linda Hutcheon, *A Poetics of Postmodernism: History, Theory, Fiction* (New York: Routledge, 1988), pp. 145–6.

[45]   Ibid., pp. 128–9.

[46]   Paul A. Merkley, "'Stanley Hates This but I Like It!': North vs. Kubrick on the Music for *2001: A Space Odyssey*," *The Journal of Film Music* 2, no. 1 (Fall 2007): 1–32. This article was the winner of an ASCAP Deems Taylor Award in 2008. The quoted phrase

Roger Hillman's book, *Unsettling Scores: German Film, Music, and Ideology*, Merkley denies the applicability of hermeneutic methodology to the study of music, whether film music or other:

> As the modern philosopher Gadamer[47] has pointed out, the hermeneutics of texts do not function in the same way as those of poetry or music; no one would interrupt a poem or a piece of music because they have "gotten the message" and need to hear no more. Yet if we follow Hillman, the audience is not listening to the music for its own sake, but only for a specific reference it makes that relates to a narrative. As a consequence, it is clear that in this kind of study the musical pursuit takes a back seat to the text-referential; music is studied mainly where it informs the audience on verbal points.[48]

Merkley presents his review as a rebuttal to "postmodern" (that is, hermeneutic) approaches: "Central to post-modern literary theory is the proposition that texts, and by extension music and images, are interpreted in different ways (and all may be valid)."[49] Although Merkley is critical of postmodern intellectualism, his description of it is true: pluralistic interpretations rather than monolithic theories. As Robert Morgan has indicated, postmodern pluralism has been manifest not only in scholarly fields but also in creative domains, including music, as testified by the diverse compositional styles and techniques that emerged during the 1960s such as "quotation music, minimalism, and new forms of music theatre, along with a host of other compositional innovations." Morgan argues that such diverse styles and techniques have replaced the "two principal 'orthodoxies' of the 1950s—serialism and indeterminacy."[50]

> Here one can recognize an important differences between postmodernism and "classical" modernism: the latter remained largely committed to preserving

---

in the title, "Stanley Hates This but I Like It!" is what Alex North's orchestrator, Henry Brant, wrote on the score, on the first page of the cue of Reel 7-1, "Moon Rocket Bus." A photocopy of this page is included in Merkley's article, p. 18.

[47]   Hans-Georg Gadamer (1900–2002) was a German philosopher, best known for his book *Truth and Method* (*Wahrheit und Methode*) published in 1960. In this book, he focused on the concept of philosophical hermeneutics.

[48]   Paul A. Merkley, review of Roger Hillman, *Unsettling Scores: German Film, Music, and Ideology*, in *Journal of Film Music* 2, nos. 2–4 (Winter 2009): 275. It seems to me that Merkley's concept of hermeneutics could be more broadened and sharpened, for it is not limited to the textual and verbal references. But it is beyond the scope of this study to delve into the complexities of hermeneutics. What seems to be Merkley's misrepresentation of Hillman's book will be discussed later in the chapter.

[49]   Merkley, review of Hillman, *Unsettling Scores*, p. 277.

[50]   Robert Morgan, "Postmodernism and the Present," in *Modern Times: From World War I to the Present*, ed. Robert Morgan (Englewood Cliffs, NJ: Prentice Hall, 1993), p. 28.

at least the appearance of stylistic coherence, and thus to the projection of a consistent voice from composers, writers or painters. (In music, for example, one finds throughout the first half of the century an almost obsessive attempt to maintain traditional values of coherence and consistency, in spite of major disruptions in compositional language.) Postmodern art, on the other hand, not only gives up the attempt to create coherence and consistency but, as often as not, makes fun of the very pretense of doing so.[51]

Not only did what has been known as the "new musicology" (for lack of a better term) emerge at the same time as postmodernism in the mid-1960s but, more importantly, it also shares its main ethos. Lawrence Kramer has noted:

> Much of what has been dubbed "the new musicology" has evolved through postmodernist critiques of the formerly (and, if truth be told, still currently) dominant models of musicological knowledge, which for want of better names can be called formalism and positivism.[52]

And he defines the new musicology as

> a musicology in which the results of archival and analytical work, formerly prized in their own right, would become significant only in relation to subjective values—which is not to say the values of an atomized private inwardness, but those of a historically situated type of human agency. Such a musicology would satisfy the demand for human interest, not by making good on music's lack of meaning but by ceasing to entertain the illusion that such a lack ever existed.[53]

According to postmodernist views, music is a culturally and socio-politically conditioned and constructed product rather than an autonomous masterpiece embodying universal, timeless values. Thus Gary Tomlinson exhorts musicologists to "abandon the myth of music's autonomy by broadening 'the horizons of our musical pleasure' and welcoming the complex situatedness of musical utterances in webs of extramusical forces."[54] As we saw above, Schoenberg demanded absolute musical autonomy when MGM attempted to offer him a commission for scoring a film: "an absolute guarantee that not a single note of my score will be altered." But as argued by such postmodern scholars as Andreas Huyssen, an absolute musical autonomy is an illusion: "The irony of course is that art's aspirations to autonomy, its uncoupling from church and state, became possible

---

[51]   Ibid., p. 30.

[52]   Lawrence Kramer, *Classical Music and Postmodern Knowledge* (Berkeley: University of California Press, 1995), p. xiv.

[53]   Ibid., p. 25.

[54]   Gary Tomlinson, "Musical Pasts and Postmodern Musicologies: A Response to Lawrence Kramer," *Current Musicology*, no. 53 (1993): 19.

only when literature, painting and music were first organized according to the principles of market economy. From its beginnings the autonomy of art has been related dialectically to the commodity form."[55]

In his review of Roger Hillman's book *Unsettling Scores*, Paul A. Merkley problematized the narrowness of Hillman's theory in terms of its applicability: "music chosen for film from pre-existing classical repertoire is a subject too narrow to support a theory ... Theory should be robust enough to stand for a broad spectrum of examples, not just unusual cases." Merkley deplores the tendency in film music criticism that focuses an "increasing amount of attention on peculiarities with the result that theorists are not so much theorizing as describing odd cases of the use of music. Indeed, it seems that the more scholars are innovative in narrative theory, while their examples are interesting, the less their arguments apply to most film music."[56] By this statement, Merkley is searching for and endorsing monolithic master theories. It is not Hillman's intention to provide such a theory. Instead, his book proposes *one of the possible ways* to interpret the classical pieces used in the films he examines. And Hillman clearly defines the scope of his book at the beginning of his introduction: "This study looks at the use of classical music in film, focusing on films of the New German Cinema of the 1970s and early 1980s."[57] It is true that the use of pre-existing music is more unusual than using "original" scores in Hollywood films, especially during its classical era, but European films have been different. If one insists on the lack of legitimacy of "unusual cases" as the object of scholarly investigation, isn't one reinforcing the status quo that marginalizes, if not totally silences, the voices of the "Other"? Would it be too much paranoia if one saw in the marginalization of "odd cases" the implicit danger of promoting an intellectual totalitarianism?

Intentionality and the Death of the Author

Merkley problematizes the kind of film-music studies that ignore filmmakers' intentions. "A glaring example" he mentions is the Nietzschean interpretations of Stanley Kubrick's *2001: A Space Odyssey* that are based on the title of Strauss's tone poem (*Also sprach Zarathustra*). He discredits these interpretations by presenting the "evidence" that Kubrick, at a very late stage of production, asked a relative to suggest a fanfare of short length, "nothing more."[58] The privileging of "evidence" evokes Arthur Mendel's disquisition on "Evidence and Explanation,"

---

[55]   Huyssen, *After the Great Divide*, p. 17.

[56]   Merkley, review of Hillman, *Unsettling Scores*, p. 275.

[57]   Roger Hillman, *Unsettling Scores: German Film, Music, and Ideology* (Bloomington: Indiana University Press, 2005), p. 1.

[58]   Merkley, review of Hillman, *Unsettling Scores*, p. 276.

which became a target for critique by such scholars as Joseph Kerman.[59] It could not be more reasonable for me if what Merkley advocates is a *balance* between "hermeneutic" and "empirical" studies (for lack of better terms). But reading between the lines of his review suggests that he privileges the latter type of methodology: for instance, he calls it a "mistake" if a study overlooks the production history that informs us of "the creators' intentions and terms of musical composition and performance." Furthermore, he argues in his concluding remarks that "[a]ll of the theoretical work will advance when it is placed within the crucible of production studies, a line that also holds promise for new media."[60] There is no doubt that considering filmmakers' intentions—whether film directors, composers, or other practitioners involved in film production—is crucial in film and film-music studies, as in any musicological works. But if one does not allow for methodological pluralism, it would promote intellectual totalitarianism.

Essentialist esteem for authorial intention can be, again, contextualized within the discourse on modernism versus postmodernism. The sanctification of intentionality is rooted in the notion of the "Author-God" (the author as God), which, according to Michel Foucault, is a creation of modernism founded upon the Enlightenment belief in the human being as autonomous, rational, and subjectively willing.[61] Jacques Derrida maintains that the concept of the Author-God will disappear with the poststructuralist demystification of Enlightenment Man. From a poststructuralist view, the author is no longer the only source for the meaning(s) of his or her work. Roland Barthes argues that the meanings of any text are to be found in its destination, not its origins; in its reception, not its production; in the reader, not the author. Hence his declaration of "the birth of the reader" in his article "The Death of the Author":

> Classic criticism has never paid any attention to the reader; for it, the writer is the only person in literature. We are now beginning to let ourselves be fooled no longer by the arrogant antiphrastical recriminations of good society in favour of the very thing it sets aside, ignores, smothers, or destroys; we know that to give writing its future, it is necessary to overthrow the myth: the birth of the reader must be at the cost of the death of the Author.[62]

---

[59]   Arthur Mendel, "Evidence and Explanation," in *Report of the Eighth Congress of the International Musicological Society*, vol. 2 (New York: Bärenreiter, 1962), pp. 2–18; Joseph Kerman, *Contemplating Music: Challenges to Musicology* (Cambridge, MA: Harvard University Press, 1958).

[60]   Merkley, review of Hillman, *Unsettling Scores*, pp. 276–7.

[61]   Michel Foucault, "What Is an Author?" in *Foucault Reader* (New York: Pantheon Books, 1984), p. 119.

[62]   Roland Barthes, "The Death of the Author," in *Image, Music, Text*, trans. Stephen Heath (New York: Hill and Wang, 1977), p. 148.

In regards to the modernist esteem for the author's intentionality, I find another interesting phenomenon, or hierarchy, in film music criticism: when the filmmaker's intention contradicts or competes with historical accuracy, the latter is privileged over the former, as in the dominant musicological responses to Milos Forman's *Amadeus*. In spite of the filmmaker's *intention* that the film be not "a screen biography but a fantasia on events in Mozart's life," there was a stream of attacks on the film's historical inaccuracy. Completely silencing Forman's and Shaffer's voices, many music historians were outraged at the falsification of historical facts, ranging from Salieri's standing in for Franz Xaver Süssmayr and the distortion of the conducting tradition of opera in Mozart's time[63] to the misrepresentation and cheap sentimentalization of the weather on Mozart's funeral day: according to the records of the Vienna weather bureau for December 7, 1791, uncovered by Nicolas Slonimsky, "it was a mild day and there was neither blizzard nor rain."[64] An extreme case is Jane Perry-Camp's three-page article, basically a listing of factual errors in the film.[65]

Gérard Corbiau's *Farinelli* (1994), a biopic about the eighteenth-century castrato Carlo Broschi (1705–82), is another film that stirred up criticism because of its historical inaccuracies. What is at stake in this biopic is the climactic scene of the film, where Farinelli performs "Lascia ch'io pianga" from Handel's opera *Rinaldo*. Farinelli did perform in a Handel opera in London, but it was not *Rinaldo* but a revival of *Ottone*.[66] The employment of "Lascia ch'io pianga," however, was not a product of the film director's historical ignorance but a directorial choice for a particular purpose: having been fascinated with the two arias from *Rinaldo*—"Lascia ch'io pianga" and "Cara sposa"—for a long time, Corbiau thought that they would be the most powerful music for the climax of his *Farinelli*.[67] It is thought-provoking that even after having found that Corbiau is not a musicological illiterate, John Higgins still describes the director as "unrepentant" of his historical distortion.[68]

---

[63] In the eighteenth century, operas were conducted by two people: the concertmaster, who was responsible for the orchestra; and the keyboardist, who was in charge of the singers. See Brown, "*Amadeus* and Mozart," p. 61.

[64] Igor Kipnis, "Amadeus and Genius: Circuses, Courts, and Commissions," *Chamber Music Magazine* 7, no. 3 (1990): 19.

[65] Jane Perry-Camp, "*Amadeus* and Authenticity," *Eighteenth-Century Life* 9 (October 1994): 116–19.

[66] A liberal adaptation of *Ottone* was produced by the Theatre of the Nobility in 1734, in which Farinelli performed a secondary role, Adelberto, while the title role was sung by Senesino, another celebrated eighteenth-century castrato.

[67] This information was included in the film's production notes dated April 1995 in the collection of the library of the British Film Institute, where I conducted arhival studies in the summer of 2005.

[68] John Higgins, "The Voice That Never Grew Up," *The Times*, October 30, 1995.

Ellen T. Harris praises Katherine Bergeron's article on Corbiau's film by describing it as offering "a wonderfully acute and perceptive analysis of this film as a portrait of a castrato."[69] Even this "acute and perceptive analysis," however, is not devoid of inaccuracy, although it does not diminish the validity of the author's main argument. The scene in which Farinelli sings "Ombra fedele" is a simulation (or replacement) of Farinelli's 1734 debut in London—his legendary performance of "Son qual nave," an aria from the 1734 pasticcio *Artaserse*. At the end of this performance, it is known that a woman, often known as "Lady Rich," shouted a "blasphemous" cry: "One God, One Farinelli!"[70] Bergeron notes that there is no one who cries "One God, One Farinelli" in Corbiau's film;[71] but there is, although it is not one woman, as in the history, but the entire audience who repeats this cry at the end of the *Rinaldo* sequence. Corbiau's displacement of the cry from the historically correct moment (the performance of "Son qual nave") to the *Rinaldo* sequence was motivated by his intention to intensify the climatic effects of this sequence, which is the central scene of the film.[72] If creative artists carry "poetic licenses"—that is, the license to kill factual truth when it stands in the way of poetic or dramatic truth, as Robert Marshall argues[73]—why can film directors not be endowed with such license? If such opera composers as Rimsky-Korsakov (for *Mozart and Salieri*), John Adams (for *Nixon in China*, *The Death of Klinghoffer*, and *Doctor Atomic*), Richard Danielpour (for *Margaret Garner*) and Anthony Davis (for *X: The Life and Times of Malcom X* and *Amistad*) are granted poetic license, why not Milos Forman and Gérard Corbiau? "I'm not a historian," Corbiau states, "and I believe, very strongly, that this is not the purpose of film … All artistic projects require a certain amount of creative licence."[74]

Unlike Higgins, Harris not only exonerates the historical falsification in the *Rinaldo* scene but even praises Corbiau's *Farinelli* by describing it as "surprisingly true to the known fact": she claims that even the presence of white stallions, a visual refrain associated in the film with Farinelli's traumatic memory of his castration,

---

[69]   Ellen T. Harris, "Twentieth-Century Farinelli," *Musical Quarterly* 81 (Summer 1997): 182.

[70]   Lady Rich's cry appears as the banner in William Hogarth's satirical drawing of Farinelli, included in the second piece of the series *The Rake's Progress* (1735). See Daniel Heartz, "Farinelli Revisited," *Early Music* 18 (1990): 438.

[71]   Katherine Bergeron, "The Castrato as History," *Cambridge Opera Journal* 8 (July 1996): 181.

[72]   This information was included in the film's production notes dated April 1995 in the collection of the library of the British Film Institute, where I conducted archival studies in the summer of 2005.

[73]   Robert Marshall, "Film as Musicology: *Amadeus*," *Musical Quarterly* 81, no. 2 (1997): 173–4.

[74]   An unpublished interview included in the production file of *Farinelli, Il Castrato*, Margaret Herrick Library of the Academy of Motion Picture Arts and Sciences. Neither the date of the interview nor the interviewer's name is given.

can be loosely connected to the historical Farinelli's interest in breeding Hungarian stallions while he was in Spain.[75] What is puzzling to me is that nowhere in the main body of Harris's article is the film director's name mentioned. "*Farinelli* the film disappoints." Thus begins her article, and the film director's name is only identified in a footnote.[76] Isn't the absence of the author's name unimaginable, if not impermissible, when one discusses an opera? Would it have been just a careless mistake, which can happen in any scholarly work, or could it be a revelation of some subconscious attitude? And could that subconscious attitude be the denial that film directors are creative artists, just as they are denied "poetic license"? The possibility of such a subconscious orientation brings me back to the issue discussed earlier in this chapter: the underlying disdain for film that is projected by modernist elitism against mass culture. In the following section, I discuss another issue in film music criticism in light of postmodernism versus modernism: the advocacy of the original score—the music composed specifically for a particular film—against the compilation score, which includes pre-existing music such as opera excerpts.

Original Score versus Compilation Score: Originality and Postmodernism

Royal S. Brown: "What do you think about the use of already existing music in a film?"

Bernard Herrmann: "I think it's stupid. What's it got to do with the film? Nothing. Cover it with chocolate ice cream, that's about it!"[77]

Herrmann's skepticism about the compilation score represents the dominant position shared by many film music composers. A notorious case—probably the most controversial one—that infuriated many composers was Stanley Kubrick's replacement of Alex North's original score for *2001: A Space Odyssey* with the pre-existing music he had used for the temp-track,[78] such as Richard Strauss's tone poem *Also sprach Zarathustra*, Johann Strauss's *Blue Danube*, and György Ligeti's *Atmosphères*. Jerry Goldsmith, the Oscar-winning composer whose film scores include five *Star Trek* films, three *Rambo* films, and *Total Recall* described Kubrick's soundtrack as an "abominable misuse of music." "The use of the *Blue Danube* waltz," he continued, "was amusing for a moment but quickly became

---

75   Harris, "Twentieth-Century Farinelli," pp. 180–81.

76   Ibid., p. 186.

77   Brown, "Interviews: Bernard Herrmann," p. 291.

78   Temp-track is a soundtrack consisting of pre-existing music from various sources that is created for temporary use in early previews or screenings of a film before an original score is composed.

distracting because it is so familiar ... It is a mistake to force music into a film."[79] Goldsmith conducted the first commercial recording of North's original score, released by Varèse-Sarabande in 1993 (VSD 5400). In scholarly studies of film music, too, the focus had long been original scores: it is not until the beginning of the twenty-first century that the compilation scores began to draw scholarly attention, promoted by such studies as *Changing Tunes: The Use of Pre-existing Music in Film*, edited by Phil Powrie and Robynn Stilwell; Michal Grover-Friedlander's *Vocal Apparitions*; Roger Hillman's *Unsettling Scores*; Dean Duncan's *Charms That Soothe*; and Marcia Citron's *When Opera Meets Film*.[80] A seminal event that stimulated studies of pre-existing music in film was an international conference held at Stanford in 2003, entitled "Reviewing the Canon: Borrowed Music in Films," organized by Tobias Plebuch.

In spite of the rapidly growing body of studies of the compilation score, a group of scholars have adamantly given priority to the original score. A passage from the editorial introduction to the inaugural issue of *The Journal of Film Music* states, "[T]he *value* of original background music as a special art (and craft, i.e. film composing) is *relativized* (if not trivialized) when categorized along with music and uses of music from which it differs *sui generis*—namely the use of existing music." Although the author—the journal's editor—presents this passage in a hypothetical voice, the undertones of his positional essay underscore his privileging of the original score.[81] He also suggests that source music (i.e., diegetic music) should be excluded from film music.

> Indeed, composers and film makers alike (as in the case of *Rear Window*) have not infrequently used source music to create a mood or achieve a dramatic effect as an alternative to underscoring. But it is nonetheless arguable that creating a mood or achieving a dramatic effect with music is only a *necessary* but not *sufficient* condition for music in films to constitute film scoring, because by definition, underscoring is not source music.[82]

The tension between the defenders and detractors of the compilation score can be contextualized in modernist versus postmodernist concepts of originality. Fredric

---

[79]   Quoted in William Penn, "Music and Image: A Pedagogical Approach," *Indiana Theory Review* 11 (Spring/Fall 1990): 51.

[80]   Powrie and Stilwell, eds, *Changing Tunes*; Michal Grover-Friedlander, *Vocal Apparitions: The Attraction of Cinema to Opera* (Princeton, NJ: Princeton University Press, 2005); Hillman, *Unsettling Scores*; Dean Duncan, *Charms That Soothe: Classical Music and the Narrative Film* (New York: Fordham University Press, 2003); and Marcia Citron, *When Opera Meets Film* (Cambridge: Cambridge University Press, 2010).

[81]   William H. Rosar, "Film Music—What's in a Name?" *The Journal of Film Music* 1, no. 1 (2002): 14.

[82]   Ibid., p. 10.

Jameson considers the modernists' emphasis on originality to be rooted in their esteem for, or more precisely their aspiration to, uniqueness:

> The great modernisms were … predicated on the invention of a personal private style, as unmistakable as your fingerprint, as incomparable as your own body. But this means that the modernist aesthetic is in some way organically linked to the conception of a unique self and private identity, a unique personality and individuality, which can be expected to generate its own unique vision of the world and to forge its own unique, unmistakable style.[83]

Such poststructuralists as Michel Foucault and Roland Barthes have radically renovated the traditional notion of originality. In "The Death of the Author," a kind of poststructuralist manifesto, Barthes contends that the "text" is fundamentally a "tissue of quotations,"

> drawn from the innumerable centers of culture … the writer can only imitate a gesture that is always anterior, never original. His only power is to mix writings, to counter the ones with the others, in such a way as never to rest on any one of them. Did he wish to *express himself*, he ought at least to know that the inner "thing" he thinks to "translate" is itself only a ready-formed dictionary, its words only explainable through other words, and so on indefinitely.[84]

Barthes's specialized definition of the "text" needs to be clarified, for it is a central concept for his skepticism of originality. He differentiates "text" from "work": the meaning of the "work" is closed and fixed by the author, while a "text" is "not a line of words releasing a single "theological" meaning (the "message" of the Author-God) but a multi-dimensional space in which a variety of writings, none of them original, blend and clash."[85] The concept of the text is more thoroughly theorized in another article by Barthes, "From Work to Text." Using a semiologian's terminology, Barthes contrasts "work" with "text": "The work closes on a signified … The Text, on the contrary, practices the infinite deferment of the signified."[86]

One of the main reasons for avoiding pre-existing music on the soundtrack is that its own identity is so strong that it tends to distract the audience from concentrating on the film. In other words, it is too audible to be an "unheard melody"— Claudia Gorbman's metaphoric definition of film music based on the principle of "inaudibility" in conventional film scoring. Leonid Sabaneev, a composer, musicologist, and music critic, expressed this principle as follows:

---

[83]   Fredric Jameson, "Postmodernism and Consumer Society," in Hal Foster, ed., *The Anti-Aesthetic: Essays on Postmodern Culture* (Port Townsend, WA: Bay Press, 1983), p. 114.

[84]   Barthes, "The Death of the Author," p. 146.

[85]   Ibid.

[86]   Barthes, "From Work to Text," in *Image, Music, Text*, p. 158.

In general, music should understand that in the cinema it should nearly always remain in the background: it is, so to speak, a tonal figuration, the "left hand" of the melody on the screen, and it is a bad business when this left hand begins to creep into the foreground and obscure the melody.[87]

Royal S. Brown argues that in recent films from the postmodern period, music tends to stand as an "image in its own right" and as a kind of "parallel emotional/ aesthetic universe." What is important in this type of film music is the "ecstasy of musicality" rather than what music signifies as a sonic support for the filmic narrative. This changed role of film music can explain the increasing presence of pre-existing music on soundtracks since the 1960s,[88] for its strong audibility does not matter any more. Brown relates the "ecstasy of musicality" to the postmodern reversal of the hierarchical relationship between sign and referent at the semiotic level: what is privileged is the sign, not its referent, the material presence of the signifier rather than what it signifies.[89] Another source that can help in theorizing the non-referential use of film music is Hans Ulrich Gumbrecht's plea for an appreciation of the materiality of the signifier, not in place of but in addition to the decoding of the signified, which has long been privileged in Western intellectual history.[90] The musical privileging of the signifier over the signified is comparable to Andy Warhol's non-mimetic use of the body in such films as *Sleep* (1963) and *Kiss* (1963). In these films, images are excruciatingly repeated, accumulated, and exaggerated through a series of close-ups of sleeping bodies and kissing couples, and in this process Warhol's cinematic bodies are deprived of a signifying function.[91]

Codetta

In his editorial essay entitled "Film Studies in Musicology: Disciplinarity vs. Interdisciplinarity," William H. Rosar traces the term "film musicology" and provides his definition of it.[92] As with his earlier editorial essay in the inaugural

---

[87]   Leonid Sabaneev, *Music for the Films: A Handbook for Composers and Conductors*, trans. S.W. Pring (London: Pitman, 1935), p. 22; quoted in Gorbman, *Unheard Melodies: Narrative Film Music* (Bloomington: Indiana University Press, 1987), p. 76. Gorbman indicates the possibility that the quote could have been made by Sabaneev's translator.

[88]   See the Prologue for the statistics of opera excerpts on soundtracks.

[89]   Brown, *Overtones and Undertones*, p. 239.

[90]   Hans Ulrich Gumbrecht, *Production of Presence: What Meaning Cannot Convey* (Stanford, CA: Stanford University Press, 2004).

[91]   Steven Shaviro, *The Cinematic Body* (Minneapolis: University of Minnesota Press, 1993), p. 202.

[92]   William H. Rosar, "Film Studies in Musicology: Disciplinarity vs. Interdisciplinarity," *The Journal of Film Music* 2, nos. 2–4 (Winter 2009): 99–125.

volume of *The Journal of Film Music*, which I discussed above, this essay shows a strong skepticism about interdisciplinary approaches to film music studies. What Rosar means by interdisciplinary is not limited to a methodological perspective but encompasses the studies of film music by non-musicologists such as Claudia Gorbman, Caryl Flinn, and Kathryn Kalinak; Rosar even distinguishes musicologists from music theorists such as David Neumeyer and James Buhler. The main purpose of his disciplinary demarcation is to avoid crossing boundaries, to protect the discipline of musicology from interdisciplinary contamination. After summarizing some major (and favorable) reviews (or "testimonials," to use Rosar's expression) of Annette Davison's book *Hollywood Theory, Non-Hollywood Practice*,[93] Rosar alludes to a negative position on interdisciplinarity through a rhetorical question:

> Whether or not earlier research on film music "ignored" film studies, as Buhler claims, is debatable and depends upon what one considers to be "film studies," but what is not clear from these testimonials written for Davison's book is how exactly the work of film musicology stands in relationship to the methodologies of musicology as a discipline, and how it relates to other musicological work—except to say that it is perceived as occupying a "site" that crosses or a "space" between musicology, film studies, and cultural studies, and that it is comprised of scholars from those areas, not just musicologists. How then is it "musicology" if at the same time it occupies a "site" or "space" outside musicology?[94]

Rosar is not alone in showing a strong skepticism towards crossing the boundaries among various academic disciplines. His editorial essay echoes Martin Mueller's reaction to *Redrawing the Boundaries: The Transformation of English and American Literary Studies*, a collection edited by Stephen Greenblatt and Giles Gunn that maps out the postmodern, interdisciplinary trend in literature; Rosar's essay is also a plea for "the *re*-redrawing of the boundaries."[95] I do see, and even sympathize with, his reservations about the ethos of postmodernism—the danger of becoming "the culture of anything goes." Fredric Jameson, one of the most prominent scholars of postmodernism, described postmodern culture as "a statue without the eyeballs," meaning it lacks the critical stance of modernism.[96] But Rosar's disciplinary demarcation is sometimes ruthlessly uncompromising: "Buhler, a music theorist," "David Neumeyer (music theorist) and Caryl Flinn (film

---

[93]　Annette Davison, *Hollywood Theory, Non-Hollywood Practice: Cinema Soundtracks in the 1980s and 1990s* (Burlington, VT: Ashgate Publishing, 2004).

[94]　Rosar, "Film Studies in Musicology," p. 100.

[95]　Stephen Greenblatt and Giles Gunn, eds, *Rewarding the Boundaries: The Transformation of English and American Literary Studies* (New York: The Modern Language Association, 1992); Martin Mueller, "Redrawing the Boundaries? Skeptical Thoughts About Literary Studies," *The Centennial Review* 38, no. 3 (Fall 1994): 606.

[96]　Jameson, "Postmodernism and Consumer Society," p. 127.

scholar)," "cultural theorist-historian Lawrence Kramer's 'postmodern agenda' for musicology, and interdisciplinary music and media scholar Anahid Kassabian's expostulations about 'rethinking' musicology."[97] A more productive way of enriching a discipline would be a "disciplinary *collaboration*," as Jennifer Fleeger has argued,[98] by avoiding territorial antagonism against certain methodologies and instead acknowledging the merits of different methodologies and perspectives. As I have argued, imposing and insisting on a certain methodology as *the* definitive one has a danger of becoming intellectual totalitarianism. Or is such a position that advocates methodological pluralism ironically promoting another form of totalitarianism—being totalitarian by opposing totalitarianism?

---

[97] Rosar, "Film Studies in Musicology," passim. Lawrence Kramer is a professional composer whose official title at Fordham University is Professor of English and Music.

[98] Fleeger, "Opera, Jazz, and Hollywood's Conversion to Sound," p. 290.

Epilogue: An Ethnographic Postscript

I had the privilege of undertaking "field work" in Nashville during the last week of shooting for *Stoker*, Chan-wook Park's first Hollywood-sponsored film[1] and his first film that uses opera as soundtrack. My field work was intended to look at the movie-making as a musicologist, to paraphrase Hortense Powdermaker's book title.[2] After the final shooting was over on October 22, 2011, Chan-wook introduced me to Nicole Kidman, who plays the title role, Evelyn (Evie) Stoker. After shaking hands with Ms. Kidman, I introduced myself to her as a musicologist specializing in film music and opera. "Oh, really? How fantastic!" responded she with a sublime smile on her goddess-like face.[3]

Unlike Nicole Kidman as Anna in Jonathan Glazer's *Birth*, a still of which (Anna at the opera house) is used as the cover image of this book, Nicole as Evie in Park's *Stoker* hates opera, while her daughter India (Mia Wasikowska) is attracted to it. One morning, India is awakened by an opera aria coming from outside of her bedroom: Charlie (Matthew Goode), Evie's mysterious brother-in-law, is strolling under Indie's bedroom window, whistling "Stride la vampa," Azucena's signature aria from Verdi's *Il trovatore*.[4] That afternoon, Indie happens to hear the same aria from the radio, but Evie, irritated, turns off the radio.[5] "Stride la vampa" is heard one more time later in the film: Charlie whistles it when he is approaching Evie to murder her—another instance of opera in cinematic death and a strong evocation of the murder scene in Howard Hawks's *Scarface* (1932), in which the protagonist

---

[1]   Its production company is Fox Searchlight Pictures.

[2]   Hortense Powdermaker, *Hollywood the Dream Factory: An Anthropologist Looks at the Movie-Makers* (Boston: Little, Brown and Company, 1950). I'm grateful to William Rosar, who first introduced this book to me.

[3]   *Stoker* was premiered on January 20 at the Sundance Film Festival in 2013.

[4]   This aria is first heard as non-diegetic music in the scene in which India meets Charlie on the stairs of her house after her father's funeral at the beginning of the film. As Charlie leaves the house, Verdi's aria softly enters on the soundtrack as non-diegetic music and is connected to Charlie's diegetic whistling of the aria.

[5]   The singer in the recording is Viorica Cortez. The diegetic status of this aria is ambiguous at the beginning of the scene, as it is first heard when the camera is panning around the house from outside; when the camera finally zooms in the kitchen, it confirms the diegetic status of this aria by showing its sound source—a radio.

whistles an opera aria before he executes a murder.[6] "So now, you don't mind using "a cliché,"[7] Chan-wook?" I asked. A silent smile was his answer.

Fresco Opera Theatre's intriguing piece, *Ding Dong, the Diva's Dead* (2010), seems to be a theatrical enactment of the cliché of opera's kinship with cinematic death (Figure E.1). Premiered at Overture Center Playhouse in Madison, WI, in October of 2010, this imaginative work stages famous death scenes in opera as those in celebrated horror films. The company's advertisement of the work reads:

> Just when you thought it was safe to go to the opera. Dead divas, zombies, demonic possession, blood curdling screams with lots of comic relief. Fresco Opera Theatre is back with an evening of opera's death scenes reworked to settings inspired by cinema's most famous horror movies such as *Frankenstein* and *The Exorcist*.[8]

The mission of Fresco Opera Theatre is to "cultivate a new generation of opera lovers" by presenting opera "in a fresh accessible way." I am confident in predicting that an effective way of cultivating such a generation is through opera's engagement with cinema, and it is testified by the most recent work of the company: *The Good, The Bad, and The Divas*, the first "Spaghetti Western opera" with "real" Italian songs, premiered in September of 2012.[9] How "the divas" have replaced Sergio Leone's "the ugly" cannot be more tantalizing to me.

---

[6]   But in *Stoker*, it remains an attempted murder. Park's original plan was to use a different aria for Charlie's whistling: Manrico's "Di quella pira" from the same opera. But he made the change primarily for the purpose of the simplification of the soundtrack: that is, when a single aria is repeatedly used, its tune can be more easily recognizable for the film audience. Park told me that it might be a little too artificial for a coincidence that India hears the same aria from the radio on the same day, but he thinks that this unlikely coincidence can express the Verdian "fate" in the love between Charlie and Indie. There is a thematic parallel between *Il trovatore* and *Stoker*, love rivalry between the two brothers, which motivated Park's choice of the opera for his soundtrack. When I had a meeting with Park in March 2011 around the time the contract with Fox Searchlight for *Stoker* was about to be finalized, Park's original plan was to use some except from Mozart's *The Abduction from the Seraglio* and his intention for using opera was to symbolize Charlie Stoker's high-cultural taste. The composers of the original soundtrack of *Stoker* are Philip Glass, who wrote the diegetic piano music performed by India and Charlie, and Clint Mansell, whose music is used as non-diegetic background music (Mansell's score for Darren Aronofsky's 2010 film *Black Swan* was nominated for the Best Score Soundtrack for Visual Media at the 2012 Grammy Awards).

[7]   See Chapter 2 about Chan-wook Park's comments on using opera in a death scene.

[8]   www.frescooperatheatre.com/ding-dong-the-divas-dead.html (accessed 14 September 2010). An excerpt of this work is available as a YouTube clip: www.youtube.com/watch?v=rmsxIWaR76I (accessed 12 May 2012).

[9]   www.frescooperatheatre.com/the-good-the-bad-and-the-divas.html (accessed July 24, 2012). This website includes the trailer of the work.

Figure E.1   Fresco Opera Theatre's *Ding Dong, the Diva's Dead*

"The Metropolitan Opera: Live in HD" series, too, demonstrates opera industry's efforts to build a new and larger audience by engaging with cinema. In the Met's press release about the series, Peter Gelb, the Met's general manager, noted:

> The Met has launched an array of new initiatives that are designed to broaden the public appeal of opera. The company's new media partnerships and expanded union agreements provide unprecedented distribution opportunities and better ways to reach new audiences. The HD movie broadcasts provide a front row seat to the unique spectacle of live opera.[10]

By echoing the cliché phrase used in the new movie advertisement, the heading of the Met's press release, "'Metropolitan Opera: Live in HD' *Now Playing at a Theater Near You*" (italics added), stresses its affinity with cinema. In his announcement of the Met series, Tom Galley, chief operations and technology officer of National CineMedia (the Met's US cinema partner for the series), particularly addressed its association with "Hollywood":

---

[10]   Peter Gelb, quoted in "'Metropolitan Opera: Live in HD' Now Playing at a Theater Near You," The Metropolitan Opera's press release, November 15, 2006, www.metoperafamily.org/metopera/news/press/detail.aspx?id=2719 (accessed 7 February 2012). Although there are other venues for this series, such as arts centers and college campuses, commercial movie theaters have been the primary venue.

Our theaters have always presented the best that Hollywood offers, and we are
excited to be able to bring U. S. audiences the best in opera and other areas of
arts and entertainment through the technology of our Digital Content Network.[11]

"The Met: Live in HD" series was inaugurated with Julie Taymor's English
production of Mozart's *The Magic Flute* on December 30, 2006, the year of the
250th anniversary of the composer's birth. It seems that this anniversary year
stimulated the film industry's abduction of Mozart from the opera theater to the
movie theater, as the release of a series of Mozart-related films has been remarkable
since 2006. Kenneth Branagh's *The Magic Flute* (2006) is a liberal cinematic
production of Mozart's opera (i.e., an "opera-film" such as Joseph Losey's *Don
Giovanni* [1979]). An abridged English version like Taymor's Met production,
Branagh's film transports Emanuel Schikaneder's original setting of the story to
the period of World War I: Tamino is a soldier and he is already married to Pamina
at the beginning of the film; and Papageno is a man who uses his underground
pigeons to detect poison gas; Sarastro is in charge of a field hospital, who wishes
to protect world peace; and the Three Ladies appear as hospital nurses. Most of
the characters are played by classically trained singers: Joseph Kaiser as Tamino
and René Pape as Sarastro, for instance. *Magic Flute Diaries* (2008), directed by
Kevin Sullivan, centers around the opera singer Tom/Tamino (Warren Christie),
who is cast in the leading role of Mozart's opera in a new production in Salzburg
and falls in love with a mysterious diva, Masha (Mireille Asselin), who performs
Pamina. Although Sullivan's film is not an opera-film, its soundtrack is replete with
Mozart's *The Magic Flute*. Carlos Saura, the director of *Carmen* (1983), the first
film in his *Flamenco Trilogy*, created another Mozart-related film, *I, Don Giovanni*
(2009). It is a fictionalized biopic of Lorenzo Da Ponte (Lorenzo Balducci), and
Mozart (Lino Guanciale) appears as a secondary character. The main event of the
plot, the making of *Don Giovanni*, is presented from the viewpoint of the librettist
and the opera is portrayed as a reflection of da Ponte's own life, and Mozart's
music permeates the soundtrack.[12]

In light of the process of the mutation of opera's cultural status in the United
States, as examined by Lawrence Levin, cinema's aggressive abduction of Mozart
from opera—the metaphor by which I mean opera's increasing engagement
with cinema whether as soundtrack or "Live in HD"—can be regarded as a
manifestation of the de-sacralization of opera. And its de-sacralization might be a

---

[11]   Tom Galley quoted in ibid.

[12]   René Féret's *Mozart's Sister* (2010) is another Mozart-inspired film. Like
Saura's *Don Giovanni*, it is a liberal biopic, whose characters include Mozart but
whose protagonist is Nannerl Mozart, the composer's elder sister, who was an
accomplished singer, violinist, and harpsichordist. The plot focuses on Nannerl's
musicality, her frustrated attempt at composition, and her suffering from gender
discrimination. In Féret's soundtrack, however, Mozart's music is minimal;
instead, Marie-Jeanne Serero's original film score is dominant.

globalizing phenomenon, as I have heard about the strong popularity of the Met's "Live in HD" series in the foreign countries I'm familiar with, such as the UK and South Korea, and I have found the use of opera as soundtrack to be surprisingly accelerated in recent Korean cinema. Like in Hollywood films, the range of the genres opera is imported to is wide. In Sang-soo Im's melodrama *The Housemaid* (2010), "La mamma morta" from Umberto Giordano's *Andrea Chénier* serves as a sonic emblem for upper-class people. In Jee-woon Kim's serial-killer film, *I Saw the Devil* (2010), a cannibalistic serial killer plays Carmen's "Habanera" from a boombox as a kind of "background music" to accompany his dissection of a living female victim.[13] Cheol-Su Park's mystery *301, 302* (1995) joins Jonathan Demme's *Philadelphia* in using opera to signify gayness, as Violetta's aria "Ah, fors' e lui" from Verdi's *La traviata* suggests a subtle homoerotic emotion between the two female protagonists, who are neighbors in a condominium: Yun (Sin-Hye Hwang), an anorexic writer who lives in room no. 302, and Song (Eun-Jin Pang), a housewife living in room no. 301, who is obsessed with cooking and feeding Yun with what she cooks.[14] Perhaps, opera's evocation of gayness in film has become a cliché beyond Hollywood. In *Strawberry and Chocolate* (1993), a Cuban film co-directed by Tomás Gutiérrez Alea and Juan Carlos Tabío, Maria Callas's voice functions as a fetish for the film's gay protagonist, Diego (Jorge Perugorría).

Another interesting phenomenon of the de-sacralization of opera, although not directly connected to film, is the ITV show called "Popstar to Operastar" in the UK. It is an opera-singing competition among celebrity pop singers, the first season of which started in January of 2010. There are eight participants in each season, and each participant is coached by a professional opera singer. The competitions are live performances in front of an audience in a television studio, whose staging always includes a neon-lit signboard saying "OPERA." The show is also televised live. The judges consist of such international opera, crossover, or rock singers as Rolando Villazón, Katherine Jenkins, and Meat Loaf. The winners of the first and second series were Darius Campbell and Joe McElderry, respectively. The show includes special performances, such as a duet by a contestant and a judge, in addition to the singing for competition (Figure E.2a). Like the phenomenon of opera-as-soundtrack, the British "Popstar to Operastar" also shows a glimpse of globalization, having been imported to Canada in a similar TV show "Bathroom Divas: So You Want to Be an Opera Star?" and to South Korea in "Opera Star" (Figure E.2b).[15]

---

13 Both titles are available from Netflix for streaming.

14 The ending of the film is creepy: Yun offers her body as an ingredient for Song's cooking. When a policeman visits Song to investigate Yun's disappearance, Song is eating what she has just cooked with a new ingredient.

15 In these TV shows of opera-singing contests, the songs chosen for competition are not limited to opera arias but extended to popular tunes such as Agustín Lara's "Granada" in the first series of "Popstar to Operastar" in 2010, and Lucio Dalla's "Caruso" in the 2011

(a)

(b)

Figure E.2   (a) Darius Campbell singing "The Impossible Dream" with Rolando
              Villazón as a special performance during the final competition of the
              2010 season of "Popstar to Operastar"; (b) Ki-Yong Park, the winner
              of the 2012 season of "Opera Star," singing "Una voce poco fa"[16]

Like the Met's "Live in HD" series, "Popstar to Operastar" and its sister shows
in Canada and South Korea are not intended for a high-cultural audience, for
whom opera is a sacralized product, but an effort to bring opera to the general
public by grafting it onto popular culture. Myleene Klass, a host of "Popstar to
Operastar," noted: "We're not here to please the purists. They are not going to like
this show at all. They don't like there being a crossover with the mainstream or
even the term 'pop opera.'"[17] One of the judges in the same program, Katherine
Jenkins, confirmed the show's intent to challenge the high cultural status of opera:

competition of "Opera Star." These popular tunes are sung in "operatic" singing style in the
competition. "Caruso" is well known for Dalla's duet with Luciano Pavarotti.

[16]   Park's winning song was "Caro nome" from Verdi's *Rigoletto*.

[17]   "Popstar to Operastar Gets Set for Primetime," *STV Entertainment*, January 15,
2010. http://entertainment.stv.tv/tv/150782-popstar-to-operastar-a-flop (accessed September
14, 2012).

"Core critics will not be happy but then they don't have to watch it. They're not going to be happy when you make something accessible to the masses."[18] And in Jenkins's purist "core critics," one can definitely include Stravinsky and Schoenberg, considering the former composer's claim that "the mass adds nothing to art" and for the latter's conviction that something "for the masses" such as film is incapable of functioning as "pure art."[19]

For a musicologist specializing in the opera–cinema encounter, the globalizing phenomenon of the de-sacralization of opera's cultural status—opera's intimate rather than intimidating relationship with the masses—is an exhilarating benefit in that a variety of people in diverse areas can be your informants and supporters. It was the person who was sitting next to me on the plane from Charlotte, NC, to Rome on June 29, 2012 that informed me of the opera excerpts in *The Iron Lady*. During our short greeting conversation after boarding, she discovered my profession and the areas of my specialization along with the purpose of my trip to Rome—to present a paper at the 19th congress of the International Musicological Society (and my paper was indeed related to the cultural status of opera and film music). While she was watching a movie on the individual screen, which I later found to be *The Iron Lady*, she poked me, saying, "Here is another example for your research." It was "Casta diva," a recording by Maria Callas. Bellini's aria is first heard in the film as an un-visualized (i.e., off-screen) diegetic performance of *Norma* that the young Margaret Thatcher (Alexandra Roach) and her husband-to-be Denis (Harry Lloyd) are watching at an opera house. The aria comes back as non-diegetic music in the film's climactic scene when Thatcher announces her resignation: after her announcement, she is slowly walking down on the corridor, the sides of which are decorated with red roses; for a brief moment of the sequence, diegetic sounds are silenced, submerged in Callas's voice—the moment to suggest the most enhanced emotional state in the film and the moment when Thatcher is identified with the opera's heroine Norma, the high-priestess of the Celts, the "chaste diva."

I asked my informant if she was conversant with opera and if she liked "Casta diva." Her answer was negative. "But at least I was able to tell the song was from an opera," she remarked, "because operatic singing is so distinctive; I mean, so unnatural." In this book, I restricted my research to strictly opera, but perhaps, inquiries into opera as soundtrack can be extended to "operatic" songs, such as Maria Callas's rendition of Heinrich Proch's "Deh torna mio bene" in Werner

---

18   Ibid. Many of the performances of "Popstar to Operastar" are available as YouTube clips. For Darius Campbell's duet with the judge Rolando Villazón as a special performance at the final competition of the first series, see www.youtube.com/watch?v=kAvSjYEoRZ8 (accessed September 14, 2012); for "Nessun dorma" sung by Joe McElderry, the winner of the second series, see www.youtube.com/watch?v=2xG1N51OfpM (accessed September 14, 2012).

19   For details, see Chapter 6, pp. 154–5.

Schroeter's last film *Nuit de chien* (2008),[20] for the distinctiveness of "operatic" singing—its unnaturalness; that is, the geno-song of the voice[21]—engenders similar effects. In fact, the person who introduced Schroeter's film to me, who is a professional musician, a violinist, mistook Proch's song for an opera aria, a motivation for him to recommend the film for my research.[22]

The methodology I adopted in this book for exploring opera's versatile functions as soundtrack is obviously interdisciplinary. Although the last chapter reveals my serious reservation about Bill Rosar's adamant advocacy of "disciplinarity" against "interdisciplinarity" (it might sound like my version of Tarantino's *Kill Bill*), I do share some of his frustrations with interdisciplinary methodology and my admiration for the depth of his knowledge and analytical vigor has never been diminished in spite of our different methodological preferences. I criticized Paul Merkley's methodological "position" in the same chapter, but there is no doubt that his article about Kubrick's *2001* is a magnum opus that more than deserves the ASCAP Deems Taylor Award. I am immensely indebted to Bill Rosar for the preparation of this manuscript and my scholarship in general: he is the person who awakened me to the joy of an anthropological investigator beyond that of an armchair scholar.

It was in the summer of 2005 when I first conducted archival research in the Hollywood areas. Bill connected me to the music librarians of the major film studios. Paramount was the first studio that I visited. When Bob Bornstein, the then music librarian, brought me the music files of *Foul Play*, how touched I was to see the handwritten notes by Ruby Raksin, younger brother of David Raksin, on the conductor's score (Ruby was the orchestrator of the soundtrack). My feeling of being privileged was no less than how I felt to see Handel's handwriting in a document that I examined at the British Library during my archival studies for an essay on Gérard Corbiau's *Farinelli* film. On my way out of the music library, I strolled around Paramount studios and I did touch the Bronson Gate, wishing for good luck on this manuscript.[23]

---

[20] *Nuit de chien* is the original title. Its German title is *Diese Nacht*.

[21] For detailed discussion of geno-song vs. pheno-song, please see Chapter 1.

[22] In the CD version of Léo Delibes's opera *Lakmé*, featuring Mado Robin, Proch's song is included as a bonus track, along with two arias from Bellini's *La sonnambula*. See *Mado Robin sings "Lakmé,"* Decca Music Group Limited, 2005. It is a digitized version of the 1952 original Decca recording of the opera.

[23] The name "Bronson" in the Bronson Gate at the Paramount studio, located on the corner of Bronson Street and Melrose Avenue, was the inspiration when Charles Bronson changed his original surname from Buchinsky to Bronson, respecting the suggestion of his agent who was worried that his exotic Eastern European family name might be an obstacle for the advancement of his career. Since the actor became a celebrity movie star after the change of his surname, there has been a superstitious belief that touching the Bronson Gate would bring you good luck.

On July 27, 2005, I had lunch with Bill at Musso & Frank Grill at 6667 Hollywood Boulevard—a historic restaurant built in 1919, frequented by many Hollywood celebrities, including Charlie Chaplin, Humphrey Bogart, and the Warner brothers. The restaurant is still popular among today's movie stars, some of whom even have their favorite tables: table 24 for Tom Selleck and table 28 for Al Pacino, for instance. When I made a reservation for lunch with Bill, I wanted Al Pacino's favorite table but it was already booked. Our conversation over lunch was long and full of argument—no wonder that we were talking about disciplinarity vs. interdisciplinarity!—and we were literally kicked out of the restaurant because it was closing at 2 p.m. We continued our argument on the street until our faces were almost cooked by the sun: Bill got a parking ticket but not me, although my parking meter was also expired (Bill's parking ticket was more expensive than the lunch I treated for him!). Although we disagreed on many things, we reconfirmed and appreciated one thing: our shared passion for music, movie, and movie music.

It was Cronenberg's *M. Butterfly* that inspired my inquiries into opera as soundtrack. I saw it Saturday evening during the AMS weekend in Montreal in 1993. I went to the movie without knowing anything about its story and during the last sequence of the film—M. (Mister) Butterfly's operatic suicide—I was literally transfixed, just like the Shawshank prisoners in Darabont's film. That was the moment when Berlioz's description of the power of music came to my mind:

> I feel a delicious pleasure in which the *reasoning* faculty has no share; the habit of analysis arises spontaneously later and brings forth admiration; … my arteries throb violently; tears, which ordinarily signal the end of the paroxysm, often only indicate an advancing condition that is far from having reached its peak. In such cases, there are spasmodic muscular contractions, a trembling of all the limbs, a *total numbness of feet and hands*, a partial paralysis of the optical and auditory nerves; I cannot see, I barely hear; vertigo …[24]

But unlike in Berlioz's case, what gave me "vertigo" was neither Puccini's music alone nor Jeremy Irons's powerful onscreen image alone, but opera's presence in cinematic death—bloody, grotesque, and violent yet poetic.

Opera's de-sacralization through its frequent presence as soundtrack must be a deplorable phenomenon for some people, definitely for the Korean diva—one of the most renowned and significant deities in the history of opera in Korea—whom I interviewed late September of 1977 when I was preparing an article about Maria Callas's death for my high school's journal (she died on September 16, 1977). The diva remarked that Callas's demise was a great loss for the whole of humanity, whereas Elvis Presley's death, which happened to be exactly a month before Callas's *Götterdämmerung*, was ignorable. I was then a classical-music supremacist, as were most of the teenagers trained in classical music in South

---

[24]   Hector Berlioz, quoted in Piero Weiss and Richard Taruskin, eds., *Music in the Western World: A History in Documents* (New York: Schirmer Books, 1984), p. 350.

Korea at that time, and even for me, there was something wrong in the Korean diva's comments on the pop divo's death and her operatic elitism. When I saw the Elvis impersonator singing Verdi's "La donna è mobile" in the *Rigoletto* episode of Don Boyd's *Aria* (1987), I couldn't help recollecting my interview with that Korean diva, whose own *Götterdämmerung* coincided with the year of the birth of my article on Boyd's *Aria*. Now that opera is a conspicuous inhabitant of soundtrack and even the Metropolitan operas are available at "a theater near you," as the Met advertises for its "Live in HD" series, it might be time for Michael Daugherty, or someone else, to compose a sequel to "Elvis Everywhere": "Opera Everywhere"—everywhere because movie theaters are everywhere. I hope that *Opera as Soundtrack*—a long journey from opera as drama, long in terms of the distance between opera's status as drama and soundtrack—will stimulate new debates in exploring the opera–cinema encounter, and, in so doing, serve the goals of Ashgate's Interdisciplinary Studies in Opera series.

Select Bibliography

Abbate, Carolyn. "Music—Drastic or Gnostic?" *Critical Inquiry* 30, no. 3 (Spring 2004): 505–36.

—— *In Search of Opera*. Princeton, NJ: Princeton University Press, 2001.

—— "Opera; or, the Envoicing of Women." In *Musicology and Difference: Gender and Sexuality in Music Scholarship*, ed. Ruth A. Solie, 225–58. Berkeley: University of California Press, 1993.

—— *Unsung Voices: Opera and Musical Narrative in the Nineteenth Century*. Princeton, NJ: Princeton University Press, 1991.

Abel, Sam. *Opera in the Flesh: Sexuality in Operatic Performance*. Boulder, CO: Westview Press, 1996.

Adorno, Theodor. *In Search of Wagner*, trans. Rodney Livingstone. London: NLB, 1981.

Adorno, Theodor, and Hanns Eisler. *Composing for the Films*. 2nd ed. With a new introduction by Graham McCann. London: The Athlone Press, 1994.

Altman, Rick. *Silent Film Sound*. New York: Columbia University Press, 2004.

Altman, Rick, and Richard Abel, eds. *The Sounds of Early Cinema*. Bloomington: Indiana University Press, 2001.

Altman, Rick, ed. *Sound Theory Sound Practice*. New York: Routledge, 1992.

Andres, Geoff. "Interview with Wong Kar-Wai." *Time Out*, January 5, 2005, 22–3.

Antheil, George. "An Interview with George Antheil." *Film Music Notes* 10, no. 2 (November–December 1950): 4–5.

Ariès, Philippe. *The Western Attitude towards Death: From the Middle Ages to the Present*, trans. P. M. Ranum. Baltimore, MD: Johns Hopkins University Press, 1976.

Arnheim, Rudolph. *Film as Art*. Berkeley: University of California Press, 1957.

Auslander, Philip. *Liveliness: Performance in a Mediatized Culture*. New York: Routledge, 1999.

Austern, Linda. "Sing Againe Syren: The Female Musician and Sexual Enchantment in Elizabethan Life and Literature." *Renaissance Quarterly* 42, no. 3 (Autumn 1989): 420–48.

Balázs, Béla. *Theory of the Film: Character and Growth of a New Art*. New York: Dover Publications, 1970.

Barthes, Roland. *Music, Image, Text*, trans. Stephen Heath. New York: Hill and Wang, 1977.

Bergeron, Katherine. "The Castrato as History." *Cambridge Opera Journal* 8, no. 2 (July 1996): 167–84.

Bergman, Ingmar. *The Magic Lantern: An Autobiography*, trans. Joan Tate. New York: Viking, 1988.

Biddlecombe, George. "The Construction of a Cultural Icon: The Case of Jenny Lind." In *Nineteenth-Century British Music Studies 3*, ed. Bennett Zon, 45–64. Aldershot: Ashgate, 2006.

Birringer, Johannes. *Theatre, Theory, Postmodernism*. Bloomington: Indiana University Press, 1991.

Bordwell, David, and Noël Carroll, eds. *Post-Theory: Reconstructing Film Studies*. Madison: University of Wisconsin Press, 1996.

Bradley, Edwin M. *The First Hollywood Sound Shorts, 1926–1931*. Jefferson, NC and London: McFarland, 2005.

Branstetter, Leah. "Angels and Arctic Monkeys: A Study of Pop-Opera Crossover." MM thesis, University of Cincinnati, 2009.

—— "Neoclassical Stravinsky Meets Classic Hollywood." Term paper for the Musicology Seminar, "Neoclassical Stravinsky." University of Cincinnati, December 2007.

Brecht, Bertolt. *Brecht on Theatre: The Development of an Aesthetic*, ed. and trans. John Willett. New York: Hill and Wang, 1964.

Brown, Royal S. *Overtones and Undertones: Reading Film Music*. Berkeley and Los Angeles: University of California Press, 1994.

Brunette, Peter. *Wong Kar-Wai*. Urbana and Champaign: University of Illinois Press, 2005.

Buhler, Jim, Caryl Flinn, and David Neumeyer. *Music and Cinema*. Hanover, NH and London: Wesleyan University Press, 2000.

Burr, Ty. "Wong's *2046* is a Mind-Altering Cocktail, Perfectly Blended." *Boston Globe*, August 19, 2005.

Camhi, Leslie. " Interview with Wong Kar-Wai." *New York Times*, January 28, 2001, Section 2, 11.

Cross, Jonathan. *Harrison Birtwistle: Man, Mind, Music*. Ithaca, NY: Cornell University Press, 2000.

Cavell, Stanley. *Cavell on Film*, ed. William Rothman. Albany, NY: State University of New York, 2005.

—— *A Pitch of Philosophy*. Cambridge, MA: Harvard University Press, 1984.

Chion, Michel. *The Voice in Cinema*, ed. and trans. Claudia Gorbman. New York: Columbia University Press, 1999.

—— *Audio-Vision: Sound On Screen*, trans. Claudia Gorbman. New York: Columbia University Press, 1994.

Cook, Nicholas. *Analysing Musical Multimedia*. Oxford: Oxford University Press, 1998.

Chua, Daniel K.L. "Listening to the Self: *The Shawshank Redemption* and the Technology of Music." *19th-Century Music* 34, no. 3 (Spring 2011): 341–55.

—— *Absolute Music and the Construction of Meaning*. Cambridge: Cambridge University Press, 1999.

Citron, Marcia J. "The Operatics of Detachment: *Tosca* in the James Bond Film *Quantum of Solace*." *19th-Century Music* 34, no. 3 (2011): 316–40.

—— *When Opera Meets Film*. Cambridge: Cambridge University Press, 2010.

—— *Opera on Screen*. New Haven, CT: Yale University Press, 2000.

—— "A Night at the Cinema: Zeffirelli's *Otello* and the Genre of Film-Opera." *Musical Quarterly* 78, no. 4 (Winter 1994): 700–741.

Clément, Catherine. *Opera, or the Undoing of Women*, trans. Betsy Wing. Minneapolis: University of Minnesota Press, 1988.

Crafton, Donald. *The Talkies: American Cinema's Transition to Sound 1926–1931*. Vol. 4 of *History of the American Cinema*, ed. Charles Harpole. Berkeley: University of California Press, 1997.

Daiken, Melanie. "Notes on Goehr's *Triptych*." In *The Music of Alexander Goehr*, ed. Bayan Northcott. London: Schott, 1980.

Davison, Annette. *Hollywood Theory, Non-Hollywood Practice: Cinema Soundtracks in the 1980s and 1990s*. Burlington, VT: Ashgate, 2004.

Doane, Mary Ann. *The Desire to Desire: The Woman's Film of the 1940s*. Bloomington: Indiana University Press, 1987.

—— "The Voice in Cinema: The Articulation of Body and Space." *Yale French Studies*, 60 (1980): 33–50.

Dolar, Mladen. *A Voice and Nothing More*. Cambridge, MA: The MIT Press, 2006.

—— "The Object Voice." In *Gaze and Voice as Love Objects*, ed. Renata Salecl and Slavoj Žižek, 7–31. Durham, NC: Duke University Press, 1996.

Dunn, Leslie C., and Nancy A. Jones, eds. *Embodied Voices: Representing Female Vocality in Western Culture*. Cambridge: Cambridge University Press, 1994.

Dunn, Leslie C. "Ophelia's Songs in *Hamlet*: Music, Madness, and the Feminine." In *Embodied Voices: Representing Female Vocality in Western Culture*, ed. Leslie C. Dunn and Nancy A. Jones, 50–64. Cambridge: Cambridge University Press, 1994.

Farmer, James Clark. "Opera and the New German Cinema: Between Distance and Fascination (Alexander Kluge, Werner Schroeter, Hans-Jürgen Syberberg)." PhD dissertation, University of Iowa, 2003.

Fleeger, Jennifer Lynn. "Opera, Jazz, and Hollywood's Conversion to Sound." PhD dissertation, University of Iowa, 2009.

Flinn, Caryl. *The New German Cinema: Music History, and the Matter of Style*. Berkeley: University of California, 2004.

—— *Strains of Utopia: Gender, Nostalgia, and Hollywood Film Music*. Princeton, NJ: Princeton University Press, 1992.

Fischer, Lucy. "*Applause*: The Visual and Acoustic Landscape." In *Sound and the Cinema: The Coming of Sound to American Film*, ed. Evan William Cameron. Pleasantville, NY: Redgrave Publishing, 1980.

Franke, Lars. "*The Godfather Part III*: Film, Opera, and the Generation of Meaning." In *Changing Tunes: The Use of Pre-Existing Music in Film*, ed. Phil Powrie and Robynn Stilwell, 31–45. Burlington, VT: Ashgate, 2006.

Gabbard, Krin. *Jammin' at the Margins: Jazz and the American Cinema*. Chicago, IL: University of Chicago Press, 1996.

Gallagher, Lowell. "Jenny Lind and the Voice of America." In *En Travesti: Women, Gender Subversion, Opera*, ed. Corinne E. Blackmer and Patricia Juliana Smith, 190–215. New York: Columbia University, 1995.

Garber, Marjorie. *Vested Interests: Cross-Dressing and Cultural Anxiety*. New York: Harper Collins, 1993.

Goehr, Lydia. *The Quest for Voice: Music, Politics, and the Limits of Philosophy*. Berkeley: University of California Press, 1998.

Goldmark, Daniel. *Tunes for 'Toons: Music and the Hollywood Cartoon*. Berkeley: University of California Press, 2005.

Goldmark, Daniel, Lawrence Kramer, and Richard Leppert, eds. *Beyond the Soundtrack: Representing Music in Cinema*. Berkeley: University of California Press, 2007.

Goldmark, Daniel, and Yuval Taylor, eds. *The Cartoon Music Book*. Chicago: A Cappella Book, 2002.

Goldsmith, Melissa Ursula Dawn. "Alban Berg's Filmic Music: Intentions and Extensions of the Film Music Interlude in the Opera *Lulu*." PhD dissertation, Louisiana State University, 2002.

Gorbman, Claudia. "Music in *The Piano*." In *Jane Campion's "The Piano,"* ed. Harriet Margolis, 42–58. Cambridge: Cambridge University Press, 2000.

—— *Unheard Melodies: Narrative Film Music*. Bloomington: Indiana University Press, 1987.

Goyios, Charalampos. "Living Life as an Opera Lover: On the Uses of Opera as Musical Accompaniment in Woody Allen's *Match Point*." *Senses of Cinema* 40 (2006). http://archive.sensesofcinema.com/contents/06/40/match-point. html (accessed August 19, 2010).

Grover-Friedlander, Michal. "The Afterlife of Maria Callas's Voice." In *Operatic Afterlives*. New York: Zone Books, 2011.

—— *Vocal Apparitions: The Attraction of Cinema to Opera*. Princeton, NJ: Princeton University Press, 2005.

—— "*Phantom of the Opera*: The Lost Voice of Opera in Silent Film." *Cambridge Opera Journal* 11, no. 2 (July 1999): 179–92.

Gumbrecht, Hans Ulrich. *Production of Presence: What Meaning Cannot Convey*. Stanford, CA: Stanford University Press, 2004.

Gunning, Tom. "The Cinema of Attractions: Early Film, Its Spectator and the Avant-Garde." In *Early Film*, ed. Thomas Elsaesser and Adam Barker. London: British Film Institute, 1989.

Günther, Renate. *Marguerite Duras*. Manchester and New York: Manchester University Press, 2002.

Hamm, Charles. *Music in the New World*. New York: W.W. Norton, 1983.

Harris, Ellen. "Twentieth-Century Farinelli." *The Musical Quarterly* 81, no. 2 (Summer 1997): 180–89.

Hillman, Roger. *Unsettling Scores: German Film, Music, and Ideology*. Bloomington: Indiana University Press, 2005.

Hunter, Mary. "Opera *In* Film: Sentiment and Wit, Feeling and Knowing: *The Shawshank Redemption* and *Prizzi's Honor*." In *Between Opera and Cinema*, ed. Jeongwon Joe and Rose M. Theresa, 93–120. New York: Routledge, 2002.

Hutcheon, Linda, and Michael Hutcheon. *Opera: The Art of Dying*. Cambridge, MA: Harvard University Press, 2004.

—— *Opera: Desire, Disease, Death*. Lincoln and London: University of Nebraska Press, 1996.

Huyssen, Andreas. *After the Great Divide: Modernism, Mass Culture, Postmodernism*. Bloomington: Indiana University Press, 1986.

Inglis, Ian, ed. *Popular Music and Film*. London and New York: Wallflower Press, 2003.

Jameson, Fredric. *Postmodernism or the Cultural Logic of Late Capitalism*. Durham: Duke University Press, 1991.

Joe, Jeongwon. "Reconsidering *Amadeus*: Mozart as Film Music." In *Changing Tunes: The Use of Pre-Existing Music in Film*, ed. Phil Powrie and Robynn Stilwell, 57–73. Aldershot: Ashgate, 2006.

—— "Hans-Jürgen Syberberg's *Parsifal*: The Staging of Dissonance in the Fusion of Opera and Film." *Music Research Forum* 13 (1998): 1–21.

—— "Opera on Film, Film in Opera: Postmodern Implications of the Cinematic Influence on Opera." PhD dissertation, Northwestern University, 1998.

——, and Sander L. Gilman, eds. *Wagner and Cinema*. Bloomington: Indiana University Press, 2010.

——, and Rose M. Theresa, eds. *Between Opera and Cinema*. New York: Routledge, 2002.

Jost, François. "The Voices of Silence." In *The Sounds of Early Cinema*, ed. Rick Altman and Richard Abel. Bloomington: Indiana University Press, 2001, pp. 48–56.

Kalinak, Kathryn. *Settling the Score: Music and the Classical Hollywood Film*. Madison: University of Wisconsin Press, 1992.

Kassabian, Anahid. *Hearing Film: Tracking Identifications in Contemporary Hollywood Film Music*. New York: Routledge, 2001.

Kauffmann, Stanley. "Stanley Kauffmann on Films: Scene Change." *The New Republic*, January 30, 2006.

—— "The Abduction from the Theater: Mozart Opera on Film." *Yale Review* 1 (January 1993): 92–104.

Kerman, Joseph. *Opera as Drama*. New and revised ed. Berkeley: University of California Press, 1988.

Kivy, Peter. "Music in the Movies: A Philosophical Inquiry." In *Music, Language, and Cognition*, 62–87. Oxford: Oxford University Press, 2007.

Koestenbaum, Wayne. *The Queen's Throat: Opera, Homosexuality, and the Mystery of Desire*. New York: Poseidon Press, 1993.

Kramer, Lawrence. "Music, Metaphor and Metaphysics." *The Musical Times* 145 (Autumn 2004): 5–18.

—— *Classical Music and Postmodern Knowledge*. Berkeley: University of California Press, 1995.

Laing, Heather. "Wandering Minds and Anchored Bodies: Music, Gender and Emotion in Melodrama and the Woman's Film." PhD dissertation, University of Warwick, 2000.

Lastra, James. *Sound Technology and the American Cinema: Perception, Representation, Modernity*. New York: Columbia University Press, 2000.

Lawrence, Amy. *Echo and Narcissus: Women's Voices in Classical Hollywood Cinema*. Berkeley, University of California Press, 1991.

Lee, Nathan. "Bleeding Men and the Women Who Love Them." *New York Sun*, August 5, 2005.

Leonardi, Susan J., and Rebecca A. Pope. *The Diva's Mouth: Body, Voice, Prima Donna Politics*. New Brunswick, NJ: Rutgers University Press, 1996.

Levin, David J. "Is There a Text in This Libido?" In *Between Opera and Cinema*, ed. Jeongwon Joe and Rose M. Theresa, 121–32. New York: Routledge, 2002.

—— *Richard Wagner, Fritz Lang and the Niebelungen*. Princeton, NJ: Princeton University Press, 2000.

Levine, Lawrence. *Highbrow/Lowbrow: The Emergence of Cultural Hierarchy in America*. Cambridge, MA: Harvard University Press, 1990.

Levinson, Jerrold. "Film Music and Narrative Agency." In *Post-Theory: Reconstructing Film Studies*, ed. David Bordwell and Noël Carroll, 248–82. Madison: University of Wisconsin Press, 1996.

Liebman, Roy. *Vitaphone Films: A Catalogue of the Features and Shorts*. Jefferson, NC and London: McFarland, 2003.

Lindenberger, Herbert. *Situating Opera: Period, Genre, Reception*. Cambridge: Cambridge University Press, 2010.

—— "Why (What? How? If?) Opera Studies?" In *Operatic Migrations: Transforming Works and Crossing Boundaries*, ed. Roberta Montemorra Marvin and Downing A. Thomas. Aldershot, England and Burlington, VT: Ashgate, 2006.

—— "From Opera to Postmodernity: On Genre, Style, Institutions." In *Postmodern Genres*, ed. Marjorie Perloff. Norman: University of Oklahoma Press, 1989.

Link, Stan. "Going Gently: Contemplating Silences and Cinematic Death." In *Silence, Music, Silent Music*, ed. Nicky Losseff and Jenny Doctor. Aldershot: Ashgate, 2007.

Locke, Ralph P. "Music Lovers, Patrons, and the 'Sacralization' of Culture in America." *19th-Century Music* 17, no. 2 (Fall 1993): 149–73.

Ludlam, Charles. *Galas: A Modern Tragedy*, in *The Mystery of Irma Vep and Other Plays*. New York: Theatre Communications Group, 2001.

Martin, Philip. "Perplexing Beauty is the Lure to *2046*." *Arkansas Democrat Gazette*, October 7, 2005.

McClary, Susan. *Feminine Endings: Music, Gender, and Sexuality*. Minneapolis: University of Minnesota Press, 1991.

—— Afterword to Jacques Attali's *Noise: The Political Economy of Music*, trans. Fredric Jameson. Minneapolis: University of Minnesota Press, 1985.

McDonald, Keiko. *Japanese Classical Theater in Film*. London and Toronto, ON: Associate University Presses, 1994.

Merkley, Paul A. "'Stanley Hates This But I Like It!'": North vs. Kubrick on the Music for *2001: A Space Odyssey*." *The Journal of Film Music* 2, no. 1 (Fall 2007): 1–32.

Metz, Christian. *The Imaginary Signifier: Psychoanalysis and the Cinema*. Bloomington: Indiana University Press, 1977.

—— *Film Language: A Semiotics of the Cinema*. Chicago, IL: University of Chicago Press, 1977.

Mueller, Roswitha. *Bertolt Brecht and the Theory of Media*. Lincoln and London: University of Nebraska Press, 1989.

Murray, Steve. "Between Past and Future and Memory and Regret." *Atlanta Journal-Constitution*, September 2, 2005.

O'Brien, Charles. *Cinema's Conversion to Sound: Technology and Film Style in France and the U.S.* Bloomington: Indiana University Press, 2005.

Ogasapian, John, and N. Lee. *Music of the Gilded Age*. Westport, CT: Greenwood Press, 2007.

Perriam, Chris, and Ann Davies, eds. *Carmen: From Silent Film to MTV*. New York: Rodopi, 2005.

Poizat, Michel. *The Angel's Cry: Beyond the Pleasure Principle in Opera*, trans. Arthur Denner. Ithaca, NY: Cornell University Press, 1992.

Powdermaker, Hortense. *Hollywood the Dream Factory: An Anthropologist Looks at the Movie-Makers*. Boston, MA: Little, Brown and Company, 1950.

Powrie, Phil, and Robynn Stilwell, eds. *Changing Tunes: The Use of Pre-Existing Music in Film*. Aldershot: Ashgate, 2006.

Preston, Katherine K. *Opera on the Road: Traveling Opera Troupes in the United States, 1825–1960*. Urbana and Chicago: University of Illinois Press, 1993.

Raksin, Diavd. "Hollywood Strakes Back: Film Composer Attacks Stravinsky's 'Cult of Inexpressiveness.'" *The Musical Digest* (January 1948). www.filmmusicsociety.org/news_events/features/2003/101003.html (accessed February 7, 2006).

Rosar, William H. "Film Studies in Musicology: Disciplinarity vs. Interdisciplinarity." *The Journal of Film Music* 2 (Winter 2009): 99–125.

—— "Film Music—What's in a Name?" *The Journal of Film Music* 1, no. 1 (2002): 1–18.

—— "Stravinsky and MGM." In *Film Music 1*, ed. Clifford McCarty, 109–122. New York: Garland, 1989.

Rosolato, Guy. "La Voix: entre corps et langage." *Revue Française de psychanalyse* 38, no. 1 (January 1974): 75–94.

Ross, Alex   "Whistling in the Dark." *The New Yorker*. February 18, 2002. www.
      newyorker.com/archive/2002/02/18/020218crat_atlarge (accessed May 22, 2009).
—— "The *Ring* and the *Rings*—Wagner vs. Tolkien." *The New Yorker* 79, no. 40
      (December 2003): 161–5.
—— "Opera and Film." *The New York Times*. March 12, 1995.
Salter, Hans J. Interview with Warren Sherk. Typewritten Manuscript, 1987.
      Margaret Herrick Library of the Academy of Motion Pictures, Arts, and
      Sciences.
Schoenberg, Arnold. "Art and the Moving Pictures," "The Future of the Opera,"
      and "Opera: Aphorisms." In *Style and Idea: Selected Writings of Arnold
      Schoenberg*, trans. Leo Black. Berkeley and Los Angeles: University of
      California Press, 1985.
Schroeder, David. *Cinema's Illusions, Opera's Allure: The Operatic Impulse in
      Film*. New York: Continuum, 2002.
Shaman, William. "The Operatic Vitaphone Shorts," *ARSC Journal* 22, no. 1
      (Spring 1991): 35–94.
Sheppard, William Anthony. *Revealing Masks: Exotic Influences and Ritualized
      Performance in Modernist Music Theater*. Berkeley: University of California
      Press, 2001.
Silverman, Kaja. *Acoustic Mirror: The Female Voice in Psychoanalysis and
      Cinema*. Bloomington: Indiana University Press, 1988.
Silvio, Teri. "Chinese Opera, Global Cinema, and the Ontology of the Person:
      Chen Kaige's *Farewell My Concubine*." In *Between Opera and Cinema*, ed.
      Jeongwon Joe and Rose M. Theresa. New York: Routledge, 2002.
Simpson, Alexander Thomas, Jr. "Opera on Film: A Study of the History and
      the Aesthetic Principles and Conflicts of a Hybrid Genre." PhD dissertation,
      University of Kentucky, 1990.
Sjogren, Britta. *Into the Vortex: Female Voice and Paradox in Film*. Urbana and
      Chicago: University of Illinois Press, 2006.
Smart, Mary Ann. "The Silencing of Lucia," *Cambridge Opera Journal* 4, no. 2
      (July 1992): 119–41.
Smith, Jeff. *The Sounds of Commerce: Marketing Popular Film*. New York:
      Columbia University Press, 1998.
Smith, Matthew Wilson. *The Total Work of Art: From Bayreuth to Cyberspace*.
      New York: Routledge, 2007.
Somerset-Ward, Richard. *Angels and Monsters: Male and Female Sopranos in the
      Story of Opera*. New Haven, CT: Yale University Press, 2004.
Sterne, Jonathan. *The Audible Past: Cultural Origins of Sound Reproduction*.
      Durham, NC: Duke University Press, 2003.
Stilwell, Robynn. "'I just put a drone under him …': Collage and Subversion in the
      Score of *Die Hard*," *Music and Letters* 78, no. 4 (November 1997): 551–80.
——, "Hysterical Beethoven," *Beethoven Forum*, 10, no. 2 (2003), pp. 162–82.

Storey, John. "Expecting Rain: Opera as Popular Culture." In *Popular Culture and High Culture: An Analysis and Evaluation of Taste*, ed. Herbert J. Gans. New York: Basic Books, 1975.

Stravinsky, Igor. "Igor Stravinsky on Film Music (as told to Ingolf Dahl)." Introduction by Ingolf Dahl. *The Musical Digest* (September 1946). www.filmmusicsociety.org/news_events/features/2003/101003.html (accessed February 7, 2006).

Swed, Mark. "'Il Trittico,' the Los Angeles Opera: Filmmaker Woody Allen Helps Deliver Great Comic Puccini." *Los Angles Times*, September 8, 2008. www.latimes.com/entertainment/news/arts/la-et-trittico8-2008sep08,0,7203446.story (accessed February 7, 2012).

Symcox, Peter. "The Four Faces of Opera." *Opera Quarterly* 3 (1985): 1–18.

Tambling, Jeremy. *Wong Kar-Wai's "Happy Together."* Hong Kong: Hong Kong University Press, 2003.

—— "Towards a Psychopathology of Opera," *Cambridge Opera Journal* 9, no. 3 (1997): 263–79.

——, ed. *A Night in at the Opera: Media Representations of Opera*. New Barnet: John Libby, 1994.

—— *Opera, Ideology and Film*. Basingstoke: Palgrave Macmillan, 1987.

Teo, Stephen. *Wong Kar-Wai*. London: BFI Publishing, 2005.

Tomlinson, Gary. *Metaphysical Song: An Essay on Opera*. Princeton, NJ: Princeton University Press, 1999.

Turk, Edward Baron. "Deriding the Voice of Jeanette MacDonald: Notes on Psychoanalysis and the American Film Musical." In *Embodied Voices: Representing Female Vocality in Western Culture*, ed. Leslie C. Dunn and Nancy A. Jones, 103–19. Cambridge: Cambridge University Press, 1997.

Vasse, Denis. *Le Poids du réel, la souffrance*. Paris: Éditions du Seuil, 1983.

—— *L'Ombilic et la voix: Deux enfants en analyses*. Paris: Éditions du Seuil, 1974.

Weiner, Marc A. "Why Does Hollywood Like Opera?" In *Between Opera and Cinema*, ed. Jeongwon Joe and Rose M. Theresa. New York: Routledge, 2002.

Wilk, Rona M. "'Vox populi': Popularization and Americanization of Opera." PhD dissertation, New York University, 2006.

Wilkins, Robert. *Fireside Book of Death*. London: Time Warner Paperbacks, 1992.

Wlaschin, Ken. *Encyclopedia of Opera on Screen: A Guide to More Than 100 Years of Opera Films, Videos, and DVDs*. New Haven, CT: Yale University Press, 2004.

—— *Opera on Screen*. Los Angeles: Beachwood Press, 1997.

Wong, Kar-Wai. "Interview." *New York Times*, January 28, 2001.

Ziegle, Aaron. "Reshaped and Redefined: Watching Cocteau's *La Belle et la Bête* with Auric and Glass." *Music Research Forum* 26 (2011): 45–74.

Žižek, Slavoj. *Organs without Bodies: Deleuze and Consequences*. New York: Routledge, 2004.

—— *The Fragile Absolute*. London and New York: Verso, 2000.

——— "'I Hear You with My Eyes'; or The Invisible Master." In *Gaze and Voice as Love Objects*, ed. Renata Salecl and Slavoj Žižek, 90–127. Durham, NC: Duke University Press, 1996.

Žižek, Slavoj, and Mladen Dolar. *Opera's Second Death*. New York: Routledge, 2002.

Zumthor, Paul. *La lettre et la voix: De la "littérature" médiévale*. Paris: Éditions du Seuil, 1987.

Index